D0031825

REFINERY TOWN

Previous titles by Steve Early

Embedded with Organized Labor:
Journalistic Reflections on the Class War at Home

The Civil Wars in US Labor: Birth of a
New Workers' Movement or Death Throes of the Old?

Save Our Unions: Dispatches from a Movement in Distress

REFINERY TOWN

Big Oil,
Big Money,
and the
Remaking
of an
American City

STEVE EARLY

Foreword by
Senator Bernie Sanders

BEACON PRESS
BOSTON

BEACON PRESS
Boston, Massachusetts
www.beacon.org

Beacon Press books
are published under the auspices of
the Unitarian Universalist Association of Congregations.

20 19 18 17   8 7 6 5 4 3 2 1

This book is printed on acid-free paper that meets the uncoated paper
ANSI/NISO specifications for permanence as revised in 1992.

Text design and composition by Kim Arney

Library of Congress Cataloging-in-Publication Data

Names: Early, Steve, author.
Title: Refinery town : big oil, big money, and the remaking of an American
    city / Steve Early.
Description: Boston : Beacon Press, [2017] | Includes bibliographical references.
Identifiers: LCCN 2016021632 (print) | LCCN 2016034085 (ebook) |
    ISBN 9780807094266 (hardcover : alk. paper) | ISBN 9780807094273 (ebook)
Subjects: LCSH: Richmond (Calif.)—Politics and government—21st century. |
    Municipal government—California—Richmond—History. | Business and
    politics—California—Richmond—History. | Company towns—California—
    Richmond—History. | Petroleum industry and trade—Political aspects—
    California—Richmond—History. | Community development—California—
    Richmond—History.
Classification: LCC JS1351.R25 E27 2017 (print) | LCC JS1351.R25 (ebook) |
    DDC 979.4/63—dc23
LC record available at https://lccn.loc.gov/2016021632

*To Dorothy D. Early,
a local news gatherer and
"women's page" editor
when there still was
such a thing*

CONTENTS

TO CHANGE U.S. POLITICS, WE NEED MORE CITIES LIKE RICHMOND, CALIFORNIA

PRIOR TO THE 2016 DEMOCRATIC PRIMARIES, I made a series of out-of-state trips to discuss the economic issues facing the United States that were propelling me toward a presidential campaign. Then and later, I met with local progressive leaders, many of whom were running for mayor or city council, the state legislature, or Congress. At "town meetings" throughout the United States, we discussed how we could work together for real change in our country.

Richmond, California, is one place I visited where such movement building was already underway. In this century-old refinery town, a determined band of municipal reformers was battling America's second-largest oil company for control over city hall.

Over the past decade, Chevron has made more than $200 billion in profits, ripping off Americans at the gas pump, even as it has paid hundreds of millions in fines for violating health and safety laws and polluting our air and water. In 2014, the $3 million it spent against progressive candidates in Richmond provides a vivid example of how the Supreme Court's *Citizens United* decision has totally corrupted the electoral process in the United States.

Corporations and wealthy individuals, like the Koch brothers, are free to spend unlimited amounts of money on local, state, and federal elections. The biggest financial players in our 2016 election cycle were the billion-aire- and millionaire-funded super PACs unleashed by *Citizens United.* Fewer than four hundred families have contributed the majority of all the money raised by candidates and super PACs combined. According to media reports, a single family spent more than either the Democratic or Republican Parties.

Candidates favored by big business no longer have to pass the hat among thousands of individual donors. Nor must they rely on the pro-ceeds of such fund-raising to pay basic campaign expenses. Instead, the "independent expenditures" made by a handful of wealthy individuals will cover these costs for them. In a city the size of Richmond, a single corporate check signer will pick up the tab on behalf of Big Oil, Big Soda, Big Banks, or whatever other corporate interest is threatened.

The price our country pays for this trend is that super PAC–backed candidates are clearly unaccountable to the rest of us. In office, these politicians will, in bipartisan fashion, shower the wealthy with more tax breaks while cutting programs that help working families. As former pres-ident Jimmy Carter points out, this system of "unlimited political bribery" represents "a complete subversion of our political system."

Fortunately, as Richmond writer and longtime labor activist Steve Early reveals in this book, there are local success stories in the fight to keep corporate giants like Chevron from just buying elections. The inspiring electoral victories in Richmond would not have been possible without the prior development of a multi-issue, multi-racial progressive organization. Our country obviously needs a great deal of change at the state and federal levels. But laying a solid local foundation, like activists in Richmond have done, is an important first step toward overcoming working-class alien-ation from politics and resulting low voter-turnout rates.

Refinery Town is based on one city's experience, but it reflects the les-sons of grassroots organizing elsewhere, including in Vermont. After my four terms as mayor of Burlington, our collective city hall achievements provided a platform for statewide movement building in the decades since.

Progressives now have far greater representation in our state legislature than in any other in America. Wherever we have more elected officials responsive to the people, that encourages wider citizen participation and helps thwart our national drift toward oligarchy, a government owned and controlled by a handful of extremely wealthy families.

We need to start engaging at the local and state levels in an unprecedented way. Hundreds of thousands of volunteers helped make history in our 2016 presidential campaign with their phone calling, door knocking, personal donations, and rally participation. Today, many remain deeply concerned about the future of our nation and their own communities.

That's why many are now going to run for school boards, city councils, county commissions, state legislatures, and governorships. State and local governments make enormously important decisions. Without an ongoing political revolution, conservative politicians and corporations like Chevron will continue to wield undue influence in Richmond and in Washington.

Since June 2016, thousands of progressives have gone to our website—berniesanders.com/win—to learn how they can become candidates themselves or support others running for office. My supporters have launched a new organization, called Our Revolution, to help transform American politics and make our political and economic systems responsive to the needs of working families. Based on the energy and enthusiasm generated in 2016, I have no doubt that this new organization will help win significant numbers of local and state elections, if many more people become involved.

We know that taking over city hall in Richmond or any other city won't, by itself, keep big money out of politics. It can't stop climate change, eliminate economic injustice and racism, or stop law enforcement abuses. Addressing those problems requires broader movement building, national and global in scale. But local progress is still possible wherever we have government that represents all of us, not just the 1 percent. This timely book offers ideas and inspiration for making change where it counts the most—among friends, neighbors, and fellow community members.

—Senator Bernie Sanders

FROM COMPANY TOWN TO PROGRESSIVE CITY

ON THE EVENING OF NOVEMBER 4, 2014, there wasn't much for liberals and progressives to celebrate anywhere in the United States. Federal election turnout reached its lowest level in seventy years. When the results of midterm congressional races were tallied, Democrats lost the US Senate. Republicans added to their already substantial majority in the House of Representatives. At the state level, Democratic and Republican governors hostile to workers' rights and strong unions were reelected for another four years. Whether the issue was income inequality, Wall Street greed, workers' rights, mistreatment of immigrants, misbehavior by police officers, campaign finance reform, or the future of the planet, the outlook was bleak—at the federal level and in many states.

I had made a well-timed move to Richmond, California, three years before this election debacle. When the polls closed there in 2014, labor and community activists, environmental justice campaigners, police reformers, gay rights advocates, anti-foreclosure fighters, and defenders of the foreign-born were all partying like they lived in another country. In reality they were just fortunate to reside in a city where more than a decade of local organizing made it possible to defeat candidates funded by one of the richest corporations in the world.

Refinery Town is a work of narrative journalism about the emergence
and success of Richmond's municipal reform movement. It examines one
city's efforts to confront local manifestations of serious national and global
problems. Within these pages is the story of how a largely nonwhite,
working-class community of 110,000 spawned a vibrant culture of resistance to corporate power and its many toxic externalities, after more than
a century of political dominance by Big Oil and other business interests.
As Richmond has transformed itself into a much-applauded progressive
city, it has even upstaged such longtime venues for Left Coast activism as
Berkeley, Oakland, and San Francisco.

Unlike its better-known Bay Area neighbors, Richmond was once
a prototypical company town. The city was run by public officials installed by global energy giant Chevron, local developers, or their building
trades and public safety union allies. Richmond's landscape was marked
and its air fouled by one of the largest refineries in California. On its
way to political metamorphosis, the city experienced the full range of
late-twentieth-century urban woes. Deindustrialization, joblessness and
poverty, substandard schools and housing, drug trafficking, street crime,
and gang violence all contributed to one of the highest homicide rates per
capita in the country. Cronyism and corruption in city hall led to financial
mismanagement and near bankruptcy; big cuts in jobs and services resulted. Relations between police and the community deteriorated due to
officer-involved shootings, beatings, and checkpoints set up to detain immigrant drivers without documentation, in a city now 40 percent Latino.

Fortunately Richmond's changing demographics produced a new generation of progressive elected officials who were committed to democratizing and revitalizing the city. Over the course of a decade they changed
municipal politics and steadily improved city hall administration. Today
Richmond activists populate an array of city commissions, departments,
and programs dealing with public safety, city planning, job creation,
shoreline preservation, urban agriculture, parks and recreation, and the
arts. Richmond has undertaken a series of creative municipal initiatives,
many of which are now being embraced elsewhere.

In November 2014, the city council got a bigger left-liberal majority, despite $3.5 million in corporate spending against candidates seeking

further progress in Richmond. As recounted in this book, a group known as the Richmond Progressive Alliance (RPA) helped engineer that victory and played a catalytic role throughout Mayor Gayle McLaughlin's eight years in city hall. The RPA is simultaneously an electoral formation, a membership organization, a coalition of community groups, and a key coordinator of grassroots education and citizen mobilization around multiple issues. Unusual in the fractious and marginalized US left, the group unites liberal Democrats, socialists, independents, and third-party voters affiliated with the California Greens or Peace and Freedom Party.

RPA candidates have distinguished themselves locally by their refusal to accept business donations, while welcoming the support of progressive unions. The Alliance relies on membership dues, door-to-door canvassing to expand its grassroots base, and, in election years, small individual donors and modest public matching funds for its city council and mayoral candidates. RPA work with labor and community allies has created strong synergy between activist city hall leadership and grassroots organizing. In a fashion worthy of emulation elsewhere, the group has become an effective local counterweight to the previously untrammeled exercise of corporate power.

Under McLaughlin's leadership, Richmond was the largest city in the country with a Green mayor, and the scene of high-profile battles with Big Oil, Big Banks, and Big Soda. The city council tackled environmental hazards arising from oil refining and crude-oil rail shipment through the city. Richmond extracted higher taxes from Chevron and sued the giant oil company over damage caused by a major refinery fire in 2012. A community mobilization led by environmental justice groups and the RPA helped the city win $90 million in financial concessions from Chevron in return for approving a refinery modernization project that both critics and proponents hoped would improve safety and reduce pollution.

Richmond residents joined coalitions fighting global warming, and cross-border alliances formed in response to Big Oil's worldwide misbehavior. As mayor, McLaughlin traveled to Ecuador, as guest of President Rafael Correa, to forge relationships of solidarity with peasant farmers suing Chevron for environmental damage. Tom Butt, her more moderate successor, met with mayors from around the world during the 2015 UN

Climate Change Conference in Paris. While national leaders negotiated carbon emissions curbs, municipal officials compared notes on renewable energy projects, stricter pollution standards, and sustainable public transit. When Butt returned from Paris, he sought ways to further reduce Richmond's reliance on Pacific Gas and Electric by promoting cleaner energy alternatives.

Richmond also made national headlines by threatening to use the power of eminent domain to block home foreclosures. This creative but soon-thwarted effort to secure debt relief for underwater mortgage holders was an emergency response to Richmond's high foreclosure rate. These lender decisions led to abandoned homes and neighborhood blight. Now, just several years later, as the local housing market rebounds and gentrification creeps in, low-income tenants face higher rents and possible displacement. So RPA members and the Alliance of Californians for Community Empowerment (ACCE) are fighting to make Richmond the first California municipality in thirty years to regulate rents and evictions.

Richmond voters and city council members have also raised the minimum wage and defeated a major development scheme based on casino gambling. They have opposed raids by federal immigration officials and created a municipal ID card to aid undocumented residents. They enacted a "ban the box" ordinance to ease the reentry of former prisoners into the community by curbing discrimination against job applicants with a criminal record. At a time when many cities have been wracked by violent crime and out-of-control police officers, progressive leaders in Richmond hired a visionary gay police chief, who increased public safety through real community policing.

All of this activity is part of a larger municipal reform trend, which emerged during a period of political deadlock at the state and federal level. The revival of local progressive politics is not unrelated to the dashed hopes and lowered expectations of the Obama era. During Obama's presidency, Congress has displayed near terminal gridlock—except when the president was engineering bipartisan victories in the form of free trade or federal budget deals opposed by his own labor, environmental, and minority community base. The track record of his successor, even if a fellow Democrat, may not differ all that much.

. . .

FORTUNATELY, BETTER THINGS ARE happening in the municipalities of the land. Innovative elected leaders have deployed the limited resources of local government to fight poverty, inequality, and environmental degradation at a moment when government at higher levels has failed to address such problems or made them worse. "The more local jurisdictions that tackle these issues, the more momentum there is for statewide and eventually national action," argues one former city councilor, a proponent of paid parental leave in San Francisco.[1]

This public policy creativity is now much celebrated across the political spectrum. After visiting "smaller town America" for the *Atlantic*, author and journalist James Fallows agreed that "strong mayors" can succeed, while presidents and legislators seem ever more pathetically hamstrung. As Fallows observed: "The more you see of national politics in this era, the worse you're likely to feel. The more we see of small cities, the better."[2] In their Brookings Institution study, *The Metropolitan Revolution*, Bruce Katz and Jennifer Bradley confirmed that a wide range of US "cities and metros are fixing our broken politics and fragile economy."[3]

CityLab, a widely read blog by city theorist Richard Florida, now bubbles over with online "conversation and debate among the leading voices on urbanism . . . people who are creating the cities of the future." In his book celebrating "rising cities," Yale professor Benjamin Barber argues that city hall leaders, at home and abroad, are doing such a good job that our governance would be better "if mayors ruled the world."[4] According to Barber, municipal leaders from Bogota to Delhi are "responding to transnational problems more effectively than nation states mired in ideological infighting and sovereign rivalries." Since Barber's book appeared, one country falling into his category of "dysfunctional nations," Spain, has spawned a new city-based formation called Podemos. Its supporters forged movement-driven coalitions that elected new female mayors and more city council members committed to direct citizen participation in Barcelona and Madrid.

Because of their catalytic role, mayors are lionized above all, generating better press than US politicians with far higher national profiles. As the *San*

Francisco Chronicle notes, "With polls showing that three-quarters of American voters have little confidence in Congress and two-thirds worry about the country's direction, experts say it may be the roll-up-your-sleeves mayors, tackling issues like climate change, education and police brutality, who are in the best position to shake up the national agenda."[5] When the US Conference of Mayors gathered in San Francisco in 2015, President Obama himself applauded the hands-on, results-oriented approach of its members. "Mayors get the job done," he told their annual meeting. "It's not sufficient to blather on—you actually have to do something."[6]

LIE FACTORY FOES

Doing something that encroaches on powerful private interests is unpopular with those adversely affected. So city hall progressives, whether in Richmond, Seattle, or New York City, face well-financed resistance to many of their initiatives. Mirroring national trends, direct business spending on Richmond politics—combined with far larger independent expenditures by corporate PACs—gives favored candidates a fund-raising advantage of 30 to 1 in our local "nonpartisan" races. Elsewhere in the country, the energy industry alone spent more than $721 million on advertising, lobbying, and midterm election campaigning in 2014. Defying this national trend, voters in Richmond handed Big Oil its biggest election defeat in municipal history on November 4 of that year. The Richmond story is therefore a timely and compelling case study of what it takes to overcome big money in politics in our post–*Citizens United* era.[7]

The corporate counter-campaigns described herein have their roots in a California political struggle that occurred during the Great Depression. Eighty years before Big Oil tried to take down Richmond's Green mayor, Gayle McLaughlin, and her city council allies, a Bernie Sanders–like socialist named Upton Sinclair faced similar business-funded, consultant-crafted attacks throughout the Golden State. The famous muckraking author was a political outsider who captured the Democratic Party nomination for governor in 1934 based on a forward-looking plan called End Poverty in California (EPIC).

Sinclair centered his EPIC campaign on poor and working-class voters whose jobs, homes, or savings were disappearing. He proposed "production for use" rather than for profit, through worker co-ops and large-scale public job creation, which the Roosevelt administration had yet to embrace as a federal government response to the Depression. Republicans, conservative Democrats, and their corporate backers were horrified by Sinclair's growing popular following. Kenneth R. Kingsbury, the president of Standard Oil of California (now Chevron) sent thousands of his shareholders a pamphlet predicting that "Sinclairism" would destroy property values, stock prices, and business in general.

To prevent that, Standard Oil and other business clients turned to the country's first professional political consulting firm, founded by Clem Whitaker and Leone Baxter. The firm, Campaigns, Inc., employed traditional public relations techniques and innovative new approaches to mass communication and social persuasion. Like progressive candidates in modern-day Richmond, Sinclair was demonized and red-baited in a torrent of negative advertising. He was smeared in thousands of expensive billboards erected throughout the state.[8] As historians including Jill Lepore report, Hollywood studios concocted scary anti-Sinclair newsreels—presented as actual reporting on his campaign—and screened them in movie theaters before feature films.[9] To ruin Sinclair's image among newspaper readers, Whitaker and Baxter combed his novels for controversial quotes from fictional characters and fed these snippets to reporters and columnists, who then attributed them to the author himself.

After losing to incumbent GOP governor Frank Merriam (by only 250,000 votes out of two million cast), Sinclair penned a book-length postmortem on his gubernatorial race.[10] In it he reflected on the mass media manipulation that discredited his proposals to reduce poverty and inequality and improve the quality of life in California. Over eighty years later, Whitaker and Baxter may be long dead but they have many successors in what is now a multibillion-dollar political consulting industry. In campaigns run against candidates, legislation, or referenda that might produce better government, fairer taxation, stronger environmental protection, or a healthier California, these "communication specialists" operate what Sinclair called a "lie factory." The twenty-first-century result, even as measured by data-driven academics, is oligarchy, not democracy: "Economic elites and organized groups representing business interests have substantial independent impacts on U.S. government policy, while mass-based interest groups and average citizens have little or no independent influence."[11]

In *Refinery Town*, we meet many such citizens, although not all of them are "average." In fact, some are every bit as ornery and unorthodox in their views as Upton Sinclair. Following in the footsteps of earlier campaigners for social and economic justice, these activists have challenged the status quo, locally and nationally. In their serial bouts with corporate power, Richmond's modern-day progressives have done more than adopt a defensive crouch. They have found ways to go on the political offensive, rallying friends and neighbors in the process. After lost rounds, in which they were pummeled badly, they rebounded and continued the fight.

Refinery Town is by no means a comprehensive history of my new hometown or the final word on any number of important topics. Much of its subject matter—whether corporate political spending, industrial pollution, public safety reform, or housing affordability—could fill volumes. A sizeable body of existing literature on municipal reform, produced by journalists, academics, urban planners, and actual practitioners of city politics can be accessed in this book's online bibliography.[12] Some of my Richmond neighbors, especially those most immersed in public policy detail, may find my rendering of complex local disputes lacking in sufficient detail, subtlety, or historical sweep. On the other hand, some out-of-towners may feel at times like they've acquired more local knowledge than they need or want!

I also realize that the particularity of Richmond could make this story seem overly exceptional. Hopefully, readers will find sufficient examples of citizen action that are timely, relevant, and reproducible elsewhere. Regardless of who occupies the White House, municipal reform movements like the one profiled in this book will remain a necessary vehicle for progressive activism. Over time, these efforts can help curb the decline in electoral participation that has left millions of poor and working-class Americans with little or no political voice.

In national elections, those with the most donor clout—what Bernie Sanders calls "the billionaire class"—are well positioned to win, whether their preferred candidate comes in first or second. Those of us dissatisfied with such outcomes have few short-term options other than expanded grassroots work in the trenches of local politics, labor organizing, or social movement building. As Sanders wound down his own 2016 presidential primary campaign, he strongly encouraged the first approach. "What we need," he said, "is a 50-state strategy, which engages people—young and working class people—to stand up and run for school board, to run for city council, and the state legislature, so government, at all levels, starts listening to ordinary people instead of campaign contributors."[13]

Much citizen activism in the United States is already focused on local improvements—like community co-ops, bike paths, urban gardens, historical preservation projects, and other sustainability efforts. In Richmond, such urban landscape changes have occurred in the context of political insurgency. The manifestations of that, as reported here, have been controversial and much contested. But the many positive results so far pose this question: If a badly scarred industrial city, long dissed and dismissed by its upscale neighbors, can undergo a municipal renaissance, why not other less disadvantaged communities? I hope that this portrait of "Progressive Richmond," warts and all, will provide inspiration and ideas for those attempting to remake their own hometowns, new and old.

ONE

A REFINER'S FIRE

AS RECENT HOME BUYERS IN RICHMOND, my wife and I were not yet focused on Chevron's historic intertwining with our new hometown. We acquired a surprisingly affordable home, just over the hill from a century-old refinery. The seller was a Chevron engineer headed for retirement in a San Diego condo. We noticed a disclaimer or two about our proximity to his former employer, but this legal notification was carefully buried in a big pile of standardized real estate agent and mortgage company paperwork that included a lot of other fine print.

Like starry-eyed California gold seekers in the nineteenth century, our gaze was distracted from any possible downside to leaving stodgy old New England after thirty-two Boston-area winters. As our realtor joked, we were about to become residents of "the Richmond Riviera." It had such a sunny, temperate Mediterranean-style microclimate that no one ever complained about anything—except possibly a neighbor with building plans that might obstruct a waterfront vista. Our own view of downtown San Francisco and Marin County landmarks like Mount Tamalpais was simply breathtaking.

The only major piece of Chevron Corporation property visible between us and much pricier Marin was a 4,200-foot pier extending out into the sparkling waters of San Francisco Bay. The 600-ton oil tankers unloading there, with their pumps humming away quietly, were often quite beautiful at night. Their illuminated superstructures made them look like carnival rides or a circus that had sailed into port from the Pacific, via the Golden Gate, whose famous bridge glittered farther off in the distance, between Angel Island and the Marin peninsula known as Tiburon.

On a bright, sunny August afternoon, six months after moving in, my wife was outside, tending to our new garden. A concerned neighbor across the street spotted her among the plants, opened her front door, and shouted: "You shouldn't be outside! Don't know you know there's a 'shelter in place'?"

"What's that?" Suzanne asked. She soon found out by looking up and over the hill behind our house, where an eruption worthy of Mount Vesuvius was underway. A major pipe rupture and fire had occurred at the Chevron refinery. Nineteen workers—the first responders to this emergency—narrowly escaped death at the scene of the accident. As the conflagration continued, a towering plume of toxic smoke spiraled up and then over much of downwind Richmond, reaching several other East Bay communities as well.

For Richmond mayor Gayle McLaughlin, August 6, 2012, was turning out to be the day she and other local Greens had long warned about. Sitting down for dinner at her modest rental home a few miles away from Chevron, sixty-one-year-old McLaughlin started to get panicked calls from residents reporting that a huge dark cloud was hovering over them. Richmond police chief Chris Magnus soon confirmed the accident location, as did company officials calling from the scene of the fire.

In Richmond, when fossil fuel disaster strikes, city hall issues an official order directing everyone affected to take cover in their own homes, a self-help procedure known as "sheltering in place." Doors must be closed and windows taped shut, if possible. Under the ranking system used by Contra Costa County to calibrate its response to refinery emergencies, the Chevron fire was judged to be a Level 3 incident, the highest level of danger. Unfortunately, the county's warning system did not quickly share this bad news. Robocalls to eighteen thousand nearby residents took many hours to complete, due to outdated software.

Many area residents decided that "sheltering in place" wasn't working well enough for them and headed for the nearest emergency room or clinic instead. About fifteen thousand sought medical treatment for respiratory complaints and other problems in the wake of the fire. Locking our doors and leaving gardening tools behind, my wife and I jumped into the car and sought refuge with friends in nearby Berkeley. That well-known university town, in neighboring Alameda County, had higher home prices and more distant bay views but fewer industrial neighbors like Chevron.

The 2012 fire was not the first refinery accident to occur locally or in other parts of the globe where Chevron operates. But its dramatic scale, negative health effects, and adverse economic impact made it a modern milestone in Richmond's often-fraught relationship with its biggest employer. The fire caused a $1.86 billion drop in the city's assessed property values, reducing tax revenues from Chevron itself, other businesses, and homeowners. It revived long-standing concerns about Chevron's environmental impact and workplace conditions. It stirred new restiveness about job safety among refinery workers whose union had waged a nearly hundred-year struggle for greater autonomy from the company. And, as Chevron spent heavily on public relations damage control, Richmond residents were subjected to many post-fire reminders of the company's historical dominance of local affairs.

As a forty-year veteran of labor and political organizing, I should have expected that a company with robber baron roots might have tangled with its own workers or downwind neighbors a few times before. Upon closer inspection, I learned that for much of the twentieth century, Richmond refinery bosses and lobbyists were skillful at winning local hearts and minds. To achieve its business goals, Chevron (formerly Standard Oil of California) has employed more than a century's worth of corporate paternalism, targeted philanthropy, slick publicity, and political patronage. During some past labor conflicts, a little picket-line repression was helpful too. The company's modern-day game plan reflected the same sophisticated multifaceted approach it has used for decades.

When Standard Oil opened for business in 1905, present-day Richmond consisted of grain fields, cattle farms, and a duck-hunting marsh adjacent to its low range of knolls rising from the bay. As California historian Gray Brechin notes, "Ohlone Indians once found the place so rich in food that they had, over thousands of years, built a gigantic pile of clam and mussel shells at the mouth of a creek there."[1] The Ohlones were long gone by 1900 when the Atchison, Topeka, and Santa Fe Railroad arrived. Its workers built a tunnel and laid track to Ferry Point, making Richmond the site of San Francisco Bay's second transcontinental railhead.

In 1912, the San Francisco chamber of commerce sent a delegation across the bay, by ferry, to check out business opportunities in what Richmond's founders hoped would become "the Pittsburgh of the West." Their "trade excursion" took them to the highest point along the city's thirty-two miles of still undeveloped shoreline. Looking east, they could admire not only one of the biggest refineries in the world but "the great car shops of Pullman, the Enterprise foundry, the plant of the Western Pipe and Steel Company of California . . . and other industrial concerns that have found cheap fuel, light and power, convenient transportation, and other favorable conditions."[2]

Within a few years, Richmond's population neared ten thousand. Its roster of brand-name companies included American Radiator, Standard Sanitary, Stauffer Chemical, and the California Wine Association, which for a time operated the biggest winery and storage plant in the world on Richmond's Point Molate. As Brechin points out, living downwind from so much manufacturing and refining was already becoming a problem for residents of West Contra Costa County and beyond because "the prevailing winds through the Golden Gate drove the smoke, ashes, and dust rich in heavy metals and asbestos, along with the stench of petrochemicals and acids, back upon the town."

Among Richmond's nascent hazards was the little matter of explosions—and not just those occurring at Standard Oil. Forced out of San Francisco and Berkeley because of local concerns about the safety of its dynamite making, the Giant Powder Company relocated to Richmond's Point Pinole. Between 1880 and 1960, two billion pounds' worth of explosives were manufactured there, within the city limits. "This was the dynamite that helped build the west," explains Point Pinole park ranger Dave Zuckerman, when he conducts tours of the 2,300-acre site today. "We like to say it was a 'booming business.'"[3]

Leading the industrial transformation of Richmond, Standard Oil started out small, on just six hundred acres, making kerosene for export to Asia. Soon there was no bigger refinery in the state and only two larger ones in the entire world. The facility was supplied by a 283-mile pipeline pumping crude to Richmond from the oil fields of Bakersfield, California, directly to the East Bay. Over time, oil pipelines, processing units, and storage tanks spread out over three thousand acres overlooking the San Francisco and San Pablo Bays. Processing capacity today is 240,000 barrels of crude daily, which can generate as much as $25 billion in sales, 10 percent of the company's worldwide total in recent years. The company now operates in 180 countries and is ranked sixteenth on *Fortune*'s Global 500 list. In 2014 it was number three on *Fortune*'s list of the five hundred top US corporations.

WHITE-COLLAR CRIMINALS

Standard Oil's original owners, the Rockefeller family, were not particularly law-abiding or labor-friendly people. They were founding members of an industry that "has always been wealthy, powerful, and feudalistic."[4] The Rockefeller rap sheet includes major white-collar crimes and multiple homicides involving union members on family-owned properties. Federal antitrust action led to the breakup of the original Standard Oil trust in 1892, when founder John D. Rockefeller Sr. was still in charge.

Two decades later the company regained "such monopolistic power that it was able to drive down the prices of crude oil it bought from producers on the one hand and drive up prices of products sold to consumers on the other hand."[5] The Supreme Court upheld a second divestiture of the family business. This reorganization created several dozen new companies, none of which remained smaller for long. Among them were the separate Standard Oils of New Jersey and New York (now reunited as Exxon-Mobil) and Standard Oil of California (later renamed Chevron).

On picket lines from New Jersey to Colorado, Rockefeller-owned firms could be counted on to unleash deadly violence against striking workers. The murder of thirty-three coal miners and their family members on April 14, 1914, by the Colorado Fuel & Iron Company—the Ludlow Massacre—was such a public relations disaster that John D. Rockefeller Jr. hired Ivy Lee, a pioneering corporate publicist and crisis communications handler, to buff up his personal and corporate reputation. But that didn't stop similar killings of sixteen protesting workers, by police and hired gunmen, in Bayonne, New Jersey, during Standard Oil refinery strikes that occurred in 1915–16.

Public revulsion turned John D. into a much-detested national figure. So the Rockefellers launched "a massive philanthropy campaign, donating large sums to various causes," to refurbish the family's image.[6] In Richmond, this calculated community-mindedness was already underway in 1906, when the San Francisco earthquake sent refugees fleeing across the bay to Richmond's Ferry Point. From there they were ushered to wooden dormitories in Rockefeller Camp, a haven for the homeless funded by a $100,000 donation from the Standard Oil founder.

In other cities at the time, workers were turning away from corporate paternalism and charity toward political involvement. The Socialist Party attracted nearly one hundred thousand members, in part by challenging local business interests for control of city hall. As political scientist Peter Dreier reports, about twelve hundred socialists were elected to public office and used their municipal positions to improve services including housing, sanitation, and street repair. Socialist mayors presided over Minneapolis, Butte, Flint, Schenectady, and seventy-five other cities in twenty-four states.[7]

These left-wing gains were reversed when the federal government cracked down on socialists opposed to US involvement in World War I. To curb radical influence, many cities, like Richmond, made their elections nonpartisan and switched to the city manager form of government. The number of elected, full-time "strong mayors," whether socialist or not, was reduced. More city council members became part-time and limited "to setting general policies carried out by trained professionals."[8]

Similar preventive measures also kept Standard Oil in Richmond union-free for half a century. The first bid for bargaining rights occurred during World War I, when organized labor broadly made membership gains. However, as labor historian Harvey O'Connor observes, the newly chartered Local 38 of the Oil Workers International Union (OWIU) proved to be "no match for the most ruthless enemy of labor in California. In 1918, all its officers and outstanding members were fired."[9] Union sympathizers in the Richmond refinery were not able to regroup until World War II started.

One obstacle in the intervening years was Big Oil's skillful deployment of its nationwide Employee Representation Plan (ERP). This system of plant-level committees, which included hourly workers and supervisors, operated firmly under the control of management. As part of its "union substitution" strategy, the company introduced a pension plan, sickness benefits, and paid vacations; it sponsored parties, picnics, sports leagues, and social centers for its employees. When the Great Depression hit and other towns became destitute, "Standard Oil helped keep Richmond alive," one local admirer recalls. Refinery wages may have been cut, but "workers were still able to keep their homes and jobs in the area."[10]

New Deal labor legislation forced Big Oil to convert its workplace committees into employee associations, less obviously dominated by management. The Congress of Industrial Organizations (CIO) began its successful late-1930s drive for unionization of auto, steel, and other basic manufacturing industries. But the struggle for collective bargaining rights in Richmond took longer because from 1942 to 1950 Standard Oil continued to prop up its company union as a tame, in-house alternative to the CIO-affiliated OWIU.

In 1946, after a representation election setback two years earlier, the OWIU finally defeated the not-so-independent Independent Union of Petroleum Workers (IUPW) and a craft union competitor from the American Federation of Labor (AFL). The OWIU made important contract gains in Richmond but was then decertified locally after a statewide strike in 1948. That walkout by fourteen thousand refinery workers at Shell, Union Oil, Standard of California, Richfield, and Texaco did not go according to plan:

> Violence was provoked in the Los Angeles Harbor area and at Richmond. Injunctions began to rain down on the hapless strikers. Damage suits running to $28,000,000 were filed against OWIU and its locals. A hysterical press played up a back to work movement. The union ranks began to break. . . . The strike was settled on company terms and hundreds of OWIU's best members were victimized. . . . Union Oil slashed gaping holes in the Long Beach and Rodeo locals by farming out its maintenance work to an outside firm that made a backdoor agreement with the AFL.[11]

In Richmond, the results were disastrous. Standard Oil mobilized anti-union workers and a hostile local press, provoking picket-line scuffles that led to the firing of sixty-two union activists (about two-thirds of whom later won reinstatement). Richmond police used tear gas against strikers. The company refused to cooperate with OWIU members on an orderly shutdown of the refinery during the strike and withdrew recognition of their union. The National Labor Relations Board stepped in, unhelpfully, to hold a decertification vote sought by an AFL union rival of the OWIU. This opening was exploited by the non-striking IUPW, which won the election. After two years of difficult shop-floor rebuilding, the Oil Workers finally regained their lost bargaining rights, by the narrow margin of 955 to 904, in June 1950. "Once again," reports O'Connor, "the banner of industrial unionism waved over the most redoubtable fortress of open shoppery in California."

Unfortunately (and with lasting consequences for labor-management relations over the next sixty-five years), the Richmond refinery remained, technically speaking, an "open shop." Elsewhere in basic industry, by some point in the era after World War II, most national contracts negotiated by other CIO unions contained "union security" clauses. These obligated every union-represented employee to pay either membership dues or the equivalent in "agency fees" to help cover the cost of collective bargaining and individual representation. Standard Oil insisted that its employees remain free to quit the union and pay nothing for its services. To this day, when union leaders take independent and sometimes controversial positions on health and safety enforcement or environmental protection, refinery supervisors are able to quietly agitate among bargaining unit employees about getting out of the union that is "working against their interests."

Contracting out is management's other method of undermining workplace solidarity. The industry-preferred mix of directly hired workers and contract labor (even if unionized) makes it hard to maintain uniform standards for job training and safety. As one industrial union official explains, "Contractors can be working in one place one day, and then in another area the next. They get only a basic level of training to come into the refinery. Over the years, the companies have compensated for the attrition of [our] membership by backfilling with contractors. The level of training has obviously dropped off because of that."[12]

The OWIU was created because most refinery workers wanted strong wall-to-wall union organization, not the old craft union system of separate bargaining units for machinists, painters, pipefitters, electrical workers, and boilermakers. Big Oil's preference for farming out maintenance work has maintained that fragmentation and perpetuated company union influence. In modern-day refineries, this takes the form of conservative building trades unions, always eager to support Big Oil in politics and policymaking.

A TENUOUS EXISTENCE

Even with its world-class refinery, rail infrastructure, San Francisco Bay ferry connection, and deepwater port, Richmond never achieved anything close to Pittsburgh-like scale before World War II. It also remained a predominantly white working-class city. African Americans numbered less than three hundred when Richmond reached its prewar population peak of twenty-four thousand. According to Shirley Ann Wilson Moore, in her definitive history *To Place Our Deeds: The African American Community in Richmond, California, 1910–1963*, these black residents "lived a tenuous existence on the outer edges of the city's industrial vision, trapped at the bottom of its economic and social hierarchy. . . . While pre-war Richmond managed to avoid the race riots that plagued other American cities after World War I, Klan parades and minstrel shows reinforced the racial status quo."[13]

Richmond's prewar scale and racial status quo were both transformed between 1941 and 1945. With massive federal funding, California steel maker and dam builder Henry Kaiser hired thousands of workers from all over the country to build cargo ships in four newly constructed Richmond shipyards. For half a decade, this extraordinary industrial complex dwarfed even the Standard Oil refinery, which fueled the Kaiser-built vessels steaming off to war from the port of Richmond. The city was one of many World War II boomtowns, ballooning to a population of 133,000 within just a few years. By 1945, there were fifty-five defense-related plants in the Richmond area.

After Pearl Harbor and US entry into the war, Kaiser's mission was launching ships "faster than the enemy could sink them." His company revolutionized the labor process by breaking it down into many little pieces. Richmond's Liberty and Victory ships were assembled like Legos, using mass production techniques pioneered by Henry Ford in the auto industry. The Kaiser operation built 747 vessels in three years, eight months, with the help of equipment like a giant whirley crane brought down from the Grand Coulee Dam. The company's motto was "Ten down the ways in 31 days"; its fastest-built vessel took only four days, fourteen hours, and twenty minutes to complete, from the laying of its keel to launching into the bay.

In an era when group health coverage and on-site day care were virtually nonexistent, Kaiser became a pioneer. The Richmond shipyard's child development center later became a model for the federal government's Head Start program in the 1960s. Kaiser also created one of the first prepaid medical plans—funded by payroll deductions from Richmond shipyard workers—and built a field hospital in Richmond. In the postwar era, this innovative form of job-based medical insurance for workers and their families grew into the Kaiser Permanente health system, which now covers more than nine million patients in California and other states. Kaiser continues to brand itself, in the face of some union dissent, as the nation's most labor-friendly health maintenance organization.

Driven by wartime labor shortages, Henry Kaiser's best-known form of workplace social engineering—and the one that left a lasting mark on Richmond—was his hiring of African Americans for blue-collar jobs long restricted to white males. Kaiser recruiters targeted young African Americans eager to escape post-Depression hardship and Jim Crow constraints in Oklahoma, Arkansas, Texas, Louisiana, and Mississippi. The results of that affirmative action stood in sharp contrast to Standard Oil's employment record. The Richmond refinery's wartime workforce of three thousand initially included just nine African Americans. By 1944, after federal government prodding, its nonwhite head count rose to only 114.[14]

Betty Reid Soskin's family arrived in the East Bay from New Orleans more than a decade before the wave of southern black immigration encouraged by Kaiser. She became one of the thousands of African American workers who gained unprecedented job opportunities in Richmond during its wartime boom. Hired at age nineteen, she spent four years commuting from Oakland to a clerical job at the boilermakers' union, where she kept track of its huge influx of new dues-paying members.

Now ninety-four and a Richmond resident, Soskin still reports to work at the Rosie the Riveter WW II Home Front National Historical Park. The visitors' center there is located near the former shipyard site, between Marina Bay and Richmond harbor. Uniformed in a dark turtleneck, green shirt and slacks, and a vest with her gold name tag and badge, Soskin gives local history talks and leads Richmond tours. The nation's oldest full-time national-park ranger, she also sports a brown, broad-brimmed Smokey the Bear hat.

Although a federal employee since 2006, Soskin pulls no punches when it comes to "home front" history. She reminds her audiences that A. Philip Randolph, leader of the Brotherhood of Sleeping Car Porters, had to threaten a march on Washington to win a Roosevelt administration ban on racial discrimination in defense industry hiring. "The Double V campaign launched the modern civil rights movement," she points out, noting that her own wartime employer balked at accepting black members because it was "a Jim Crow union." In Richmond, African Americans were initially hired at Kaiser as "helpers and trainees," with black men finally gaining access to other shipyard jobs in 1943 and black women the following the year. Richmond's waterfront army of new welders was only fully integrated, out of necessity, in the final months of the war in 1944–45.

African Americans were required to pay full dues to the conservative AFL-affiliated International Brotherhood of Boilermakers. Based on race, they were denied voting rights, couldn't file grievances, and were consigned to the union auxiliary that employed Soskin. Nevertheless, as Shirley Ann Moore reports, their segregated Local A-36 served as a transitional vehicle to "union consciousness" for black workers with no prior labor movement experience. It became an "institution through which African American workers began to challenge workplace discrimination." Rank-and-file activists formed Shipyard Workers Against Discrimination (SWAD), which picketed the Boilermakers' Richmond office in 1943 to protest the union's failure to provide equal representation. SWAD was a forerunner to the Richmond branch of the NAACP, established a year later and soon its most active affiliate on the West Coast.

By the end of the war, 20 percent of the Richmond shipyard workforce of one hundred thousand was African American. At the Ford automotive assembly plant in Richmond, blacks represented a similar percentage of a new United Auto Workers bargaining unit. Prior to 1941, when Ford was still operating on a nonunion basis in Richmond, management had been even more hostile to minority hiring than Standard Oil. A sign posted outside had clearly stated: "No Mexicans or Black Workers Wanted."[15]

Throughout the war, no children of black workers were ever enrolled in Kaiser's child development center. Eighty percent of Richmond's black residents lived in hastily constructed public housing units that were racially segregated. After World War II, Soskin and her husband faced racial discrimination themselves when they bought a home in an all-white suburb east of Oakland. They received anonymous warnings and neighborhood hostility when they moved in, but they stuck it out. Soskin raised four children, got active in Democratic Party politics, and eventually became a Richmond field staffer for a California state legislator.

Thousands of other African Americans sought postwar acceptance in the very place they had been "invited to participate in making ships," as Richmond minister Alvin Bernstine describes their Kaiser recruitment. Members of Bernstine's family, originally from Louisiana, founded the Bethlehem Missionary Baptist Church, where Alvin serves as pastor today. As Bernstine recounts in his book *A Ministry That Saves Lives*, the congregation experienced phenomenal growth because of the massive immigration of southern blacks. These arrivals worked in the shipyard and other defense industries, started small businesses and new churches, and "always believed that Richmond and the Bay Area would see value in including them in the benefits of California living."[16]

But not everyone saw African Americans as "value added" to Richmond in the postwar era. As Lucretia Edwards, a longtime neighborhood leader recalled, "It was assumed by the pre-war original 'core community' that the shipyard workers would return to the far-flung states and towns from which they had come. But this, of course, did not happen. . . . The chaos of life in a town with a quadrupled population was compounded, post-war, by unemployment. . . . [M]any of the residents who came as shipyard workers had no feeling of participation in the life of the City. . . . They might experience strong emotional feelings of pride and commitment to the neighborhood in which they lived, but, for the city of Richmond, their feelings ranged from indifference to annoyance."[17]

Annoyance turned to anger when Richmond's fourteen thousand African Americans became victims of renewed housing and job discrimination and wholesale displacement efforts. By 1945, Richmond had the largest public housing program in the nation, with a population of seventy-three thousand.[18] Its federally funded projects became a major postwar battleground because of decisions made by the powerful Richmond Housing Authority (RHA). In the late 1940s and early 1950s, nonwhite public housing tenants were showered with eviction notices warning that their apartment buildings were about to be torn down. The RHA's demolition plans were protested by the local NAACP because they appeared clearly designed by Richmond's then all-white city leadership to reduce its African American population. Tenants responded by signing petitions and attending mass meetings, picketing the RHA, and organizing rent strikes, all of which slowed the process. Nevertheless, by 1953, all seventeen of the public housing projects near Richmond harbor had been dismantled.

Private housing options in the city were far more limited for blacks than whites, as navy veteran and American Legion post vice-commander Wilbur Gary discovered. He tried to move his wife, Borece, and their seven children from the Harbor Gate wartime housing project when it was scheduled for destruction in 1953. The new home he bought, through a black real estate agent, was located in Rollingwood, a subdivision of eight hundred single-family homes that had been occupied by white defense workers during the war. The family was greeted by neighbors who planted a white KKK-style cross on their lawn. The office window of their realtor was shattered by a brick. In order to "restore harmony to our community," the Rollingwood Improvement Association, a group of fellow homeowners, tried to buy the Garys out, offering them one thousand dollars more than their purchase price before they could even move in.

On the night of March 7, 1952, after the family did move in, a menacing crowd of four hundred white men and teenage boys gathered outside the Gary family's home to jeer, throw stones, and hurl racist insults at their new neighbors. They listened to the county sheriff read parts of a recent US Supreme Court decision outlawing restrictive covenants of the sort that white homeowners wrongly assumed would continue to protect Rollingwood from newcomers of the wrong color. They were similarly unmoved by the arrival of three white ministers who carried a US flag and a copy of the Constitution. The sheriff's department made no arrests and little effort to disperse the threatening crowd.

Fortunately, hundreds of Bay Area progressives, both black and white, mobilized and came to the scene that night, and for several nights thereafter, to defend the Gary family. Among the first to arrive were Jessica Mitford and Buddy Green, two left-wing activists from the East Bay branch of the Civil Rights Congress (CRC). According to Mitford, author of *The American Way of Death*, their quick consultation with the besieged family led to "a many-pronged approach: physical protection of the house, trade union resolutions demanding police protection, [and] leaflets to be drawn up by the CRC, and distributed throughout the Bay Area."[19] The NAACP mobilized its members as well. And soon even a few brave white neighbors began to welcome the family.[20]

Community and labor campaigners for the Garys also pressured the Richmond city council to ban segregation in local public housing. A special council session heard complaints about housing, joblessness, and other problems facing the city's African Americans. A contemporary survey of private businesses in Richmond showed that 30 percent refused to employ blacks at all; another 40 percent would only consider them for menial jobs.[21] Richmond's own exclusionary hiring practices came under fire too. At the time it had no nonwhite firefighters and only two black police officers.

A COMMUNITY FOR ALL?

African Americans became the majority of homeowners in Parchester Village, a four-hundred-unit development of single-family homes constructed in 1950 by Fred Parr, a white real estate developer. Now located within the Richmond city limits, this neighborhood was built in a then unincorporated area between the Standard Oil refinery and the old Giant Powder Company site. It was marketed as a "community for all Americans" but it was far from downtown and lacked public services. Few whites bought homes and moved in after they discovered it was racially mixed.

Even when African Americans could find better postwar housing, in a place like Parchester Village (where all the streets were named after prominent African American ministers and historical figures), further plant shutdowns put good union jobs beyond their reach. In the mid-1950s, Ford decided to relocate its Richmond production to a new plant in Milpitas, a San Jose suburb fifty miles away. As Richard Rothstein of the Economic Policy Institute writes: "The United Auto Workers negotiated an agreement with Ford permitting all Richmond workers to transfer, with their seniority rights intact. White workers were able to take advantage of this agreement, because inexpensive single-family home subdivisions were blossoming in the Milpitas area. Black workers, however, could not, because these subdivisions were open to whites only."[22] Community representatives urged Ford management in Detroit to address the housing needs of Richmond African Americans who might want to transfer. The company responded that "it was only interested in building automobiles" and "unconcerned with workers' housing problems."

Jobs and housing were still big civil rights issues when Martin Luther King Jr. spoke out against racial discrimination before a large crowd in the Richmond Auditorium in 1963. By the mid-sixties there was mounting racial tension at Richmond High School between black and white students. At the time, the latter still outnumbered the former by two to one. In March 1966, a school fight spilled out into the streets, resulting in rock-throwing and vandalism along Macdonald Avenue, as African American students headed home to their respective neighborhoods on the north and south sides of the city. "Emotions ran so high that Richmond's police chief issued an order to 'shoot all looters,' an action approved and defended by many citizens," according to Lillian Rubin, a UC-Berkeley sociologist and resident of the area.[23] A dusk to dawn curfew was imposed and additional police were mobilized and deployed from surrounding communities.

Forty Richmond religious leaders—including ministers, priests, and rabbis—urged law enforcement restraint. In an open letter, they called for greater sensitivity to "the underlying causes of lawlessness and tensions," which included African American exclusion from better housing, education, and employment. Two years later, however, in 1968, National Guard troops were deployed in Richmond during three days of rioting after a white reserve police officer shot and badly wounded an unarmed black fifteen-year-old. Retail outlets along Macdonald Avenue were the target of looting and fire-bombing. In its World War II heyday and even into the 1950s, the city's main thoroughfare had banks, restaurants, theaters, hotels, chain stores like Macy's and J. C. Penney, smaller shops, and a bowling alley. But what was left of Richmond's once-vibrant business district in the late 1960s never recovered from this second uprising and its aftermath.

Downtown businesses that reopened soon faced fatal competition from the city's shiny new Hilltop Mall. Built in the early 1970s on the site of a former Standard Oil storage tank farm, the mall offered chain store shopping far from the newly perceived dangers of downtown Richmond. Its one hundred acres lay in close proximity to new residential development along the corridor of Interstate 80, on the safe, secure, predominantly white outskirts of the city.[24] The project was sold to the city council and the Richmond Planning Commission as a big job creator. Both rejected a competing plan for downtown renewal favored by the Richmond Redevelopment Agency.

Chevron was positively "giddy over the opportunity to jump into the real estate game," planning at the time to build more than a thousand luxury housing units. "The idea," explained Chevron spokesman Robert Brooks, "is to have a self-contained community where people can live, work, and play without leaving Hilltop." For many residents, even Hilltop wasn't far enough away from downtown. Working-class whites left Richmond in growing numbers for more racially homogenous communities like San Pablo, El Sobrante, and Pinole. In November 1968, San Pablo gave Alabama governor George Wallace his greatest presidential-campaign support anywhere in California—21.7 percent of the vote. Support for Wallace in Pinole and El Sobrante wasn't far behind at 19.1 and 15.1 percent respectively.

RADICAL RICHMOND

While this political polarization was occurring, the same radical currents flowing through the rest of the Bay Area in the 1960s and 1970s also affected Richmond. The Bay Area Revolutionary Union (RU), a group created by students opposed to the Vietnam War, sent "cadre" to Richmond because its leader, the son of a prominent East Bay judge, much admired its "proletarian character." "When I was at Berkeley High," RU founder Bob Avakian recalls, "people would say, 'Richmond High! Even the white guys are tough over there.'" In his memoir *From Ike to Mao and Beyond*, Avakian describes how Richmond young people aiding the United Farm Workers "went down to the local Safeway, which was being boycotted by the union, and trashed it," resulting in "dozens of them being busted." In October 1969, RU members worked with local Black Panthers to organize a Richmond High School walkout timed to coincide with a national campus "moratorium" against the Vietnam War.

Avakian describes this "very militant demonstration" as "one of the high points of our work in Richmond." It did not lead to any local electoral engagement, however, a path to "state power" rejected by the RU as insufficiently revolutionary. The Richmond branch of the Black Panther Party for Self-Defense (BPP) had more indigenous roots and greater staying power. The BPP did its first local organizing in the spring of 1967, just six months after the party's founding in Oakland. The Panthers soon became nationally known for their public display of loaded weapons during a lobbying visit to the California State Capitol in Sacramento when Ronald Reagan was governor. The BPP delegation was protesting a bill that soon restricted open gun-toting, a dramatic form of street theater premiered in North Richmond in late April 1967.

Earlier that same month, North Richmond resident Denzil Dowell, a twenty-two-year-old construction worker, was fatally shot by a deputy sheriff while allegedly fleeing a burglary. In a sequence of events still familiar in major US cities nearly fifty years later, Dowell's death was quickly deemed "justifiable homicide" by the authorities. "I believe the police murdered my son," his mother told the Panthers. Seeing an opportunity to organize against police brutality, the Panthers called for a street rally at the corner of Third and Chesley in North Richmond. Fifteen BPP activists showed up in their signature black berets and leather jackets, armed with twelve-gauge shotguns, M1 rifles, and various sidearms.

In its prime, the BPP operated first in a church on Bissell Avenue and then out of a North Richmond home that functioned as a community center. There, twenty-five to forty-five kids were fed every day as part of the free breakfast program that was an organizational hallmark of the Panthers everywhere. Bobby Bowens, a new Panther recruit and recently returned military veteran, helped organize the free distribution of twenty-five hundred pairs of shoes to people in need. Panther volunteers did testing, door-to-door, for sickle cell anemia and hypertension. They also started a "liberation school" that held classes on Saturdays, because, as Panther Bill Jennings recalls, "African American history was just not taught in Contra Costa County public schools."[25]

In 1969, after heavy rain, much of North Richmond's one and a half square miles was badly flooded. Panther volunteers waded through its streets to help people stranded at home and on their front porches reach a Red Cross evacuation center. This latest misery, inflicted on an unincorporated residential area long neglected by local and county officials, illustrated why, in the Panthers' view, North Richmond needed to become an independent city. Neighborhood people would then be in "control of their own police force, their own school system, and they will have the power to tax the businesses in the area, like Standard Oil."[26] To this end, the party registered hundreds of new voters to insure that residents could sign petitions, vote on ballot measures, and serve on what would otherwise be all-white juries. In four cities—Richmond, Oakland, San Francisco, and Berkeley—the party gathered signatures to trigger a citywide vote on "community control of the police."

As BPP cofounder Bobby Seale described this plan forty-five years later, members of an elected civilian review board would investigate shootings by officers, reports of unnecessary force, and other misconduct allegations instead of leaving that task to the police themselves and county prosecutors. But only in Berkeley did this controversial plan even make it onto the ballot.[27] In Richmond, local Panther activity petered out, as the national organization splintered and fell victim to widespread police repression. Other black activists, like the late Fred Jackson—whose name now adorns North Richmond's main street—continued the work of advocating for the poor, the imprisoned, and those unfairly treated by the police.

To this day, North Richmond remains a troubled, crime-ridden, unincorporated neighborhood of thirty-seven hundred. It has no municipal voting rights and even less community control over the police than residents of Richmond (which also lacks the authority to run its own public schools or set property tax rates for Chevron). North Richmond law enforcement is still handled—with inadequate staffing and many unsolved homicides—by the county sheriff, based in Martinez, twenty miles away.[28]

In Richmond overall, "liberal coalition politics" emerged in the 1960s. This was shaped, according to Shirley Ann Moore, by "the optimism of the civil rights movement and a rising tide of Democratic voter registration." The city's white political establishment was challenged by George Livingston, a thirty-one-year-old shipyard worker and Richmond Planning Commission member, and lawyer George Carroll, a local NAACP leader. Both won city council seats, and in 1964, the council unanimously chose Carroll to be Richmond's mayor, the first black person to hold that office.

With Democrats controlling the city council after 1963 and Republicans on the run, it appeared, writes Moore, "that black Richmondites had finally won a place on the civic agenda and would now be in a position to shape it." In other cities with large minority populations, sixties social movements and subsequent community organizing led to what Pierre Clavel calls "progressive urban politics." Insurgent Democrats in Gary, Cleveland, Chicago, Hartford, and other cities challenged machine politicians. After they gained city hall influence, as Clavel describes in several books, "these cities experimented with radically new forms of participation, public enterprise, property regulation, service structure, and neighborhood involvement. Many of their programs had a populist tone reminiscent of the great democratizing movements around the turn of the century."[29]

This was not the political trajectory of Richmond, despite African Americans there achieving near majority status by 1980. By the turn of the century, Richmond did have a black mayor (and city manager) of its own, every department head in the city was black, and so was the city council majority. "But, unfortunately, it turned out to be a bust," one community leader told me.[30] A corporate-backed African American political machine, aligned with conservative, self-serving, and predominantly white police and firefighter unions, dominated city government. Cronyism, corruption, and bureaucratic incompetence became deeply entrenched and much intertwined. "The city was pretty much run by the business interests Chevron cultivated," says Tom Butt, a liberal reformer from Point Richmond first elected to the council in 1995. "That was the reality of it."

STRIKING BIG OIL AGAIN

After the strike setbacks of 1948, oil workers in Richmond and other refinery towns had to confront another reality—namely that their "industry had learned how to operate, at least to a partial extent, with the use of supervisors, contractors, and other non-union personnel."[31] Just setting up a picket line no longer meant that an oil refinery would be shut down. So, in 1969, the Richmond refinery union then known as Local 1-561 of the Oil, Chemical, and Atomic Workers (OCAW) tried a different approach when its members struck for a new contract.

Management responded, like it did twenty years before, by getting a court order that severely limited worker picketing. G. T. ("Jake") Jacobs, the elected leader of the local, issued a call for outside help from UC-Berkeley, San Francisco State, and other local campuses, an overture that was controversial with some fellow officers and members. Radical students from Berkeley and other Bay Area campuses trooped to Richmond to join oil worker picket lines. The national office of Students for a Democratic Society (SDS) expressed its solidarity by declaring a nationwide boycott of Standard Oil. The strikers were featured in publications like the *Guardian* and *New Left Notes*. Jacobs hailed this worker-student fraternization as "the dawning of a new era."

Four years later, OCAW's daring cultivation of new allies became the hallmark of its nationwide strike against Shell Oil. In January 1973, four thousand Shell workers walked out because their employer would not agree to workplace health and safety committees, newly created in the rest of the industry. With help from other unions and consumer organizations, the strikers called for a nationwide boycott of Shell products. Virtually all the nation's environmental groups backed the struggle, which generated much favorable publicity about the connection between worker and community exposure to the same refinery hazards.

Tony Mazzocchi, the visionary labor environmentalist who led the Shell strike, continued to promote this "blue-green alliance" in the 1980s and 1990s. Among OCAW-represented refinery workers, Mazzocchi recruited and trained a national network of health and safety coordinators. At Chevron, local union activists were encouraged to work, whenever possible, with the environmental justice movement, led in Richmond by the West County Toxics Coalition (WCTC). As Antonia Juhasz recounts in *The Tyranny of Oil*, lifelong resident Henry Clark helped form the WCTC in 1986. Its goal, Clark told her, was to "get Chevron to invest their profits in pollution prevention equipment and to reduce its impact on our community. There's asthma in our community, skin rashes, there's cancer, and this company makes a profit at our expense."[32]

In its public jousting with Chevron, the Toxics Coalition got the company to admit it would "like nothing better than massive buffer zones," as opposed to increasingly restive downwind neighbors in North Richmond, Parchester Village, and the Iron Triangle section of the city (so named for its rail lines on three sides). But refinery spokesperson Hal Holt was fatalistic about the possibility of improving "process safety," as it is called today. "We're working in an industry that has a lot of machinery, a lot of people," he explained. "Occasionally, machines break down, and occasionally people make mistakes."[33]

In 1988, Henry Clark ran for Chevron's board of directors at a shareholders meeting in San Francisco. Clark's campaign enabled him to press WCTW's demand for direct negotiations between the company and the community on health and safety issues in Richmond.[34] "We don't negotiate with community groups," Holt responded. "That's not what we do. There are duly constituted agencies that represent the public, and that's who we deal with."[35]

Over the years, those "duly constituted agencies" had their hands full at Chevron in Richmond. From 1989 to 1995, Juhasz notes, "there were more than three hundred reported accidents at the refinery, including major fires, spills, leaks, explosions, toxic gas releases, flaring, and air contamination." In her muckraking account of Big Oil misbehavior, Juhasz also describes several local mishaps that gave our August 2012 fire the feeling of déjà vu all over again. In March 1999, a leaking valve installed more than thirty years before ignited a massive explosion, releasing a huge plume of sulfur dioxide smoke.

Ten thousand residents were told to remain inside for several hours, while those in the closest neighborhoods were evacuated. A column of thick, acrid, foul-smelling smoke rose high in the air, cloaked the refinery and then began to drift slowly to the southeast. . . . Hundreds of people flooded local hospitals complaining of breathing difficulties and vomiting.[36]

Eight years later, in January 2007, the refinery erupted again with a boom that could be heard and flames that could be seen all the way across the bay in San Francisco. The cause this time was a leaking corroded pipe that, investigators later found, should have been replaced a decade earlier. Two workers were injured and "the five alarm fire burned for nine hours. . . . Almost three thousand people in nearby neighborhoods received phone calls instructing them to stay inside with their doors and windows shut to avoid breathing the toxic fumes."[37]

After its very similar August 2012 event, Chevron was clearly on the defensive, dealing with multiple investigative agencies, pesky reporters, and angry neighbors. Its past Clean Air and Environmental Protection Act violations and troubling Cal-OSHA inspection results added up to quite a record of California recidivism. In Richmond alone, previous fires and explosions had resulted in $877,000 worth of penalties for "willfully failing to provide protective equipment for employees," eight of whom were injured, along with local firefighters. Between 1988 and 1999, the company paid $2.6 million to settle litigation over toxic emissions or wastewater releases, such as its practice of bypassing the Richmond refinery's wastewater treatment system and dumping directly into San Pablo Bay, a practice long protested by Greenpeace.

Chevron's oil-drilling misbehavior in the Santa Barbara Channel resulted in an $8 million fine and pleas of guilty to criminal and civil charges in 1992. A year later it was time to plead no contest and pay a $550,000 fine for an oil spill off El Segundo. Four years after that, safety violations on its offshore drilling platform near Ventura cost the company $1.1 million to settle. In 2000, back in El Segundo, offshore loading operations in violation of the Clean Air Act were settled for $7 million. Oh, and then there was the 2001 settlement of a lawsuit over groundwater contamination in

California and nineteen other states. That one cost Chevron and its competitors $422 million. Chevron refineries in Colorado, Pennsylvania, and New Jersey had a rap sheet similar to the company's California facilities.[38]

The 2012 accident investigation conducted by the US Chemical Safety Board revealed that Chevron engineers in Richmond had recommended repair work on the corroded pipe at fault—more than a decade earlier. When the pipe burst after being prodded, the resulting vapor cloud reached an ignition source almost immediately, creating a huge fireball followed by a thousand-foot column of toxic smoke and gas. "This was a near-miss that was totally preventable," said Ron Espinoza, an official of the United Steel Workers, which now represents Richmond refinery workers after absorbing the OCAW in 2005. "It was also inevitable, given the way these companies are running the refineries. They haven't been doing preventive maintenance, and it's getting more and more dangerous."[39]

I asked one refinery safety expert, who came to Richmond with the US Chemical Safety Board, why Chevron deferred needed maintenance work for so long. He believed the same type of accident could have occurred at any number of other refineries locally or nationally. "The culture of the industry is very cowboy, very macho," he explained. "The oil industry is arrogant, insular, and doesn't learn from other sectors. Upper management and even the safety professionals in an oil refinery are very production-oriented and know the least about refinery safety." Mike Smith, a Richmond refinery worker now employed by United Steelworkers (USW) Local 5 agrees: "The industry's record pretty much sums it up. These so-called accidents are not accidents at all. They're what happens when an industry doesn't pay attention to safety."

The biggest price that Chevron paid for the 2012 fire was its own repair and lost production costs of $5.3 million and $900 million respectively. California's Division of Occupational Health and Safety (Cal/OSHA) cited the company for eleven "willful" violations and proposed its largest fine ever—nearly $1 million. Chevron pleaded "no contest" to six criminal charges filed by state and local prosecutors and agreed to pay $2 million in fines and restitution. (By one estimate, these financial penalties equaled five minutes' worth of the company's total operating revenue at the time.)[40] Chevron was also placed on probation for three and a half years. While in that status, the company promised to inspect its piping system for other signs of corrosion, develop new pipe leak and emergency response training materials, and provide periodic reports on its implementation of these and other safety steps.

Ten months after its safety lapse, Chevron named a new general manager for the Richmond refinery. Chemical engineer and twenty-seven-year company man Kory Judd embarked on a local goodwill tour, which included a stop at the Point Richmond Neighborhood Council. Judd appeared before us with buzz-cut hair, an open-necked blue shirt, trendy leather jacket, and a folksy manner. He had a corporate PR person at his side. "We have to appreciate some of the issues and concerns the city and community have raised," Judd acknowledged. Since the 2012 accident, the company had "changed the way that we do maintenance and inspections," he assured us. In addition, Chevron had "changed protocol around responses to leaks" and was about to install new and improved air quality monitoring devices that would further protect the community.

In response to an audience question about Chevron's current or future use of crude from Canadian tar sands, transported to Richmond by rail, Judd denied that the company had any plans to unload its raw material from anything but tankers. "We've got a nice deepwater wharf," he explained, referring to the 4,200-foot East Bay landmark in front of our house. According to Judd, Chevron just wanted to "make good products and be a good neighbor." But, he emphasized, the company could not "add value to the city of Richmond" without making a "reasonable profit."

Reasonable or otherwise, Chevron's estimated Richmond profits were, at the time, about $2 billion a year. With that healthy bottom line in mind, the city council voted in late July 2013 to seek what some activists hoped would be hundreds of millions of dollars in fire-related compensation. Chevron had already reported spending millions to reimburse local hospitals for their emergency care and satisfy some claims filed by twenty-four thousand individuals affected by the fire. However, when the city also tried to negotiate a settlement, covering its claimed losses, the company's best offer never topped $10 million.

Even city councilors friendly to Chevron found this to be on the low side. So in a rare unanimous vote the council authorized hiring a high-powered personal injury firm to pursue environmental justice before a judge and jury in Contra Costa County Superior Court. Richmond's damage suit accused Chevron of "years of neglect, lax oversight, and corporate indifference to necessary safety inspection and repairs" in a facility generating $20 billion in annual revenue and 10 percent of the company's overall earnings in 2013.

THE CASE OF ECUADOR

Unfortunately, if Ecuador's courtroom battles with Big Oil are any guide, it may be quite a while before Richmond's case is resolved. Ecuadorans filed their own pesky lawsuit against Chevron in 2003 and it has since become the *Jarndyce v. Jarndyce* of global environmental litigation. The plaintiffs' claim dates back to the 1970s and 1980s, when Ecuador's Lago Agrio oil field was being exploited, under a friendly government, by Texaco, a US firm later acquired by Chevron. In the 1990s, Texaco agreed to pay $40 million to clean up the mess it made by dumping toxic waste in the Amazon rain forest. In 1998, the Ecuadoran government agreed that Texaco should be absolved of any further financial responsibility.

The indigenous people directly affected disagreed and continued to seek further compensation for their damaged flora, fauna, and water sources. Chevron has vigorously contested their class action claim, arguing that it's not liable for what Texaco did. An Ecuadoran trial court initially granted the Lago Agrio plaintiffs $8.6 billion in damages for their lost crops, farm animals, and oil-related health problems, including increased local cancer rates. On appeal, this award was boosted to $19 billion, a decision then contested by the company before the Ecuadoran National Court of Justice, the country's highest court, which scaled the damages back to $9.5 billion.

Meanwhile, the plaintiffs sought to collect their court judgment in other countries where Chevron still operates—such as Brazil, Argentina, and Canada. In September 2015, the Supreme Court of Canada upheld an appellate court ruling in Ontario permitting the Ecuadorans to proceed with their suit to seize Chevron assets in Canada to satisfy the 2011 judgment, as amended. The company's defense in Canada is likely to track the arguments made in a countersuit filed in the United States under the Racketeer Influenced and Corrupt Organizations (RICO) statute, a federal law that has been used against organized crime groups.

In that case, Chevron claimed that the original verdict in Ecuador was the product of "coercion, bribery, money laundering, and other misconduct." The federal judge presiding ruled that Steven Donziger, the brave public interest lawyer representing the people of Lago Agrio, used fraudulent and "corrupt means" to win his case. The company's top lawyer described the court's sanctioning of Donziger as "vindication of what we have been saying all along"—namely that all the earlier litigation, favoring the plaintiffs, was "a travesty of justice."

Chevron planned to use the RICO case ruling, upheld on appeal, to shield itself from further overseas collection efforts, in Canada or anywhere else. In a 2015 interview, Donziger, with little exaggeration, accused Chevron of conducting "the most well-funded corporate retaliation campaign in the history of human rights litigation." By his estimate, the company "has spent at least $2 billion on 60 law firms, 2,000 lawyers, 200 private investigators, dozens of lobbyists, and at least eight different public-relations firms."[41]

Richmond's own lawsuit was filed on the first anniversary of the 2012 fire, a day before the biggest refinery-related protest in the city's history. The rock stars of that event were Mayor McLaughlin, from the Richmond Progressive Alliance (RPA), and Vermont visitor Bill McKibben, founder of 350.org, the national environmental group that cosponsored the demonstration with the RPA. In her speech to a crowd of 2,500, McLaughlin demanded that Chevron develop "a new culture of safety" while reducing emissions, saying that "future generations have the right to live and breathe on a planet that's sustainable." McKibben looked up at the bright sky over Point Richmond and wryly observed that we were experiencing "a solar spill." The day will come, he predicted, when all that sun won't go to waste and Chevron will either be "an energy company that works on the sun and the wind or they will go out of business."

As Richmond police arrested two hundred members of the crowd who peacefully blocked the main entrance to Chevron, some protestors passed around copies of an unusual full-page ad in the weekend edition of the *Contra Costa Times*, Richmond's newspaper. It was paid for by the Ecuadoran government and expressed solidarity "with the people of Richmond on their day of protest about the disaster and its aftermath." Said the ad: "In the fight against Chevron, the people of Ecuador and the people of Richmond can deploy the most devastating weapon ever invented . . . the truth."

TWO

THE GREENING OF CITY HALL

LATE-TWENTIETH-CENTURY RICHMOND mirrored the postindustrial desola-
tion of former manufacturing centers in the Rust Belt. Once prosperous
and bustling, the city now suffered from high levels of unemployment,
poverty, family disintegration, street crime, and violence. In neighborhoods where residential housing and industrial activity once coexisted,
factory owners packed up and fled, just like local retailers did after the
downtown disturbances of the 1960s. Left behind were vacant lots and
abandoned buildings, brownfields were scattered all over town, each representing a loss of blue-collar jobs.

More than a dozen former factory sites, often lacking warning signs
and protective fencing, were not just eyesores. Due to past chemical manufacturing or storage, they were "toxic hot spots" ending up on the Environmental Protection Agency Superfund cleanup list. On Point Isabel,
just south of the former Kaiser shipyard, tens of thousands of old battery
casings lay buried beneath a shoreline park, leaching lead and other poi-
sons into a swimming beach and nearby fishing spots.

In North Richmond, liquid polychlorinated biphenyls (PCBs) from
discarded utility company equipment tainted local groundwater, thanks
to past dumping by Fass Metals. The processing and shipping of DDT
by United Heckathorn left marine sediment in Richmond harbor badly
contaminated. Stauffer Chemical, another maker of pesticides and fertil-
izers, created a residual toxic stew so hard to remediate that its former site

remains fenced off, overgrown with weeds, and undeveloped nearly two decades after production ceased there.[1] In the Blair Landfill, a shoreline parcel near the Stauffer site, radioactive material was discovered in the soil, a likely legacy of solid uranium being melted for years by Stauffer Metals, a sister company.

Deindustrialization left human wreckage behind as well. By the early 1980s, Richmond was suffering from a major crack epidemic. Assault rifles replaced handguns as the weapon of choice for drug dealers seeking to expand or simply defend their local market share. Adding to the city's illegal gun trafficking were three dozen federally licensed firearms dealers who did business from private homes within the city. Homicides increased from ten to twenty per year in the 1960s to an annual death toll of fifty in the 1980s, finally peaking at sixty-two killings in 1991, almost all drug- and gang-related.

Meanwhile, Richmond's African American community was decimated from within by the highest rate of AIDs transmission in the Bay Area, through heterosexual sex and drug use. In search of personal security, better housing and schools, or improved job prospects, middle-class blacks joined the trajectory of Richmond's earlier white flight. People moved their families to safer communities such as Vallejo, Antioch, Fairfield, or even far-off Tracy. Left behind, in disproportionate numbers, were Richmond residents one activist described as "low-income, under-educated, and criminal-justice involved."

During this troubled era, Richmond city hall was no beacon of hope. Its deepening dysfunction was due in part to Darrell Reese, a Richmond fire captain and longtime leader of Fire Fighters Local 188. Reese, a shady backroom patron of local African American politicians, "raised plantation politics to an art form," according to John Gioia, a Richmond native who is now a Contra Costa County supervisor.

City councilors depended on Reese for campaign funding and endorsements. In return, Richmond's public safety unions, including Reese's, got favored city hall treatment at the bargaining table, sometimes to the detriment of other union-represented city workers. Reese was a white Republican who lived in suburban Rodeo. Yet his stock in trade—as a part-time political consultant, fixer, bagman, and lobbyist for developers—was election year appeals to "save the black seats on the council." Meanwhile, Reese's own firefighters' local, like the Richmond Police Officers Association (RPOA), still had few nonwhite members.

Through his union political action committee, Reese wielded enough influence to pick Richmond city managers. In 1993, he helped install Floyd Johnson, who served four years before being fired for shoddy budgeting, dwindling city reserve funds, and other administrative problems. With backing from Reese, Richmond's director of employment and training, Isiah Turner, then replaced Johnson, with disastrous consequences. Turner was hired despite an employment history that included a forced resignation in Washington State after an auditor discovered his misuse of $22,000 in public funds. On Turner's watch, Richmond city finances deteriorated further, to the point of near bankruptcy.

After budget shortfalls and layoffs in 2003, Turner suddenly retired for "health reasons," followed out the door by his finance director. Just a few months later, Richmond discovered that it faced a $35 million budget deficit, which the recently departed city manager had managed to conceal. California state auditors accused Turner of "deliberately misrepresenting both the size of the city's reserves and its annual expenses."[2] The city's full-blown fiscal meltdown led to two hundred layoffs and budget cuts, which closed libraries, parks, some fire stations, and senior services.

In many places, such a long-brewing mess, born of cronyism, corruption, and incompetence, would have deepened popular cynicism about city government. In Richmond, instead, an "unlikely group of Greens, Latinos, progressive Democrats, African Americans, and free spirits" formed a "new Richmond political coalition united over ideals rather than power and personalities," as then city councilor Tom Butt described this favorable development. The group included residents committed to "civil rights, the environment, education, open government, and quality of life issues," people who wanted to challenge old guard politicians when five city council seats were up for grabs in 2004.

Spearheading this effort was fifty-three-year-old Juan Reardon, a burly, gray-bearded immigrant from Argentina. Reardon's youthful involvement in left-wing politics had led to his exile abroad after a mid-1970s military coup in his homeland. In the late 1980s, he immigrated to the

United States and got a graduate degree in epidemiology and biostatistics at UC-Berkeley. Reardon first became familiar with local problems while doing data collection during Richmond's drug-related HIV-AIDs epidemic. He moved to the city in 1999, helped raise funds and equipment for Cuban hospitals, and lobbied to create an official sister-city relationship between Richmond and Regla, a refinery town near Havana. During Ralph Nader's presidential campaign in 2000, Reardon joined the California Green Party and pulled together some of its most active local members.

Calling themselves the Richmond Alliance for Green Public Power and Environmental Justice, Reardon's group opposed construction of a municipal power plant next to the Chevron refinery. Proponents claimed that this oil-fueled facility would meet all of the city's own electricity needs, as well as generate millions in new revenue when the surplus power was sold to customers elsewhere via Pacific Gas & Electric. The project was killed after the Greens turned out surprisingly large crowds to speak and protest against the additional pollution it would create. They urged the city to explore alternative energy solutions instead. Working with existing environmental groups, like the West County Toxics Coalition, their alliance also pushed Richmond to adopt a stronger industrial safety ordinance to reduce the risk of refinery fires and explosions or chemical spills.

Reardon and his fellow activists launched a yearlong campaign against police harassment of homeless people after the city council banned sleeping and camping in public places. They supported that part of Richmond's rapidly growing Latino population accused of vagrancy when seeking work on the sidewalk outside our local Home Depot outlet. To give these workers a collective voice, Reardon helped them create the Richmond–El Cerrito Day Laborers Association. Its protest activity led to an unusual ten-point agreement between the association and the Richmond Police Department (RPD). In writing, the RPD agreed to treat day laborers more politely, respect their right to be on public property, and pursue their complaints about wage theft.

Organizing around such issues "showed what a little group of people could accomplish," Reardon recalls today. But members of the group, soon to be rebranded the Richmond Progressive Alliance, realized they needed more allies, like liberal Democrat Tom Butt, within local government. That required getting themselves elected to office or appointed to city positions where they could directly affect policymaking.

Given Richmond's financial distress and city hall dysfunction, the municipal voting scheduled for November 2004 created a timely opening. RPA founders originally hoped to field a full five-candidate slate for the council that would reflect the city's racial and ethnic diversity. Andres Soto, a graduate of Richmond High School and nearby Contra Costa Community College, had deep roots in the community and was ready to run, particularly on the issue of police misconduct.

In 2002 Soto and his two sons were among several dozen Latinos arrested during Richmond's Cinco de Mayo festival. Soto, a city and later county employee, who once contemplated a career in law enforcement, questioned the RPD's heavy-handed dispersal of a celebratory crowd. As a result, he was roughed up, pepper-sprayed, and charged with resisting arrest and assaulting a police officer. A Latino community mobilization, orchestrated by Soto, led to a Richmond Police Commission finding that excessive force was used. A commission investigator recommended that one officer responsible be fired. On the day of his own trial, all charges against Soto were dropped.

Other potential candidates, from the black community, were less eager to be tethered to a common political platform developed by local radicals. Tony Thurmond, a liberal Democrat who now represents Richmond in the California Assembly, met with RPA founders and sought their endorsement of his planned 2004 council race. However, in return for that support, he wasn't willing to spurn corporate donations—required, then and now, of all RPA-backed candidates.[3]

Soto's only RPA running mate ended up being a newcomer to Richmond, a fifty-two-year-old Chicago native named Gayle McLaughlin. Before relocating to California in 2000, McLaughlin had been active in the Central America solidarity movement and supported Jesse Jackson's Rainbow PUSH Coalition. The daughter of a union carpenter, she studied psychology in college and worked after graduation as a postal clerk, teacher, and caregiver for disabled children and the elderly. As a member of the Young Socialist Alliance, she got to know Peter Camejo, then a leader of its parent organization, the Socialist Workers Party. Camejo later joined the California Green Party and twice ran as its candidate for governor.

In California, McLaughlin joined the Greens too and met fellow members like Juan Reardon. As a movement person, she had never considered running for office herself. However, she had decided, after arriving in Richmond, "that it was time to put down roots and get involved in local work." Both Camejo and Reardon encouraged her to run for city council. Reardon agreed to serve as her campaign manager, which required becoming a self-taught expert on the mechanics of local campaigning.

Soto and McLaughlin kicked off their joint campaign with public forums featuring speakers from out of town. Matt Gonzalez, a Green Party member on the San Francisco board of supervisors who had just lost a close race for mayor, came to Richmond, as did US congressman Dennis Kucinich, then campaigning for the Democratic presidential nomination. Six hundred people turned out to hear speeches by Kucinich, McLaughlin, Soto, and an up-and-coming Bay Area environmental justice campaigner named Van Jones. McLaughlin challenged the crowd to "begin right here and now to build a progressive future for our polluted, our corrupted, and our life-threatened city."

To reinforce McLaughlin and Soto's message that "another Richmond is possible," the RPA convened a first-ever "People's Convention." Three hundred residents set local policy goals that included repealing the city's anti-homeless ordinance, taxing Chevron more heavily and punishing its "industrial pollution events," strengthening police oversight by the community, fighting for affordable housing and public access to Richmond's shoreline, enacting rent control and "just-cause" eviction protection, establishing a living wage, and fully "investigating the current city budget crises and the governmental mismanagement" responsible for it.

Soto's campaign for "new leadership, new ideas, and new ethics" garnered far broader labor and political support than the lesser-known McLaughlin. A registered Democrat, he was endorsed by the Contra Costa County labor and building trades councils, the county Democratic Party, and local Democratic officials. Both RPA candidates were backed by ACORN, the community organization later known locally as ACCE (the Alliance of Californians for Community Empowerment), and the Service

Employees International Union (SEIU) local that represents Richmond city employees.

Soto's $175,000 settlement from a lawsuit over his Cinco de Mayo mistreatment made him persona non grata with the Richmond Police Officers Association (RPOA) and Fire Fighters Local 188. Soto regarded both as "attack dogs for corporate power," and they responded in kind. Their Keep Richmond Safe Committee spent $270,000 on advertising for its favored candidates and hit pieces aimed at Soto.

Both Soto and McLaughlin were also heavily outspent by Chevron. McLaughlin's low-budget, grassroots campaign had so little money for glossy mailers that she was not taken seriously by those smearing Soto and thus largely ignored. Yet, in a field of fifteen candidates, she placed third among the five winners, while Soto, after being severely attacked as a dangerous radical, finished sixth. As a new city councilor, McLaughlin proceeded to confound the expectations of Richmond insiders "who saw her as an ideologue ill-suited for the tedious work that elective office requires."[4]

OUTSIDER ON THE COUNCIL

After taking office in January 2005, McLaughlin championed new park projects and faster, safer cleanup of Richmond's toxic sites. On refinery-related issues, McLaughlin aided a promising but short-lived "Sunshine Alliance," which united building trades unions (that later became RPA critics) and local environmental groups. All opposed Richmond's practice of allowing Chevron to ensure its own compliance with city codes and permitting requirements through "self-inspection." Over company objections, the city council voted to make refinery construction work subject to regular city permits, fees, and independent certification—regulatory oversight that also had the effect of curbing the company's use of nonunion contractors.

McLaughlin backed a successful campaign by Communities for a Better Environment (CBE) to get the Bay Area Air Quality Management District to adopt a first-in-the-nation flare control regulation, applying to Chevron and four other nearby refineries. And, much to Chevron's additional chagrin, McLaughlin criticized Big Oil's privileged treatment as a utility user, joining Tom Butt's activism on this issue, which had begun before he joined the council in 1995.

While other Richmond residents paid, on average, about 10 percent of their tax bill for utility services, the refinery's liability was capped at $14 million a year, based on a very favorable flat rate formula. With support from some city councilors, the company balked at releasing information about its actual energy use, claiming that "business confidentiality" prevented the city from accessing such records. This bolstered McLaughlin's case for repealing the utility users' tax cap in order to generate revenue for a greatly expanded jobs program for Richmond youth.

Irma Anderson, an African American public health nurse then serving as Richmond's mayor, was not supportive of McLaughlin's ideas. The widow of a former city council member and mayor, Anderson enjoyed the support of the local industry council, the Richmond Chamber of Commerce—then headed by Chevron executive Jim Brumfield—and Chevron itself. She was dismissive of Richmond Greens, calling them "a special interest group."

To accomplish more on the council, McLaughlin challenged Mayor Anderson when she was up for reelection in 2006, creating a three-way race that included a second black candidate, former Richmond councilor Gary Bell. The incumbent collected a string of endorsements from California Democratic Party heavyweights, like US senator Dianne Feinstein and then state treasurer Phil Angelides. She raised four times more money from her business backers than McLaughlin did from her small individual donors and campaign volunteers. Chevron, the chamber, and the industry council also helped Anderson by running ads against McLaughlin criticizing her support for Measure T, a tax proposal on the November 2006 ballot.

If adopted, Measure T would have raised $10 million by imposing a manufacturers' tax on Chevron. Unfortunately, the poorly drafted measure would also have closed a local tax loophole benefiting small landlords, so Measure T foes were able to claim that its passage would trigger rent increases. Voters were bombarded with mailings declaring that "Gayle Should Fail with Her Terrible T." Measure T did fail, but McLaughlin did not. Instead she shocked and amazed the local political establishment—and surprised herself—by winning the mayoral race by 279 votes.

McLaughlin's upset victory in 2006 made Richmond the largest city in the United States with a Green mayor. Despite Chevron's win on Measure T, McLaughlin's RPA-backed campaign raised public awareness about Big Oil's long history of trying to substitute corporate philanthropy—voluntary donations to schools, libraries, and local nonprofits—for tax revenue that would be greater, if the company paid its fair share in one form or another. Future tax fights would not end so favorably for the refinery.

USING THE BULLY PULPIT

Under Richmond's city charter, the disparity between the authority of the city manager and the mayor is pretty clear. The latter is paid far less than the former—in Richmond's case, five or six times less. The city manager directs a city workforce of about seven hundred today, while the mayor's office has a staff of only two or three people. The mayor casts a single vote on the city council, presides over its meetings, and appoints, subject to council approval, members of local boards and commissions. But the mayor can also "develop and inform City residents of policies and programs which he or she believes are necessary for the welfare of the City," an agenda-setting role that Gayle McLaughlin played to the hilt during her eight years in office.

McLaughlin turned what had been a part-time job with a $45,000 salary—less than a city janitor's pay—into a bully pulpit for reform causes. In a series of battles that pitted fossil fuel defenders against local critics, the new mayor confronted industrial hazards arising from both oil refining and local railroad operations. She and her council allies waged major fights over development issues, home loan foreclosure relief, and an innovative public health initiative to curb soda consumption. Under McLaughlin, Richmond quickly became a more welcoming place for immigrants and, unlike most US cities during the same period, managed to improve relations between police and the community.

One of McLaughlin's first official appearances as mayor set the tone for her administration. In January 2007 she addressed an emergency meeting of one thousand Richmond residents protesting local raids by federal Immigration and Customs Enforcement (ICE) agents. These neighborhood sweeps, leading to deportation and detention of some undocumented

workers, made other immigrants in the community fearful of contacting
the police to report crimes. City hall began work on the creation of a mul-
tiyear municipal ID card for anyone living in Richmond who did not have
picture identification. Unveiled in 2014, this card can be used in dealings
with the police or other accessing of public services.[5]

McLaughlin helped strengthen grassroots organizing in the city by
seeding an array of city commissions, boards, and committees with like-
minded activists rarely considered for such roles in the past. Three prominent RPA members she named to the Planning or Human Rights
Commissions—Jovanka Beckles, Marilyn Langlois, and Eduardo Martinez—later ran for city council based in part on their records as city com-
missioners. Along with community advocate Nicole Valentino and union
activist Jeff Shoji, Langlois also served on the mayor's full-time city hall
staff. Through its energetic outreach work, the McLaughlin administration built ongoing relationships with a wide range of community groups
and tried to strengthen ties between city hall and Richmond's forty neighborhood councils.

One of the most important actions that McLaughlin and council allies
like Tom Butt took, even before she became mayor, was hiring Bill Lindsay as city manager. Lindsay arrived in Richmond two years after its near
bankruptcy, taking over from a former Contra Costa County adminis-
trator hired to manage the city on an interim basis. Lindsay's background
and appearance was quite different from that of the Richmond activists in
McLaughlin's kitchen cabinet. A gray-haired Yale graduate, he dresses in
such neatly pressed, buttoned-down fashion that he could easily pass for a
New England prep school headmaster or classics teacher. Before coming
to Richmond, he served as city manager of Orinda, an upscale East Bay
bedroom community not far from Walnut Creek, where he was raised.
No less than McLaughlin, however, Lindsay believed that "new ideas
can percolate up from cities" when municipal government becomes a
policy innovator. He shared Richmond progressives' strong commitment
to making city government more accountable and transparent. And, pro-
ceeding in his own brisk, business-like fashion, he was no less willing to
push the envelope when gang violence or mortgage foreclosures required
unusual policy initiatives.

Lindsay was viewed with much initial suspicion. "People just thought that Richmond would gobble me up," he told me. The city government Lindsay inherited was "viewed as a failed organization. There were not a lot of high expectations for what it could do." Among the challenges the new city manager faced was ensuring sufficient funding for public safety (now 45 percent of Richmond's general fund budget), developing better departmental leadership, and repairing municipal labor relations. During Richmond's 2004 layoffs, "people found out in the newspaper whether they were losing their jobs," he recalled. "So there was a complete lack of trust." Over time the new city manager was able to develop what he describes as "good relationships with our unions." During the always challenging process of balancing annual budgets, "they have come to the table and said, 'We want to be part of the solution.'"

In addition to better communication within the city workforce—now several hundred employees smaller than when Lindsay arrived—one hallmark of his tenure is the remarkable amount of information flowing from his office to the community. The city manager sends a weekly report, illustrated with charts, graphs, and photographs, to several thousand Richmond residents who have signed up to be on his e-mail list. He provides information for people trying to access city programs and services of all kinds, detailed updates on the work of various municipal agencies and departments, and the activities of local nonprofits serving the community.[6]

Lindsay also oversaw the drafting of "Richmond General Plan 2030." This sweeping policy document now provides guidance in the area of "land use, economic development, transportation, open space conversion, and arts and culture." In rather singular fashion, Richmond's general plan also prioritizes "community health and wellness—conditions that previous city administrators and elected officials had neglected."[7]

When Lindsay was hired, others in city hall were still bemoaning Richmond's generally unfavorable media coverage. The city had a reputation for crime, violence, and political dysfunction that was hard to shake. New business was difficult to attract and even some BART users avoided its downtown Richmond station. Lindsay's response was "If you don't want horrible press, do good work. If you get things done, you'll get good press." Over the next decade (while not always entirely avoiding controversy himself) Richmond's manager followed his own advice. As city hall administration and conditions in the city steadily improved, Richmond's turnaround became widely hailed as "one of the most remarkable stories in the Bay Area."[8]

The list of civic accomplishments under McLaughlin and Lindsay would have been much shorter if the city council majority had remained beholden to past benefactors. Jeff Ritterman, the second RPA member elected to the council, was definitely not a favorite of Richmond's corporate donor class. Then chief of cardiology at Kaiser's Richmond Medical Center, Ritterman is a former sixties radical, who sports a graying ponytail. He belonged to Physicians for Social Responsibility and aided Central American solidarity campaigns in the 1980s.

When Ritterman announced his council candidacy in 2008, he had just helped secure thousands of signatures for another ballot initiative to raise taxes on Chevron. Both Chevron and the Richmond Chamber of Commerce spent heavily to defeat this local utility tax proposal, claiming it would hurt small business. Nevertheless, 54 percent of Richmond voters favored the RPA-backed measure. In a council race more competitive than usual (because the body was being downsized from nine to seven members), Ritterman emerged as a winner.

The city's legal and political skirmishing with Chevron over taxes continued for another two years before a settlement was reached. The company agreed to make a graduated payment to Richmond totaling $114 million in return for a fifteen-year moratorium on any new local taxes.[9] Meanwhile, McLaughlin and the RPA helped keep the pressure on county tax assessors during a protracted fight triggered by Contra Costa County's 2004 decision to reassess the value of Chevron property in Richmond. The company appealed the resulting tax bills three times, leading in one case to a $23 million rebate. In late 2013, Chevron finally settled its property tax disputes, based on the refinery's 2012 assessed value of $3.28 billion.

By 2014, that meant the company was paying about $50 million in property taxes to Contra Costa County, with Richmond, its second largest city, receiving less than one-third of that amount. "Is $3.28 billion a 'fair' assessment?" asked RPA activist Jeff Kilbreth, who was one of many who lobbied the county for a better deal. According to Kilbreth, Chevron "is still going to pay property taxes based on roughly 1/3 of the Richmond refinery's true value."[10] But, he notes, that unfair result is the product of California's nearly forty-year-old cap on taxation of commercial real estate that doesn't change hands, a property tax policy badly in need of statewide reform.

NOT EASY BEING GREEN

Gayle McLaughlin presided over a city with nearly 20 percent of its population living in poverty and a local jobless rate that was, at its peak, twice the national average. During her first term, Richmond city hall tried to generate new employment, particularly for young people who might otherwise be drawn to gangs, drugs, or street crime leading to jail. The mayor took credit for attracting one thousand new jobs via businesses relocating to or starting up in Richmond. McLaughlin's enviro-friendly electoral base favored green jobs. But, without far greater federal funding for them, job creation of any kind, on the scale needed, was a major challenge. Richmond did launch the Worker Cooperative Revolving Loan Fund (WCRLF) as a grant-funded stopgap measure and demonstration that "another world is possible." The fund aided local worker-run enterprises, few and small.

The private sector had a very different job creation plan for Richmond. In 2009–10 it became the center of a heated community-wide debate about what kind of economic development was good or bad for the city. The battleground was a 422-acre section of the Richmond shoreline with sweeping views of Mount Tamalpais in Marin County, across the bay. There, at Point Molate, a wealthy East Bay developer named Jim Levine sought city approval for construction of a hotel and casino complex. In place of an abandoned winery and a former US Navy fuel depot, Levine promised to erect what local environmentalist David Helvarg caustically described as "the greenest most eco-sustainable billion dollar casino, high-rise hotel, and parking structure this side of Las Vegas."[11]

Backers of the project argued that it would generate much-needed tax revenue for Richmond, while providing thousands of new jobs in construction and then hospitality. "You put a casino out there and you'll be manufacturing money," one building trades leader predicted. Since the crash and burn of Atlantic City was several years away, such claims quickly gained traction. Casino gambling still retained considerable cachet as an engine of economic development in depressed communities. And, as Helvarg wryly observed, "moving from alcohol to petroleum to gambling" on this particular Richmond site did "make sense in terms of the continuity of human addiction."

The pro-gaming forces included many influential local players, plus a Native American ally from out of town, the Guidiville band of Pomos. They hailed from Mendocino County, had no historical connection to Richmond, and were enlisted to provide tribal cover for a piece of the action. Levine's firm, Upstream LLC, spearheaded the campaign for city hall approval, aided by a very enthusiastic Contra Costa County Building and Construction Trades Council. A majority of Richmond council members favored the project, including its senior member, Nat Bates, a declared candidate for mayor in 2010. Bates rallied his longtime supporters in the African American community, including many ministers, behind the casino idea. He promoted the project on his weekly cable TV public affairs show, which was funded, in part, by Levine. Joining this "pro-growth" faction were two surprising partners, the Sierra Club and Audubon Society. Both conservation groups got seduced by the promise of shoreline preservation outside of Richmond—funded with $48 million in slot machine revenue—if Point Molate itself was sacrificed to the developer's plan.

For much of Richmond's modern history, residents had limited access to its thirty-two miles of shoreline. Users of the waterfront like Standard Oil (now Chevron), Kaiser and other manufacturers, the Port of Richmond, and the US Navy kept things off-limits to local people, unless they were employees or uniformed personnel. Now, local hikers, bicyclists, bird-watchers, and would-be expanders of public space were not eager to trade the sound of wind and waves at Point Molate for the whir, chimes, and beeps of four thousand slot machines. As Upstream's environmental impact report confirmed, "a 182,000 square foot casino . . . up to two hotels . . . with ancillary restaurants and retail, a 150,000 square foot business, conference and entertainment center, and approximately 5,000 parking spaces" was not exactly "balanced development" of the site.[12] Organizing as Citizens for a Sustainable Point Molate, community critics stressed the traffic congestion, over-building, and visual blight that casino gambling would bring, along with its other well-documented ills.

McLaughlin and the RPA joined the opposition during an election year in which the Green mayor was seeking her second term. "Our point of view was that whatever you build at Point Molate is going to create a lot of jobs," she explained. "And we're for good, healthy, sustainable development that benefits the whole community rather than takes advantage of poor people by picking their pockets."

In the ensuing propaganda war, casino backers spent $500,000 to win voter approval of Measure U, a citywide advisory referendum on the project, held in November 2010. But operators of local card clubs, a gambling interest group already well entrenched in the Richmond area, did not want to see their own low-income customer base eroded by new slot machine competition at Point Molate. A combination of their self-interested spending, grassroots organizing, and community education produced a 57.5 percent vote against Levine's scheme. When Richmond's new city council reaffirmed those results in early 2011, the developer—apparently not a gambler himself—sued Richmond to get his $15 million "non-refundable deposit" back.[13]

Just as gambling interests were helpfully divided over the future of Point Molate, so were McLaughlin's critics when they had their opportunity to oust her. By the fall of 2010, Richmond business interests and allied labor organizations had plenty of reasons to deny her a second term. Fortunately they couldn't agree on a single candidate against her. Furious about the mayor's opposition to the Point Molate project, the county building trades council backed John Ziesenhenne, former president of the Richmond Chamber of Commerce. The construction unions even opened a campaign office in Richmond to help get him elected. City councilor Nat Bates ran with his usual strong financial backing from Chevron. Bates's other business donors included an auto importers association with a big stake in Richmond port operations and Veolia, a global firm that operates Richmond's privatized sewage treatment system.

Amid the resulting blizzard of negative ads and mailers directed at McLaughlin, the top prize for personal vilification was won by two familiar

foes, the firefighters and the police association. Their mailers detailed a
past personal bankruptcy filing by the mayor, triggered by $119,000 in
credit card and student loan debt, and trumpeted her alleged inability to
"hold down a job." The most infamous hit piece in this series disclosed
that McLaughlin had once been treated for depression and was for a time
eligible to collect social security disability benefits.

As would later prove true of Chevron-funded smears in 2014, the dark
portrait of McLaughlin painted by her political enemies seemed unrecog-
nizable to the many residents of Richmond who had personally encountered her. "Gayle is so committed and indefatigable," observes Robert
Rogers, who covered the 2010 campaign for the *Contra Costa Times*. "She's
totally authentic, and you can see the natural affinity she has with the un-
derdog, because of her own life experiences—and she draws her strength
from that."

McLaughlin's reservoir of goodwill and respect, even among those
who disagreed with her, fed the widespread backlash against those prying
into her past for political gain. She handled their disclosures with grace
and candor. She acknowledged having suffered "debilitating illnesses"
and "personal finances that suffered as a result." She urged voters to re-
member her six-year record on the city council, including her role in
achieving the city's $114 million tax settlement with Chevron. She em-
phasized her continuing commitment to "transparent and participatory
government" and curbing "the influence of large corporations and developers on public policy."

In his campaign for McLaughlin's job, her strongest opponent took a
higher road than his public safety union backers. Nat Bates claimed that
his "background as a retired probation officer provided him with unique
knowledge in fighting crime." Alienating many Latino voters, he promised to "reinstate police checkpoints and hold them on a regular basis
throughout the city to protect the safety of the community." Bates also
stressed that he was a "lifetime Democrat," with close ties to California senators Barbara Boxer and Dianne Feinstein and then congressman
George Miller, whose district included Richmond. He urged the 69 percent of the city's voters who had registered as Democrats to "stand strong
and united" against the "loyal Green Party member" who had regularly

failed to support Democratic presidential candidates but now "wants Democrats to vote for her." A tiny party such as the Greens, with only 462 registered voters in Richmond (1 percent of its total electorate), "should not control this city," he declared.[14]

Neither Green-baiting nor his allies' vilification of McLaughlin proved to be a winning strategy for Bates. The mayor was reelected with 40 percent of the vote in her three-way race. When all the ballots were counted, the results, as in 2008, reflected further erosion of Chevron influence and the emergence of a strengthened left-liberal majority. It was now composed of McLaughlin and Ritterman, their frequent allies, Democrats Tom Butt and Jim Rogers, as well as forty-seven-year-old Jovanka Beckles, a leader of the RPA (and registered Democrat) who worked for the county. Beckles's victory in 2010 was both a personal triumph and a major organizational breakthrough for Richmond progressives. In a majority minority city, their only previously successful candidates were white.

DR. RITTERMAN'S PRESCRIPTION

Amid its many charms and allures, one small downside of life in Richmond is the need for a bigger mailbox at election time. Any extra roominess comes in handy when special interest groups, with millions of dollars to spend, decide to bombard the electorate with direct mail deriding local progressives and their latest controversial schemes. During the 2012 election cycle, Big Soda became the biggest spender on such glossy, full-color junk mail. The industry's target was a much-needed public health initiative promoted by Jeff Ritterman.

Through his work as a doctor in Richmond, Ritterman became familiar with all the refinery-related health problems common among Chevron's low-income neighbors, including high childhood asthma rates, cancer clusters, and lower than average life expectancies. In his medical practice, he also treated hundreds of African American and Latino patients suffering from heart disease, type-2 diabetes, high blood pressure, and other weight-related ailments. Ritterman watched with mounting concern as a leading local cause of heart attacks and strokes began to spread to younger people in the community; nearly half the city's children were growing up overweight or obese.

Increased US consumption of sugar-sweetened beverages is a major factor in the development of obesity, type-2 diabetes, hypertension, heart attacks, strokes, and some forms of cancer. If current trends continue, nearly half of all Americans will be obese by 2030, putting a huge additional strain on US medical spending and guaranteeing a life of pain, misery, and disability for many. According to California health researchers, a tax on soda, to discourage its consumption, would produce the greatest health benefits among blacks and Latinos in the state. In Richmond, these groups represent two-thirds of the population currently most at risk for diabetes and heart disease.

In response to this public health crisis, Ritterman and the RPA launched a citywide drive to raise $3 million annually in new tax revenue for youth sports programs and health education. The funding mechanism was a penny-per-ounce tax on sugary drinks. Ritterman decided not to run for reelection to the city council, preferring instead to focus on voter education about the soda tax. In countless community meetings and forums, he explained how this new tax revenue could "provide adequate sports fields and teams for Richmond children," plus fund "programs that prevent childhood obesity, like healthy school gardens and nutrition and cooking classes in the schools."

Ritterman's cause was bravely embraced by only a few African American ministers and health workers. The Reverend Alvin Bernstine of the Bethlehem Missionary Baptist Church proudly maintains a "no fry/no soda zone" in his congregation's social hall and is quick to invoke the historical connection between sugar plantations and slavery. "The soda companies have been exploiting black people for too long—with products that have no nutritional benefit and no community economic benefit. Our people want to be healthy because healthy physicality is a sign of healthy spirituality."

Local soda tax opposition was soon ginned up by its perennial national foe, the American Beverage Association (ABA). The ABA hired Whitehurst/Mosher Campaign Strategy and Media, a high-powered Bay Area political consulting firm, whose past clients have included Governor Jerry Brown and liberal state legislator Mark Leno.[15] Whitehurst/Mosher was simultaneously working for Chevron's political action committee,

Moving Forward, which ended up spending $1.2 million on Richmond's 2012 election. Coca-Cola deployed its own lower-level Bay Area managers to personally canvass Richmond neighborhoods. Just before the 2012 election, two men from Coke knocked on my door. They were working in tandem, like a pair of young Mormon missionaries. The pamphlet I was offered by the Coke brothers was entitled *Our Position on Obesity*. It disputed claims by doctors and medical researchers that Americans are overweight because we drink too much soda.

The ABA's local consultants recruited and deployed teams of paid canvassers to distribute "Vote No on N" lawn signs in black and Latino neighborhoods. They enlisted Latino grocery store owners and hired former San Francisco mayor Willie Brown to deliver an anti–soda tax speech to NAACP members and Richmond ministers. In a West Coast replay of the industry-orchestrated minority community backlash against soft drink regulation in New York City, Measure N supporters in Richmond were accused of being racist and elitist, plus proponents of a regressive tax on low-income people. As sociology professor Edward Walker documents in *Grassroots for Hire: Public Affairs Consultants in American Democracy*, this approach is part of the broader "Uber-ization of activism." By that Walker means that when individual firms like Uber and Airbnb or a trade association like the ABA fights taxation or regulation these days, they do far more than deploy "traditional public relations tools: TV ads, robocalls, mass mailings, celebrity endorsements, and political operatives." Their campaigns also mobilize consumers, urging them to join a "social-media assault" on public officials critical of the corporate behavior or new business model in dispute. According to Walker, these new "protest-on-demand movements" blur the distinction between genuine grassroots organizing and its "astroturf" counterpart.[16]

The ABA's Richmond front group was dubbed the Community Coalition Against Beverage Taxes. It's "No on N" materials focused on the higher cost of sports drinks, baby formulas, and commercially made *horchata* and *agua fresca* (the latter two consumed largely by Hispanic residents). Campaign materials said, "Richmond needs real solutions like more jobs, better schools and safer streets. No more taxes on working people!" The Vote No campaign's paid canvassers were largely young men of color in need of a summer job. By the end of the campaign, their duties included engaging in some minor vandalism outside the Vote Yes campaign headquarters (the RPA office). An attempt by the city to mandate greater disclosure of Community Coalition funding sources did not survive an industry challenge in federal court. The ABA propaganda campaign did remain subject to California Fair Political Practices Commission (FPPC) reporting requirements, which are less stringent.

For the RPA's year-round foes, Measure N was the wedge issue from heaven. It enabled them to depict would-be soda taxers as racist, elitist social engineering agents of a local nanny state opposed even to the simple pleasures of an ice-cold Coke. As city council member Nat Bates complained to the *New York Times*: "They're using the black community to pass a measure for us without consulting us. . . . We're tired of this Progressive Alliance coming in and telling us what to do. I've renamed them 'the Plantation Alliance.'"[17] Bates's leading ally on the council, Corky Booze, questioned whether sweet potato pie, candied yams, and cupcakes might be the next targets of taxation.

The Contra Costa labor council urged its affiliates to reject Measure N because it might reduce employment for Teamster delivery drivers and bottling plant workers. "We can't make Richmond healthier with a new tax that takes money out of people's pockets," argued Don Gosney, a retired plumbers' union official. Ritterman tried in vain to remind organized labor about "the additional health care cost and loss of wages suffered by every union family member with a preventable chronic condition related to sugary drinks," Some local unions, including the Service Employees International Union Local 1021 (which shares office space with the RPA) and the Amalgamated Transit Union Local 1555, representing BART workers, heeded his message and urged their members to support the soda tax.

Overall the ABA spent about $2.5 million to defeat Dr. Ritterman's prescription for a healthier community by a 2 to 1 margin. (Ritterman and the RPA raised less than $70,000 to defend Measure N.) Ritterman went on to promote similar soda tax proposals in Berkeley, San Francisco, and Mexico. In November 2014, a majority of voters in Berkeley embraced the idea after a $650,000 Bloomberg Philanthropies grant helped pay for advertising that only the industry could afford in Richmond. According to Marion Nestle, author of *Soda Politics: Taking on Big Soda*, the Berkeley campaign became a more "inclusive effort with a very strong diverse coalition" that avoided the bad "racial dynamics of Richmond." As a result, the ABA was less able to depict the ballot measure as a "regressive tax backed by white elitists that would boost grocery bills of working class people of color."[18]

In 2012 Richmond progressives paid a heavy political price for their soda tax advocacy. For the first time since the RPA started running candidates, none of them won. The combined Richmond election spending of Big Soda and Big Oil totaled about $3.7 million—setting a local record not broken even two years later. Worst of all, Big Soda's successful racialization of the Measure N debate threw local progressives on the defensive in an election held just a few months after the Chevron fire, which should have been a boon to RPA candidacies. "We did a bad job," one RPA strategist admitted. "We did not realize what was coming and we didn't build strong enough coalitions with the black community." With Ritterman's departure from the council (and the electoral defeat of Marilyn Langlois and Eduardo Martinez), the RPA delegation was reduced to two—McLaughlin and Beckles.

AN EMINENT DOMAIN SOLUTION

Big Soda elbowed aside Big Oil as a source of local controversy only until it was time for the banksters to become the next subject of Richmond political rumbling. The burst of the housing bubble, our nation's related Wall Street meltdown, and subsequent bank foreclosures hit Richmond particularly hard. In the city's Iron Triangle neighborhood, the 2007–2008 crisis devastated housing prices, with some homes losing 75 percent of their value. Even Point Richmond, with its funky but tonier mix of apartment buildings, private homes, and, on one side of the hill, sweeping views of the bay, saw real estate prices halved.

In 2012 Richmond had nine hundred foreclosures. By the end of 2013, 50 percent of Richmond homeowners were still saddled with underwater mortgages, and many owed an amount twice the current value of their property. Foreclosures forced poor and working-class families out of their homes, often leaving vacant dwellings behind, which contributed to neighborhood blight and further depression of local property values. In the "zombie houses" of South Richmond, Santa Fe, and Coronado, squatters moved in, exacerbating problems like drug dealing, gang activity, and flight from the city by those who could afford to leave.

With no effective relief in sight from any other level of government, Richmond city hall joined forces with the Alliance of Californians for Community Empowerment (ACCE) to unveil a program they called Richmond Cares. Mayor McLaughlin accused the banking industry of creating the crisis with its "predatory lending policies" in Richmond and other cities. At the mayor's initiative, a city council majority voted to use the threat of eminent domain to force mortgage lenders to renegotiate the terms of their housing loans. That way Richmond residents who qualified for the program could hold on to their homes.

As McLaughlin explained, her approach would help "people who are underwater, who have mortgages higher than the current value of their home. The city will purchase these loans at fair market value from the banks and reset the mortgages in line with the homes' current value. Then we'll put these refinanced loans, with lower mortgage payments, into the hands of our homeowners. That way, they can continue to stay in our community and our neighborhoods will remain stable. They can avoid going into default, experiencing foreclosure and eviction, and having to walk away from their home. If lenders don't cooperate, we have the option of acquiring the properties through eminent domain, again paying fair market value."

Big mortgage holders, like Wells Fargo, Bank of New York Mellon, and Deutsche Bank, did not favor this scenario. Like the ABA trying to block a first-time-ever local soda tax, the banking and real estate industries wanted to strangle Richmond Cares in the cradle before it could become a model and precedent for other cities. An industry bid for injunctive relief in federal court was denied because the city's eminent domain powers had not yet been exercised. So the well-funded critics of Richmond Cares stepped up their nonelection-year "air war" to sway public opinion against it.

The National Association of Realtors bombarded Richmond homeowners with slick mailers warning of the dire consequences of McLaughlin's "radical scheme." Among these were redlining by Richmond's municipal bond holders and a lending institution boycott that would send property values plummeting even further. "If the eminent domain plan goes into effect, lending for new home buyers will dry up, home values will decline, and neighborhoods will be hurt," claimed one brochure from the West Contra Costa Realtors Association.

The industry's message was carefully designed to pit neighbor against neighbor: if you were paid up on your mortgage, why should you care about others in Richmond who should never have bought a home with so much borrowed money to begin with? The campaign by bankers, realtors, and builders against Richmond Cares also drove away much-needed allies on the city councils of neighboring communities. Some of these leaders had initially expressed interest in joining the anti-foreclosure fight, wielding their own eminent domain powers, and then sharing with Richmond the cost and risk of litigation.[19]

Richmond Cares generated national publicity for McLaughlin's administration, most of it favorable. Yet there was one aspect of the program that critics were quick to question, and it aroused some concern on the left as well. Just as the success of the campaign against the Point Molate casino included a strange political bedfellow—local card clubs—Richmond's proposed use of eminent domain was an idea of mixed provenance. As McLaughlin acknowledged, it was San Francisco-based "Mortgage Resolution Partners (MRP), a private company, that actually brought this idea to us. The city has a formal agreement with MRP that they will provide the funding and technical assistance in purchasing these mortgages. It will not cost the city of Richmond or its taxpayers one penny."

As Rebecca Burns reported for *In These Times*, the venture capital firm had been shopping its plan to other cities for some time. Under the terms of its proposed private-public partnership, MRP "would take a cut on each mortgage acquired through eminent domain in return for providing the necessary capital backing." In Richmond, that would mean "primarily buying mortgages where the homeowner is current on payments" but not necessarily coming to the rescue of homeowners with second liens increasing the risk of foreclosure.[20] "In an ideal world," said liberal journalist Robert Kuttner, "you would not be reliant on a renegade Wall Street group to come up with the capital, but it's what we've got for now."[21]

For its part, the ACCE did essential door-to-door work, educating and mobilizing local homeowners who were getting barraged with anti–Richmond Cares propaganda. ACCE organizers like twenty-three-year-old Melvin Willis helped them resist evictions, seek renegotiation of their mortgage loans, and protest the deceptive lending practices that victimized minority home buyers in Richmond and other cities. At a September 2013 meeting attended by three hundred people, the city council voted 4 to 3 to resist industry pressure and pursue, to the extent possible, McLaughlin's anti-foreclosure initiative. Actual use of the city's eminent domain powers required a "super majority" of five, only unattainable if voters in 2014 replaced one of the council opponents of Richmond Cares.

Richmond's anti-foreclosure initiative might have gone further if like-minded progressives had wielded greater influence in neighboring communities. Yet even the ACCE, with multiple local chapters and a statewide staff, was unable to get any other city to go as far as Richmond did. In late 2014 President Obama prevented further spread of the Richmond Cares concept when he signed a bill passed by Congress forbidding any federal role in mortgage financing of homes taken by eminent domain. As a fallback approach, McLaughlin got the Richmond council to support a "Foreclosure Prevention and Neighborhood Stabilization Program" promoted by ACCE.

Under this program banks and federal agencies would "offer their distressed mortgages first to non-profit organizations to help keep homeowners in their houses and rents low through reduced monthly payments."[22] At the US Conference of Mayors meeting in San Francisco in mid-2014, the mayors of Richmond, Berkeley, Oakland, San Jose, and fourteen other cities lobbied for this approach because "HUD, Fannie Mae, and Freddie Mac have millions of distressed mortgages on their books but don't assist families who are struggling with payments." As McLaughlin told a reporter: "There's a better path here than selling these mortgages to speculators and hedge funds."[23]

Similar networking by McLaughlin and other progressive city officials helped build Local Progress, a policy clearinghouse backed by four hundred mayors, city councilors, and county supervisors. Assisted by the Center for Popular Democracy in New York, the group offers a sixty-page guide to improving local labor and environmental standards, housing and education, policing, voting rights, and financing of elections.[24] It also holds annual conferences, with workshops and presentations by mayors like Mc-Laughlin and New York's Bill de Blasio. At these gatherings, local victories are celebrated and setbacks like that of the Richmond Cares campaign can be dissected. Local Progress strategists believe that neither street politics nor electoral victories alone will make a sufficient dent in the status quo. To counter corporate influence, progressives need what Local Progress chair Nick Licata called "an outside and inside game . . . people on the inside and people protesting on the outside to provide insiders with backbone."[25]

RICHMOND'S SISTER COUNTRY

Throughout her two mayoral terms, Gayle McLaughlin faced reoccurring objections to her international activities. Many American cities have sister-city relationships, designed to promote global understanding and cross-border solidarity. Such partnerships are either developed by local civic organizations or municipalities themselves. The latter type tend to be noncontroversial, like the sister city projects and exchanges that Richmond has conducted over the years with communities in Japan, China, and Cuba (although linking up with the Cuban refinery town of Regla was a more daring political statement at the time).

But Richmond under Gayle McLaughlin was virtually alone among North American cities in forging direct ties with another country. Its solidarity relationship with Ecuador grew out of the shared experience of environmental pollution and resulting litigation against Chevron. In mid-October 2013, at the invitation of Ecuador's left-wing populist president, Rafael Correa, McLaughlin and a small local delegation flew off to Quito, accompanied by *East Bay Express* reporter John Geluardi. After conferring with Correa at the presidential palace in Quito, McLaughlin's party flew to the hot and humid Lago Agrio rain forest, where a large media contingent awaited their arrival. With President Correa leading the way, the US visitors personally inspected one of the hundreds of sludge pits that mar the local landscape and contain millions of gallons of toxic waste. "Gayle, Gayle," Correa said, holding up his goo-covered hand. "This is Chevron. For thirty years, this is Chevron!"[26]

Correa's visitors from California then met with the mayors of Lago Agrio and neighboring Shushufindi. As Geluardi reported from the scene, residents of both communities recited a litany of health problems in the area, including skin infections, miscarriages, birth defects, and rare cancers. "Texaco—now Chevron—clearly disregarded the environment and simply disposed of its toxic products in the most cost-saving way," McLaughlin said. "They just tossed them into the rivers, streams and roads. As a result the indigenous people who drank from and bathed in the rivers, cooked their food and washed their clothes in the water, suffered monumentally and continue to suffer."[27]

During her six-day visit, which coincided with Richmond's celebration of Hispanic Heritage Month back home, McLaughlin invited members of the Union of Affected People and their courageous local lawyer, Pablo Fajardo, to visit California and report on their Chevron lawsuit. Back home, she and the RPA also arranged for a public screening of *Crude: The Real Price of Oil*, a documentary about the Ecuadoran lawsuit against Chevron. Even though it was conducted at foreign government expense, McLaughlin's fact-finding mission to Ecuador drew political flak from the usual direction.

Chevron issued a statement saying that the mayor "would better serve the citizens of Richmond" by staying home and "constructively addressing the city's most pressing issues, including jobs, education, and public safety." Chip Johnson, a columnist for the *San Francisco Chronicle*, similarly chided McLaughlin for "intertwining her personal politics with the duties and responsibilities of her elected office." In Johnson's view, holding "the company accountable for environmental damage in Ecuador seems a little bit beyond her job description."[28]

McLaughlin was typically unrepentant. "Chevron is not only polluting our air and water," the mayor said. "They're polluting our politics and legal system. So we're building an international 'union of affected people' that can turn our shared pain and suffering into the power to change things."

In March 2014 McLaughlin reached out to a group of affected people in Canada who had, like the Ecuadorans, quite a story of pain and suffering to share. At a packed public meeting organized in response to crude-by-rail shipments to Richmond, the mayor welcomed Marilaine

Savard from the Citizens Committee of Lac-Mégantic, Quebec. In French-accented English, this slim, sad-eyed woman described the federal regulatory lapses that proved fatal to forty-seven of her friends and neighbors. Nine months earlier, a runaway "bomb train"—improperly braked by its single-man crew—had barreled into Savard's rural community. The resulting derailment and explosion obliterated its entire downtown. "The oil industry is far too powerful," she told a crowd of 150, packed into RPA headquarters. "The first duty of government should be to protect citizens, not shareholders."

Locally Big Oil's clout was on display in a new form, as far as the eye could see in the sprawling Richmond rail yard located just across the street from the Chevron refinery. Operated by Burlington Northern Santa Fe Railway (BNSF), the rail yard was now filled with hundreds of black, metal tank cars. These had just carried the same volatile form of crude oil that destroyed Lac-Mégantic, all the way from the Bakken fields of North Dakota to a transfer facility located right next to Richmond's oldest residential and business neighborhood. Kinder Morgan, a major energy firm, stored up to seventy-two thousand barrels per day there, under a lease agreement with the BNSF, which is owned by Nebraska billionaire Warren Buffett. The crude-by-rail shipments were then loaded onto tanker trucks bound via local streets and a state highway for the Tesoro refinery in Martinez, California.

In 2014–2015 hazards of transporting Bakken crude were highlighted by a series of major train fires and explosions. As labor and environmental critics pointed out, the Achilles' heel of crude-by-rail everywhere is the aging condition and structural weakness of most tank cars. They were designed and used in the past for hauling less hazardous cargo. According to the Association of American Railroads' own estimate, "78,000 of the 92,000 cars now moving oil need to be replaced or retrofitted."[29] Meanwhile, the US Department of Transportation failed to mandate tank car modernization and upgrading in timely fashion. Chevron and the rest of Big Oil objected to "forcing oil producers and shippers to use newer tank cars and replace older models" because that "would impose high costs on the industry and lead to a shortfall in tank car capacity." Chevron's industry-wide lobbying arm, the American Petroleum Institute, filed a legal challenge to "new federal rules intended to improve the safety of oil-by-rail transportation," further delaying "a two year-effort to reduce the risks of moving hazardous materials on railroads."[30]

Even newer, supposedly safer tank cars have sometimes failed to protect the public from the consequences of oil train collisions, rollovers, tank car ruptures, and spills. The total amount of oil spilled in 2013 due to derailments was greater in volume than all the spills occurring in the United States during the previous forty years. One major accident in West Virginia triggered a fire that burned for five days, forced the evacuation of two nearby towns, and seriously threatened local water supplies.

Despite this alarming track record, the Bay Area Air Quality Management District (BAAQMD) board issued the permit necessary to bring Bakken crude into Richmond in secret. There was no prior notice, nor were there any public hearings or environmental impact review. Outraged when they discovered this, Communities for a Better Environment, the Sierra Club, and the Asian Pacific Environmental Network filed suit to block Kinder Morgan from operating in Richmond. The Richmond city council backed revocation of its permit and urged Congress to halt all Bakken crude shipments until tougher federal safety rules could be implemented. Unfortunately, a superior court judge in San Francisco dismissed the permitting challenge on the grounds that it wasn't timely. This unhelpful ruling was appealed but never overturned.

Seven months after Savard's visit, local environmentalists took the fight directly to Kinder Morgan's front door. With well-organized backup teams, reporters covering their action, and a legal consultant on hand, eight protestors chained themselves in pairs to a rail yard fence, using bicycle U-locks. This had the effect of blocking trucks from entering the main gate. It also created a three-hour impasse between the Richmond police and a security officer from BSNF since the trespassing occurred on railroad property beyond the RPD's jurisdiction. The railroad cop initially seemed intent on pressing some kind of federal charges, more serious than trespassing.

Thanks to the intervention of local officers, the demonstrators were allowed to leave after being identified, with no citations issued or charges pressed. Per usual when there was a protest scheduled in Richmond, Gayle

McLaughlin was at the scene—this time watching from the sidelines. As one participant from Oakland, Margaret Rossoff, reported, the mayor offered her warm congratulations. Then, adding to Rossoff's surprise, "the Richmond officers lined up to shake our hands." This parting gesture made the Sunflower Alliance member feel like she was on "a receiving line at a wedding or bar mitzvah," rather than wrapping up "a non-violent direct action protest!"[31] It was not the reception she might have gotten in her own hometown or any other place yet to undergo its own greening of city hall.

THREE

RICHMOND'S COMMUNITY POLICEMAN

FIFTY-TWO-YEAR-OLD CHRIS MAGNUS, a fair-haired Midwesterner, circulated through the crowd with no visible sign of Richmond Police Department rank. Twenty-five hundred people had just completed the largest protest march in Richmond's history, walking from downtown to the Chevron refinery. Magnus greeted people in friendly, low-key fashion. He was hatless, wearing blue jeans and a windbreaker with a barely noticeable RPD logo on it. When he approached a small group of us chatting about the large turnout, he smiled broadly. As if already attuned to the topic of our conversation, he stopped and declared, "Isn't this a terrific crowd? What a great day for our city!"

Despite his calm, even stolid, appearance, Magnus has often been described in the media as being unconventional. That characterization does apply to his personal background, which includes no other cops in the family tree. A native of Lansing, Michigan, Magnus grew up in university circles. His father was a professor at Michigan State (MSU); his mother, a local piano teacher. He first worked as a police dispatcher and later became a paramedic. After joining his hometown police force as a patrol officer, he rose to the rank of captain in sixteen years. Along the way, he earned a master's degree in labor relations at MSU. Then he departed to serve as police chief in Fargo, North Dakota.

Six years later, when Magnus was forty-five, he applied to become Richmond's new chief. That was in 2005, when the city was rightly notorious for its violent crime, youth gangs, drug trafficking, and troubled relations between police and the public. Richmond's city hall search committee wanted to hire someone who could reduce crime by reconnecting the RPD to the community it serves. Community policing, as that approach is known, now has many boosters, but a decade ago it was still little understood and not so widely embraced.

Those vetting Magnus for the chief's job in Richmond were duly impressed with his credentials as a public safety reformer. And they had good reason to act quickly since "in just one two week period in the summer of 2005, a stream of day-time shootings had left eight people dead and many more wounded. By the end of the year, Richmond would record 40 killings, making it the second most violent city in California behind Compton. . . . In response, some residents pleaded for the National Guard to be deployed to the area."[1]

Thanks to a memorable film by the Coen brothers, Magnus had some explaining to do about his previous six-year posting. As police chief of Fargo he was coming from one of the safest and whitest places in America, a community averaging one homicide every two years. As the *San Francisco Chronicle* noted, "At least four months out of the year, the weather in Fargo falls below zero, sometimes 30 or 40 degrees below zero. Police there believe the frigid temperatures may be partly responsible for the low crime rate."[2] Richmond was not much bigger than real-life Fargo. But its population was largely nonwhite, low-income, and about to experience even more homicides (forty-two) in 2006, making it one of the most dangerous cities in the United States per capita. In neighboring Berkeley there were only four violent deaths during the same period.

"I really thought Fargo would be a disqualifier for me because of the demographics of the city," Magnus said.[3] In addition, the candidate from North Dakota was not yet known for being one of the few gay police chiefs in America. If that fact had been publicized during Richmond's search process, Magnus might not have been hired, according to one city hall observer.

Fortunately, City Manager Bill Lindsay and then city councilor Gayle McLaughlin and others in city government decided to take a chance on a man now celebrated as one of the country's most effective police reformers. The department Magnus inherited had a sordid history of corruption, brutality, racial division, and hostile interaction with the public, all of which had generated a huge pile of bad press clips. In the early 1980s the stars of this horror show were a group of out-of-control white officers known as "the cowboys." Their trigger-happy behavior even gained the attention of the *New York Times* and *60 Minutes.* It also cost the city a lot of money.

In 1983, two African Americans, Johnny Roman and Michael Guillory, were fatally shot by the RPD. The families of the deceased won a $3 million damage award after filing a federal lawsuit, which alleged "a pattern of misconduct that police and city officials ignored or condoned." The plaintiffs' attorney, who worked for the National Association for the Advancement of Colored People (NAACP), thought he had negotiated a pretrial settlement worth $760,000. But that deal was rejected by five white city councilors, joined by Nat Bates. As Bates explained: "We have a department and a reputation to defend."[4]

Fortunately, some African American officers—then representing only 20 percent of the force—took the stand against their fellow officers when the Roman-Guillory case went to a jury trial in federal court. Sergeant Tony Zanotelli, then president of the Richmond Police Officers Association, denounced these witnesses as "puppets for the NAACP" and their attorneys as "blood sucking."[5] Speaking at a city hall prayer vigil, C. A. Robertson, president of Guardians of Justice, a local black officers' group, defended their actions: "Our common cause is to stand up and testify and make the city of Richmond better." To achieve that goal, black community leaders like James McMillan, a local pharmacist, called for the hiring of "a city manager and police chief with the commitment to have the police do their work properly"—a personnel change that was still two decades away in Richmond.

Long after "the cowboys" were discredited and disbanded, the RPD still deployed overly aggressive "street teams." A veteran of the department interviewed by Joe Eskenazi for *San Francisco Magazine* recalled "hopping over fences and chasing people and loving it—walking around the department like I was the baddest guy." To thwart lookouts posted on corners, this officer and others would jump out of unmarked vehicles to maintain an element of surprise—thus becoming known to civilians on the street as "Jump-Out Boys." Eskanazi's source showed him an old departmental publicity photo featuring these same scowling officers "decked out in full tactical gear and toting MP5 submachine guns." According to Eskenazi, they looked, acted, and felt like members of a paramilitary unit. At best, this pre-Magnus approach left "murderous gangs locked in a futile stalemate with police" in Richmond. Even Eskenazi's RPD source acknowledged a sense of failure: "I don't feel like we bettered the city at all, looking back."[6]

Richmond community organizer Tamisha Walker would agree. As recently as the 1990s she even feared being robbed by the Richmond police. "They'd say, 'If you don't shut up, we'll put you in the back of this car, take you somewhere, beat your ass, and no one will do anything about it.'" Meanwhile, the RPD didn't endear itself to Richmond's growing Latino community with incidents like the beating and arrest of Andres Soto and his sons on Cinco de Mayo in 2002. For too long, Soto contends, there were "not a lot of professional standards" in the hiring of new Richmond officers. As a result, "too many ex-military, thuggish cops, and rednecks" simply ran roughshod over nonwhite residents. For their part, newly hired veterans of military service abroad were shocked by the level of gun violence they encountered in Richmond. "I couldn't believe I was in an American city," recalls Ben Therriault, who spent 2005 assigned to a military police brigade in Iraq. "I thought I was back in Baghdad."

Beginning in early 2006, Chris Magnus reshuffled the RPD's command structure and promoted like-minded senior officers. As he explained much later, "If you're really committed to community policing, you have to make structural changes within your organization." As he saw it, Richmond and other cities have the choice between having "community policing officers who are this small cadre within a department that is essentially its public relations wing" or "integrating the larger expectations of community policing into the role of every officer in the department."

Magnus pushed the latter, more systemic approach. One major change was relying far less on "street teams" that would "go into high crime neighborhoods and roust anybody who's out walking around, doing whatever, with the idea that they might have a warrant outstanding or be holding drugs or something." According to the new chief, that kind of law enforcement activity, if conducted on a regular basis, only served "to alienate the whole population that lives in those neighborhoods. And 95 percent of those are good people not engaged in crime."

Magnus applied the same philosophy to Richmond's now very restrained handling of political protests, including marches and rallies, which after 2006 often included the mayor and other members of the city council. The RPD became more careful about who was picked to be part of its Mobile Field Force, the unit responsible for dealing with civil unrest or large crowds.

"I think it's really important to get the right people both commanding those teams and also on the line," Magnus said. "They need to be given very clear direction and supervision: if someone behaves badly towards you, you just smile, and you don't need to respond or take it personally. A successful event is not one where you've had to engage and get into a fight with somebody. It's actually one where everybody leaves, there's no arrests, no injuries, everyone feels they have been treated fairly and well. . . . That doesn't mean that people who are protesting necessarily have to agree with us on everything or even care for police in general. But they at least feel they are treated with respect."

On a day-to-day basis, the RPD began assigning more officers to regular beats, where they were encouraged to do more foot patrolling. The use of bicycles increased as more officers were trained and became willing to use them in their assigned neighborhoods. Under a new job evaluation system, career advancement became more closely tied to an officer's ability to build long-term relationships with individual residents, neighborhood groups, and community leaders. Richmond cops were given personalized business cards, with their work cell phone numbers and e-mail addresses, and urged to give them out. The RPD even began hosting Coffee with a Cop conversations in coffee shops and other places where residents could meet officers assigned to their neighborhoods, ask them questions, and get crime-fighting tips.

"We assign people for longer periods of time to specific geographic areas with the expectation that they get to know and become known by residents," Magnus explained. "They are in and out of businesses, nonprofits, churches, a wide variety of community organizations, and they come to be seen as a partner in crime reduction. Our idea is that you're not going to be able to just arrest your way out of crime, but that you have to develop a wide range of strategies that involve community members as partners to really improve public safety."

Magnus argues that this approach has a dual benefit. It "not only leads to better outcomes in terms of crime reduction, it also makes for police officers who are a lot more satisfied and productive over the course of their careers because they're not just arresting the same people over and over again. They're actually engaged with residents. They're seeing their work have an impact and make a difference. They're feeling appreciated and valued."

To set a strong personal example, Richmond's new chief took another unusual step when he first arrived. Although most RPD personnel live outside the city, he bought a home in the area known as the North and East neighborhood. From there he could bicycle to work and, when off duty, was never far from the daily challenges he faced on the job. At home he could hear police sirens late into the night, the occasional shot being fired, and members of his neighborhood association knocking on his door to report nearby crimes. On one occasion a neighborhood activist named Brian Lewis heard a knock on his own door and was amazed to find the chief personally checking in after Lewis's home had been burglarized.[7]

Felix Hunziker, a project manager for an architectural firm, got to know Magnus first as a North and East neighbor. In 2007, four years after Hunziker moved to Richmond, foreclosure-driven blight began to creep into the area, despite its many blocks of well-kept single-family dwellings. Vacant houses multiplied, burglaries increased substantially, several home invasions occurred, an elderly man was murdered, and someone fired twenty-three rounds into a house just up the street from Hunziker's. "Community policing was just getting off the ground," Hunziker recalls, but civilian self-help was already being encouraged.

Working with officers under Magnus's direction, Hunziker and forty other residents formed a neighborhood patrol. Equipped only with flashlights, vests, and mobile phones, they patrolled the North and East neighborhoods once or twice a week, at night. They applied the "broken windows" theory of policing to any visible signs of littering or disorder, reporting trash pile-ups to Richmond Code Enforcement (an arm of the RPD that grew from six officers to twenty-eight under Magnus). "Curbing blight was part of what we did, but the main focus was to build community," Hunziker said. "We distributed thousands of multilingual door-hanger flyers, knocked on many hundreds of doors to let people know about the N&E neighborhood council and how to start a neighborhood watch. We showed our community that people cared and they too could get involved."

Under Magnus the department began hiring and promoting more women, minorities, and Richmond residents. "When you have a department that doesn't look anything like the community it serves, you're asking for trouble, no matter how dedicated and professional your employees are," he explained. "So an ongoing mission for us here is to hire the highest quality people that represent that diversity of the community, across the board. I don't even just mean from a racial, ethnic, or gender standpoint. I mean in terms of life experiences, being connected to neighborhoods, growing up either in Richmond or cities like Richmond."

As retirements and other openings permitted, Magnus was able to personally select more than 90 of the department's nearly 140 patrol officers. Over time he appointed all but four of the RPD's forty-six supervisors as well. By 2015, only twelve officers serving on the force when Magnus arrived remained on its payroll. Budgets prepared by Bill Lindsay and approved by the city council kept the RPD at full strength during a period when fiscal pressures on neighboring cities, like Oakland, led to force reductions and what some residents believed was a related increase in crime.

The RPD changed its personnel record-keeping system while Magnus was chief, making it difficult to compare diversity figures, before and after, with total precision. But by 2014 about 40 percent of the department's 182 active police officers were white, while 60 percent were from minority groups. The RPD had twenty-six women on the force, including officers highly visible in the community, like Captain Bisa French and, until her retirement, Lieutenant Lori Curran. As Magnus explained to one reporter, "It's easier to get new people in a department than it is to get a new culture in a department."[8]

A CASE OF DISCRIMINATION?

The creativity that Magnus displayed when making personnel decisions was much applauded later. But these changes were extremely controversial at the time. His shake-up of the RPD roster threatened the old departmental hierarchy, its institutional power and perks. Internal opposition began coalescing when Magnus was still just one of six candidates for the chief's job in 2005. According to Captain Mark Gagen, a later ally of Magnus, two of his fellow officers—lieutenants Cleveland Brown and Arnold Threets—made it clear that they were going to undermine anyone picked from outside the RPD.

During Magnus's first six months in office, he created two new deputy chief positions. He filled one post with Lori Ritter, a now-retired white female officer who favored departmental change. This put Ritter in charge of Brown and three African American captains who felt passed over for promotions. Among the other black RPD veterans who were bypassed was Lieutenant Johan Simon. (While serving as a detective in the 1980s, Simon had complained on *60 Minutes* that the crime-fighting effectiveness of his white "cowboy" colleagues was being unfairly hampered.) At a command staff retreat in September 2006, internal tensions escalated, and colleagues resentful of Ritter's promotion accused her of racism.

Three months later, the attorney representing six of the seven African American police officers who later sued Magnus and the city for racial discrimination called a press conference outside RPD headquarters. The chief was publicly denounced for creating a hostile work environment for black officers, including soon-to-be-plaintiffs Threets, Brown, Simon, and Lieutenant Shawn Pickett, then in charge of RPD detectives. According to Gagen's subsequent testimony in their case, Pickett viewed Simon and Threets as "the rightful chief and deputy chief" and boasted that their lawyer's press conference would hit Magnus like a "sledgehammer." Officers (like Gagen) who sided with the chief faced verbal abuse and veiled threats. At the scene of a homicide, Pickett angrily confronted Gagen, accusing him of being a "kiss ass" for Magnus; on another occasion, Pickett called him "a little snitch bitch."[9]

Robert Rogers, then a reporter for the *Contra Costa Times*, covered the resulting state and federal court cases, which took five years to resolve.

He believes this litigation was part of the broader "struggle between what Richmond was and what it's becoming," between its old culture of patronage and insider connections, and the modern practices promoted by newcomers like Magnus and Lindsay. Rogers doubts that the aggrieved officers ever expected to go to trial. They hoped that negative publicity about Magnus would generate sufficient political pressure to trigger a coup within the department and that the new chief would be dumped as too controversial and costly for Richmond. To rally black community support, anonymous supporters of the plaintiffs distributed hundreds of copies of a DVD showing Magnus and Ritter being deposed in the case, but with their taped testimony doctored and distorted.

Vernon Whitmore was, at the time, operating the *Globe*, a black community weekly paper founded in 2004, shortly before Magnus arrived in Richmond. The *Globe* tried to provide its 25,000 African American readers in the East Bay with "good news—no shootings, no murders," its publisher explained. Yet, as a Richmond resident, Whitmore knew that the city's policing had to be drastically changed, which led him to reject appeals to racial solidarity made by critics of the chief. "The *Globe* was the only local newspaper that supported Chris Magnus," Whitmore told me, noting that he "lost some friends over it."

Other backers of Magnus, from across the political spectrum in Richmond, formed a committee to support him. The group included Mike Parker, a leading RPA activist, and Felix Hunziker, who often disagrees with the RPA and finds it too uncompromising in its views. Their ad hoc committee set up a website and encouraged residents to attend the trial, where the bias claims were heard. After deliberating in April 2012, jurors concluded that the plaintiffs were past beneficiaries of a "buddy system that facilitated their rise to the highest positions in the department through intimidation, race baiting tactics, and backroom dealing."[10] Racial discrimination was not a factor in the alleged sidelining of their careers. The plaintiffs lost every single claim, including their bid for $3 million each for "emotional distress."

During these proceedings, officers who sued Magnus and the city remained on active duty. Afterward, four of the seven retired or departed for jobs elsewhere. Some had to declare personal bankruptcy to avoid being assessed hundreds of thousands of dollars in legal costs awarded to the city by the judge. Richmond's total legal bill was about $5 million. After his courtroom victory, Magnus pledged: "We'll have to work together and show respect to each other and focus on reducing crime and working with the community."

FAIR AND IMPARTIAL POLICING?

As chief of the RPD, Magnus not only curbed explicit racism. The department sought to improve its day-to-day interaction with the public by getting new recruits and experienced officers to examine their own unconscious biases related to race, gender, ethnicity, sexual orientation, and socioeconomic status. Amid the wave of police brutality protests that swept the nation from 2014 to 2015, police critics, academic observers, and even leading law enforcement officials all agreed that unconscious bias was part of the problem.

A New York Times/CBS News poll found, not surprisingly, that four in ten blacks—and nearly two-thirds of all black men—said they felt they had been stopped by police just because of their race or ethnicity, compared to only one in twenty whites.[11] Stanford University law professor Richard T. Ford, the author of *Racial Culture*, argues that such disparate treatment is "a recurrent theme of American law enforcement." In Ford's view, the recent rash of misconduct cases involving officers from Ferguson, Missouri, to New York City is "a product of the racially divided society in which they work"—and, more specifically, their assignment to "poor, high-crime neighborhoods of color," which leads to "countless experiences that reinforce racial prejudice." Given that "many officers *will* consider race when approaching people suspected of wrongdoing," Ford believes "the best we can hope for is to limit the injury that these encounters cause. . . . Demands to root out and punish biased officers are necessary and understandable but real improvement will require comprehensive institutional reform."[12]

In a widely reported speech at Georgetown University in early 2015, FBI director James Comey similarly noted that urban police officers "often work in environments where a hugely disproportionate percentage of street crime is committed by young men of color."[13] In such a setting, he acknowledged, "no one's really color blind" and "everyone makes judgments based on race." Whether an individual officer is white or black, Comey contended, he or she views young whites and blacks differently, because the latter "look like so many others the officer has locked up."

To make policing more fair and impartial, both New York City police commissioner William Bratton and Comey called for better training, a policy panacea now almost universally embraced but still viewed with suspicion by those skeptical about police reform in general. One of the leading proponents of "fair and impartial policing" (FIP) is Lorie Fridell, a criminologist from the University of South Florida. Her public safety consulting business began to boom after Michael Brown's shooting in Ferguson, followed by the fatal choking of Eric Garner in New York City and the police killings of Tamir Rice in Cleveland, Walter Scott in North Charleston, South Carolina, and Samuel Dubose in Cincinnati, not to mention Freddie Gray's fatal "rough ride" in a Baltimore "paddy wagon" (the very name of which, as Comey noted, is an enduring testament to mid-nineteenth-century nativist bias against poor Irish immigrants, then widely considered to be nothing more than "drunks, ruffians, and criminals"). As the *Wall Street Journal* disclosed, Baltimore already ranked high among US cities incurring legal costs due to police misconduct. In 2014 the ten US cities with the largest police departments experienced a 48 percent increase in the dollar value of such settlements and court judgments over the previous year. Between 2010 and 2014, they collectively paid out $1.02 billion to civilians who suffered beatings, shootings, or wrongful imprisonment.[14]

Fridell's fellow FIP trainers include six retired police officers similarly dedicated to altering problematic behavior. Since 2010, Fridell has conducted seminars on unconscious bias for law enforcement officers from 250 local, state, and federal agencies. The Department of Justice's Office on Community Oriented Policing Services (COPS) has invested more than $1 million in FIP training, and additional funds have come from local police departments, particularly those facing costly civil rights litigation or DOJ pressure to clean up their act.

When Fridell came to Richmond in February 2015 at Chief Magnus's invitation, to help train RPD patrol officers and commanders, her visit was a homecoming of sorts. Fridell's father, Leo, was a longtime Richmond public school teacher who compiled a guide to local government for use as a social studies text. His sixty-year-old *Story of Richmond* includes an idyllic five-page section on the RPD. In it we learn that the much less diverse and more traditionally trained RPD of the last century even helped enforce the city's election-day closure of bars and liquor stores—not the most popular form of community policing in any era.

When Florida-based Fridell comes to town with her thick workbooks, academic articles, PowerPoint presentation, and small group exercises aimed at identifying and rooting out bias, the local reception is not always friendly. Police audiences "are generally somewhere between defensive and hostile," she reports, because "this is cops' least favorite topic." She believes that other experts in her field have "done a poor job of talking about bias in policing," so rank-and-file officers undergoing mandatory training report for it "expecting the same old message." In Richmond, however, she was able to reinforce attitudinal change and better practices already fostered under Magnus, for whom she had fulsome praise.

During the training, Fridell explained, in non-accusatory fashion, how "modern bias is likely to manifest as implicit bias. Implicit biases impact on our perceptions and behavior. They occur below our conscious awareness. And they manifest even in individuals who, at the conscious level, *reject* biases, prejudices, and stereotyping." She encouraged Richmond officers to continue harnessing the power of "contact theory," the idea that, when people have more positive personal contacts with others different from them, it helps erode conscious prejudices and keep implicit biases in check. "Knowing many citizens by face and name improves officers' abilities to differentiate between suspicious and non-suspicious people on a basis other than race," she said.

Tamisha Walker attended Fridell's seminar as a representative of Safe Return, a support group for the formerly incarcerated. Walker is a community organizer and mother of two, whose brother was killed in a police shooting in another city. In the four years she has worked with the RPD, she has seen that "a lot of guys get it," a perception of the police not necessarily shared by everyone locally. As she explained to a visiting NBC News crew, many of her Richmond neighbors developed an us-against-them view of local cops during their "cowboy" era. Now, she believes, the relationship between the community and law enforcement is healing. The RPD's training on unconscious bias gave her further cause for optimism, although she wished that community participation had been broader. "I think the police training, as it relates to Richmond, could go a long way toward helping officers who have not made the transition to having real community relationships," Walker told me.

Walker has spent time in jail herself. She now helps Richmond residents with a criminal record get job training, employment, and affordable housing so they don't end up homeless or back in prison. She expressed concern that past convictions can result in a continued stigmatization and disparate treatment. "Law enforcement does not view formerly incarcerated people as having rights like regular community members," she said. "When a police officer pulls over a white guy, he doesn't ask if he's on parole or probation. People in law enforcement are more biased in their dealings with people of color, particularly with those with criminal histories."

Malcolm Marshall, editor of the community newspaper *Richmond Pulse*, also attended Fridell's training. *Pulse* coverage of Magnus was generally favorable, but the forty-two-year-old African American journalist did not equate the chief with the entire department. "Of course, training can help," Marshall told me. "It's a start but not a cure-all. It's just a step in the right direction and has to be followed up. You can have a Chief Magnus, but filtering it down to the rank-and-file is another issue. I don't know if it got that deep."

A PROTESTOR IN BLUE

By 2014, change in the RPD was deep enough and public safety sufficiently improved that Richmond's homicide rate went down for the fifth straight year. The city's eleven murders represented the smallest annual number in three decades. Violent crime in general was 23 percent lower and property crime down by 40 percent since Magnus's arrival. The results of reconnecting police officers to the community looked very good, compared to the consequences of more traditional policing methods still in use elsewhere.

When those old methods failed in cities like Ferguson, Missouri, local authorities responded to ensuing civil unrest by deploying what author Radley Balko calls "warrior cops." Local law enforcement's use of hand-me-down Pentagon gear, including battlefield weapons and armored vehicles, in crisis situations became a fresh symbol of its day-to-day dysfunction. Too much US policing takes the form of military-style occupation of minority communities. The resulting "battlefield mentality" among urban police officers has, according to Balko, left them "isolated and alienated . . . putting them on a collision course with the values of a free society."[15]

In recognition of Richmond's steady progress in a different direction, Magnus was named to two Department of Justice Civil Rights Division teams investigating police in other cities. He helped prepare a DOJ report criticizing Ferguson cops for making discriminatory traffic stops that created deep resentment among local blacks long before Michael Brown was killed. After Freddie Gray died in Baltimore police custody, triggering riots in that city, Magnus joined a similar panel of experts investigating whether a "pattern and practice" of misconduct there had contributed to his death. In addition, President Obama's Task Force on 21st Century Policing sought advice from Magnus on its response to law enforcement controversies in other cities.

Testifying in Phoenix, the chief explained how a "team effort between our department and the community" had been key to Richmond's public safety improvements. On another occasion, Magnus dispatched Erik Oliver, a five-year veteran of the RPD, to the White House for a forty-five-minute meeting with Obama and Vice President Joe Biden. There, Oliver also briefed the administration on best practices for engaging police departments with their communities. When Obama's attorney general, Loretta Lynch, toured six cities noted for their "community policing, relationship building, and crime reduction," Richmond was on her schedule.

During her local visit, Lynch went to RPD headquarters, city hall, and the RYSE Youth Center. Although some RYSE members were critical of policing in Richmond high schools, Gemika Henderson praised a Richmond officer who encouraged her to succeed in school. "What was different about him?" Lynch asked Henderson. "He cared," the young woman replied. "He was a cool dude. You didn't see him as a uniform because he saw you as a person."[16] The frank exchange with Lynch at RYSE was arranged, Magnus explained, because "we are not here to say 'mission accomplished.'"

Nothing underlined that self-critical stance more than the chief's controversial role in a community vigil, sponsored by RYSE, in December 2014. About one hundred people lined up on both sides of Macdonald Avenue, the city's main thoroughfare, for four and a half hours, the period of time that Michael Brown lay in the street in Ferguson after being shot. When a young protestor handed Magnus a hand-painted sign proclaiming that "Black Lives Matter," he displayed it to passing traffic, while chatting with others at the event. "I've never seen anything like it, not in Richmond, not anywhere else," said longtime resident Mary Square. "The police chief holding a sign calling for an end to police violence. . . . I'm going to tell my kids."[17]

The chief's dramatic gesture of conciliation was praised by city officials, like Lindsay, Butt, and McLaughlin. As local commentators observed, the otherwise uneventful vigil in downtown Richmond stood in sharp contrast to the almost simultaneous street clashes between police and protestors in Berkeley and Oakland, just a few miles away, after grand juries failed to indict Brown's killer in Ferguson or the officer who fatally choked Eric Garner in New York City.

Yet, after a photo of Magnus and his sign appeared in local and national media outlets, this rare fraternization between a uniformed officer and police brutality protestors was condemned by the Richmond Police Officers Association. "Police chiefs are not above the law," declared RPOA lawyer Alison Berry Wilkinson. "While many may admire the chief for proactively engaging with the community on one of the most significant political issues of the day, by doing so in uniform, he violated the very laws he is sworn to uphold."[18]

The law invoked by Wilkinson was California's Government Code, which prohibits public employee participation "in political activities of any kind while in uniform." On Facebook and in his own press interviews, Magnus rejected her accusation. He asked his critics how it became "a political act to acknowledge that 'black lives matter' and show respect for the very real concerns of our minority communities?" The chief's local defenders also pointed out that police union officials had frequently been pictured, in uniform, in past election mailers, paid for by Chevron or RPOA itself.[19]

The RPOA criticism of Magnus was muted compared to outbursts elsewhere, directed at protestors or public officials who sided with them. Police-union lobbying, contract bargaining, or representation of individual officers is now viewed, by critics on the left and right, as an obstacle to public safety reform. As *New York Times* columnist David Brooks argues, "If you look at all the proposals that have been discussed since the cases of Michael Brown in Ferguson, Mo., and Eric Garner in New York, you find that somewhere or other around the country, police unions have opposed all of them."[20]

Within the labor movement some activists demand that unions representing cops be shunned. At the University of California, Brandon Buchanan, a graduate student employee, persuaded his 13,000-member affiliate of the United Auto Workers to seek expulsion of the International Union of Police Associations (IUPA) from the AFL-CIO. "We are seeing a number of police unions and associations criticizing black activists for addressing the needs of their communities, and actively working to cover up and dismiss issues of police brutality in their departments," Buchanan contends. "They always seem to be out there ready to defend and support the status quo."[21]

Although Magnus was a past (and future) target of union criticism himself, he took a more nuanced view, based on his own rank-and-file experience in Lansing, Michigan. There Magnus had joined other union reformers who favored "an alternative way of addressing a lot of the issues we had with management." His opposition slate defeated long-time incumbents no longer in touch with the concerns of younger officers. "This happens on a larger scale, obviously, in communities and [in] police departments in general," he explained. "You see departments go through cycles. They go with the status quo for a long time, and then all of a sudden it doesn't work anymore, and you have to have some change."

The RPOA underwent a leadership change itself shortly after its much-publicized criticism of Magnus. To clear the air about his "Black Lives Matter" sign holding, the chief held a meeting with new union president Virgil Thomas and other officers that one participant recalled "was not warm and fuzzy." Afterward, Thomas told the press that "we talked about it, and I understood what he was trying to do. He's trying to bridge the gap, like we all are." A Richmond cop for nineteen years, Thomas was among those skeptical of Magnus when he was hired. "I mean, not only was he coming from outside the department, he was coming from Fargo, of all places. But he came in with a plan and stuck to it, and the image of the city and the police has changed dramatically. Morale has improved greatly."[22]

By 2014, even Lieutenant Shawn Pickett, a former plaintiff in the race discrimination case against Magnus, was giving the chief his due. "We had generations of families raised to hate and fear the Richmond police," he said. "A lot of that was the result of our style of policing in the past. It took us a long time to turn that around and we're seeing the fruits of that now. There is mutual respect, and some mutual compassion."[23]

In local progressive circles any new respect and compassion for the police was about to be tested—due to an "officer involved shooting," in the terminology of insiders. In the wake of a tragic incident, the city's police reform progress would be questioned not only by friends and family of the deceased. They would be joined by local advocates of strengthened civilian oversight in Richmond and by police brutality critics from out of town, who saw little difference between Richmond cops and their counterparts in other cities.

A DEATH AT UNCLE SAM'S

By the summer of 2014, there had not been a fatal shooting of a Richmond resident by the police since 2007. Between 2008 and 2014, despite making thousands of arrests and confiscating, on average, one gun a day, the RPD was recording less than one officer-involved shooting of any kind per year. (Cops in nearby Vallejo, a city only slightly larger than Richmond but with similar problems, managed to kill six Vallejo citizens in 2012 alone.) On September 6, 2014, the *Contra Costa Times* ran a story, citing these and other favorable comparisons. Its headline: "Use of Deadly Force by Police Disappears on Richmond Streets."[24] Just one week later, however, there was a fatal encounter between Wallace Jensen, a Spanish-speaking officer with seven years of RPD experience, and twenty-four-year-old Richard Pedro Perez III. It took place near midnight, just outside Uncle Sam's Liquors and

Deli, in the middle of a grimy block of one-story retail buildings, between Nancy's Nail Salon and the Taqueria Chavinda, at the intersection of Cutting Boulevard, Stege Avenue, and South Thirty-Fourth Street.

Perez had been released from detention earlier in the day after a drunk-driving arrest. He was also on probation for firing a gun in a salvage lot a few blocks away, where he lived in a trailer and worked for Perez Brothers Paper Recycling, his family's firm. When Officer Jensen responded to a complaint about Perez causing a disturbance in Uncle Sam's, a store with a history of late-night loitering problems, he found the young man to be heavily intoxicated and unsteady on his feet. According to Jensen, Perez did not remain seated on the curb outside the store, as instructed, while his identity was being verified.

This led to physical grappling between the two. An "independent witness" later cited by Magnus reported that Perez "grabbed and held on to one of the officer's hands while using his other hand to simultaneously go for the officer's gun." Defenders of Perez claimed this version of events was contradicted by other unnamed witnesses. His family and friends knew Pedie, as he was called, to be kind, generous, funny, lately depressed but, drunk or sober, no great danger to anyone else.

The RPD was still a few months away from requiring all officers to wear body cameras. So there was no video record of any threatening behavior by Perez before Jensen fired three bullets into him. Surveillance camera footage, obtained from Uncle Sam's, showed Perez lurching back into the store, collapsing face-down, in the middle of an aisle. "I was afraid he was going to take my gun and kill me," Jensen told a coroner's inquest several months later.

The Perez family immediately retained John Burris, a well-known Oakland civil rights attorney, to sue the city. Burris's most famous previous case involved Oscar Grant, an unarmed twenty-two-year-old Oakland resident who died on a Bay Area Rapid Transit (BART) platform in 2009. Grant had been shot in the back by a BART police officer while handcuffed and lying face-down. The officer was later convicted of involuntary manslaughter after his lawyer argued, at trial, that his client had used his gun by mistake, instead of his Taser. The BART system agreed to a $2.8 million civil settlement with Grant's family. The shooter served

eleven months in jail. The case became nationally known after release of
Fruitvale Station, a Hollywood movie about Grant's life and death.

Pedie Perez's aunt invited Chris Magnus to her nephew's funeral, which
Magnus and Deputy Chief Allwyn Brown both attended in civilian clothes.
Magnus also deployed his considerable social media skills to disseminate detailed information about how parallel investigations of the shooting would
be conducted by the RPD's Professional Standards Unit and the Contra
Costa County District Attorney's Office. RPD maintains a website, a Facebook page, and the chief's own Twitter account to fulfill its organizational
"commitment to transparency and openness," soliciting citizen feedback
even if "questioning or critical." "One of the things we tried to convey is
that we have genuine sympathy for the family and acknowledge that the
death of this young man is tragic," Magnus said, noting that the "officer
involved had to make a very tough decision in a matter of seconds."

The RPD reported that Jensen, a member of its crisis negotiation team,
had received special training in how to handle volatile situations. Pending
the outcome of the multiple investigations into his conduct, he was placed
on paid administrative leave. The officer's shooting of Perez spawned a
public protest by about forty people at RPD headquarters. Based on the
information initially available, other Richmond activists seemed to reserve judgment because, as Mike Parker explained, "people had a lot of
confidence that the police would look into it and deal with it." City council candidates, backed by the RPA, were, at the time, touting improved
public safety and better police behavior as grounds for their reelection.

La Voz, a bilingual Richmond newspaper edited by RPA cofounder
Juan Reardon, did run an article headlined "Latino Youth Fights with
Police Officer and Is Fatally Shot"—although that was definitely not the
Perez family's preferred framing of the incident. Pedie's parents demanded
to know why Jensen didn't use his nightstick or Taser to subdue their
son, although the latter police tool is not always nonlethal, as it is said to
be.[25] Noting that Richmond had "spent more than $500,000 since 1997
to outfit police officers with Tasers and, in recent years approximately
$27,000 on new Tasers and replacement cartridges," *La Voz* asked similar
questions: "Did the officer have a taser gun available to him? If not, why
not? Did he have it and not use it? Why?"

The RPD's own investigation later confirmed that Jensen was wearing his Taser and a flashlight, which can be used as a baton. After the Contra Costa County DA ruled that Jensen had acted in self-defense, he was returned to duty, even before the RPD completed its own investigation of whether this was "justifiable homicide." (Jensen later sought and was granted medical disability retirement from the RPD.)

Members of the Oscar Grant Committee Against Police Brutality and State Repression—a group formed after the shooting of Oscar Grant—asked the RPA to host a community forum on the Perez case. RPA coordinators Mike Parker and Marilyn Langlois welcomed these visitors, plus a sprinkling of RPA members, to a Sunday afternoon meeting in late April 2015. Parker criticized the DA's exoneration of Jensen but disclaimed any RPA interest in becoming "the jury or judge in this case." As he told the crowd of about forty people, "we're extremely proud of our police chief and police department."

That civic pride was not shared by the Grant Committee. One of its Oakland-based leaders told me that any Richmond "socialist who defends Chris Magnus is a betrayer of the working class." Rather than letting the disturbing details of the Perez case speak for themselves, Grant Committee speakers, like Gerald Smith, framed a general indictment of US policing that largely ignored Richmond's own hard-won reforms. "There is a system in place to deny these dastardly crimes and cover them up," asserted Smith. "This murder is a test—this is what determines what kind of city you live in." Other Oakland visitors trained their fire on the extra layer of legal protection that cops get during investigations that might result in job-related discipline or criminal charges or both. The Grant Committee believes that this "police officer bill of rights," which applied to Jensen, should be repealed in California (and sixteen other states with similar statutes) although sympathetic legislators in Sacramento have not even been able to amend it.[26]

The most compelling speakers at the meeting were grief-stricken friends and family of the deceased, who had no political axe to grind. "I just want flat-out justice," said Rick Perez, a stocky, bearded, red-faced man wearing a blue work shirt and under it a T-shirt displaying his son's picture. "If that cop did what I think he did, we don't need cops like that." Unlike his family's out-of-town helpers, Perez acknowledged that Chris Magnus had "done a good job" in Richmond. He described Officer Jensen as "a bad apple on the force, who made a bad decision and needs to be held accountable for it." Several nights after the Grant Committee presented its case against Jensen, Richmond city councilors held their own inquiry. The subject of their "study session" was RPD methods for avoiding the use of deadly force, and investigating such incidents when they occurred. Chris Magnus was the leadoff witness, flanked by captains and lieutenants involved in both training and upholding professional standards among the department's 185 sworn officers.

In 2014, Magnus reported, the RPD responded to 122,159 calls for service. Nearly 3,000 resulted in somebody being arrested (and 357 guns being confiscated). But only 6 percent of all Richmond arrests required the use of force in some form. In those situations, a Taser was deployed about 25 percent of the time. Seventy of the 182 suspects arrested with the use of force were injured, along with 22 officers involved in detaining them. In 2014 there were 12 investigations related to allegations of excessive force. These cases involved civilian complaints made directly to the RPD or Richmond's Police Commission, or internal reviews of officer conduct initiated by the department itself.

To aid such probes, all RPD personnel with the rank of sergeant or below are now required to wear body cameras and turn both audio and video on when responding to calls for service. However, if body cam footage or other evidence results in later misconduct accusations, the public's right to information is not unlimited, Magnus warned.

"I'm a huge advocate for transparency in policing," the chief told the city council. "But I have to face some realities, as [do] our department and city. Police officers have very specific rights to due process in many different circumstances, including officer-involved shootings and other matters that could lead to disciplinary action. So we have to follow that Police Officers' Bill of Rights or we can be sued by the officer. . . . That means we're limited in what kind of information we can release at different stages of an officer-involved-shooting investigation, when that is ongoing."

Magnus and other presenters also explained how "scenario-based training," involving frequent role-playing, has augmented shooting range exercises. The RPD's new approach teaches better firearm decision making. In addition, more than a dozen officers have been trained to respond to crisis situations involving mentally ill people who threaten to harm themselves or others.

"You will see repeatedly that officers are using a wide set of skills, including good verbal, sensitivity, and de-escalation skills to gain people's cooperation," Magnus said. "The results clearly speak for themselves. We have had only two fatal officer-involved shootings in a period of ten years . . . despite the fact that we still have a lot of violence in this community. That's one of the lowest rates of force you're going to find in any urban police department in this country. And that's a testament to the kind of patience, empathy, and skill that officers use in doing their job."

The de-escalation training and alternatives to deadly force that Magnus and his command staff described are designed in part to correct deficiencies in the curricula of many US police academies. There, as the *New Yorker* has reported, new recruits may be "rigorously trained in firing weapons and apprehending suspects but not in establishing common ground with people who have had different experiences. . . . A recent survey by the Police Executive Research Forum revealed that cadets usually receive fifty-eight hours of training in fire arms, forty-nine in defensive tactics, ten in communication skills, and eight in de-escalation tactics."[27]

The RPD's briefing on its use-of-force protocols got a mixed council meeting reception. Several members of the audience, rallied by the Oscar Grant Committee, questioned the seven-month delay in getting a Professional Standards Unit decision about Officer Jensen's future. They expressed continuing doubts about the official account of what transpired at Uncle Sam's on September 14. Other speakers objected to the special treatment of police officers under investigation for alleged misconduct, a statutory constraint acknowledged in the RPD's presentation.

"That bill of rights has to go," Rick Perez told the city councilors and assembled RPD brass. "Police are citizens just like us, and if they make bad decisions, they have to be answerable for them, just like we would be. . . . All of these internal investigations you guys got are just among the blue brotherhood. It's a gang, just like the Hell's Angels. They're going to back each other the same way."

"My trust in the department is definitely broken," said Carol Johnson, a McLaughlin appointee to the city's Human Rights Commission. "We have to balance the police officers' bill of rights with our human rights, because Pedie Perez did not get due process; he just got murdered."

In their quest for justice, the Perez family also felt thwarted by the Richmond Police Commission (RPC). The commission was created by the city council in 1984 in response to the abuses of the "cowboy" era; even the RPOA agreed that this form of civilian oversight was necessary. The RPC was charged with investigating citizen complaints involving "the use of force or racially abusive treatment." But, thirty years later, its nine members were operating with limited funds and a part-time staff. Between 2005 and 2015, the commission received only a handful of complaints annually and sustained just one. When Rick Perez learned of the RPC's existence and objected to Jensen's use of force there, the RPC's own investigator (a former police chief in another city) and Richmond city attorney Bruce Goodmiller ruled that his complaint was untimely.

Goodmiller also warned RPC members like Felix Hunziker not to discuss the Perez case publicly, citing the pending lawsuit filed by Burris. In an online response titled "Justice Denied in Richmond," Hunziker questioned both of Goodmiller's actions. He argued that the commission needed greater resources and a rewrite of its authorizing ordinance to permit truly independent reviews of police misconduct in the future. Magnus favored a different and rather unusual structural reform: putting RPD internal affairs investigations under the control of a civilian. In Richmond, such probes are now handled by an Office of Professional Accountability, located in city hall rather than within the department; the OPA's first director has been previously employed as a police officer, lawyer, and judge.

Magnus remained skeptical of what even a revamped RPC could accomplish, given the constraints of existing California law. "If you have the right chief, you're going to get better results," he told me.[28] In early 2016, however, a city council majority sided with advocates of strengthened civilian oversight through the RPC. The council voted to extend its complaint filing period to 120 days from 45. The commission is now required to investigate every officer-involved civilian fatality or serious injury (that results in hospitalization for more than three days), even without a trigger-ing complaint. The RPC has been renamed the Citizens' Police Review Commission (CPRC). With the help of its own professional investigator, who can subpoena officers and question them under oath, the CPRC was authorized to conduct its own belated probe of the Perez case. As these changes made their way through the process of city council approval, All-wyn Brown, RPD deputy chief under Magnus (and later his successor), told the *East Bay Express* that he wasn't worried about having "another pair of eyes and ears for checks and balances."[29]

The city council also approved a settlement of the lawsuit filed by Burris. The Perez family received a payment of $850,000, and the city admitted no liability in the case. The Oscar Grant Committee explained that its continuing advocacy of "an independent investigation" of any police officers "inflicting harm on other community members" did not reflect "antipathy towards the RPD, but merely an effort to hold them accountable." The committee even applauded "the fine job that the ma-jority of officers are doing" and acknowledged, belatedly, that "many of the reforms implemented by Richmond have been helpful, contributing to better police-community relationships."

CEASE-FIRE—ALIVE AND FREE?

Though Officer Jensen's shooting of Pedie Perez was an understandable preoccupation of his grieving friends and family, almost all young peo-ple of color who die from gun violence in Richmond are killed by each other. At a candlelight memorial service for one such victim, a popu-lar sixteen-year-old basketball player shot in his own driveway, Magnus questioned Richmond's ability to maintain peace by making more arrests. "There are way too many illegal guns out there—and too much access to them," he said. "We need to be moved to action. Violent crime is an outcome we can all influence."

One Richmond civic network founded on that premise is Richmond Ceasefire. It includes the RPD, local churches, community groups, and concerned individuals seeking to reduce Richmond's declining but still appalling rate of violent deaths. Ceasefire sponsors periodic nighttime walks through different parts of the city, with highly visible participation

from pastors and members of religious congregations like the New Hope
Missionary Baptist Church, in North Richmond, and the Reverend Alvin Bernstine's Bethlehem Missionary Baptist Church at the other end
of town.

The act of walking, collectively and peacefully, along a route from
Bernstine's church, through nearby Richmond neighborhoods like Crescent Park and on to North Richmond or back is symbolic and significant.
Much gunplay by local gang members is turf-related, involving tit-for-tat
shootings and other dangerous forays into enemy territory. When there is
a cycle of retaliatory violence underway, daily life in affected neighborhoods or particular low-income apartment complexes becomes even more
claustrophobic, not to mention dangerous, for bystanders of all ages.

Some Ceasefire volunteers, like Valerie Duncan, have no shortage of
street cred. "I've carried pistols. I've ducked lead and bullet fire. Sold dope.
I've done all of that," Duncan told the *Richmond Confidential*, a community
news service operated by the UC-Berkeley Journalism School. As a church
member, Duncan joined the collective effort to identify younger people
most at risk of committing violent crimes and help them find a different
path. In one of his quarterly *RPD Updates*, Chief Magnus described the
available options in tough-love fashion: "Ceasefire involves doing call-ins
or making home visits to active shooters. The called in individuals are
then given a choice: accept support and services to get out of the gang life
(including job training, anger management counseling, substance abuse
services, etc.) or expect tougher police scrutiny and consequences associated with any criminal behavior."[30]

An anonymous RPD source confirmed to Joe Eskenazi that the "premise of Ceasefire is not as flattering as a Kumbaya story. It's about focusing
on 75 of the most violent people in the city—who lose their anonymity,
become paranoid, and leave."[31] For its devoted volunteers, Ceasefire work
remains a blessed obligation and never-ending grind. Anyone looking for
instant results need not apply. As Valerie Duncan notes with frustration,
"We're doing everything we can as a church—we march, we protest—and
they're still killing each other left and right."[32]

Stopping that killing is the full-time mission of Richmond's Office
of Neighborhood Safety. ONS was created in 2007, with strong backing

from Magnus, Bill Lindsay, and Gayle McLaughlin, a year after she became mayor. "We decided that Richmond would never be able to achieve its goals with this violent crime ball and chain," Lindsay recalls. "The city would never be able to move forward."

ONS receives an annual city budget allocation (now $1.1 million a year) to hire and deploy six full-time youth mentors with past prison or gang experience. Like Ceasefire volunteers, these "neighborhood change agents" try to identify Richmond youth most prone to gang membership and/or gun violence. Participants in the Operation Peacemaker Fellowship run by ONS receive eighteen months of job training, counseling, and life-skills classes, as well as financial incentives for abandoning criminal activity. Its privately funded stipends aren't much—no more than one thousand dollars monthly for a maximum period of nine months. But the novel idea of "paying kids to stay alive" helped ONS director DeVone Boggan garner almost as much national media attention as the police reforms of Chris Magnus.[33]

For example, *PBS NewsHour* reported in May 2016 that "sixty-eight men have completed the Peacemaker Fellowship so far. And according to the program, only about 20 percent have been arrested or charged for new gun crimes. Thirteen were convicted and got kicked out of the program. . . . The number of murders here in Richmond has fallen by half in the last decade—from 42 in 2006 to 21 in 2015."[34]

While these metrics arouse some doubts locally—mainly within the RPD—ONS has won high marks from the National Council on Crime and Delinquency. According to the NCCD, Richmond's crime stats improved due to a "number of factors, including policy changes, policing efforts, and an improving economic climate." But "the work of the ONS was a strong contributing factor in a collaborative effort to decrease violence in Richmond."[35] Those results were good enough for neighboring Oakland, as well as Toledo, Ohio, and Washington, DC, all of which have begun replicating Richmond's Operation Peacemaker in some fashion.

As the charismatic Boggan noted in one MSNBC appearance, "the clearance rate" of cases in cities with the most gun violence is pretty low; too many homicides never get solved. ONS-style mentoring and personal income support is proactive and preemptive if successful with particular

individuals. "Targeted youth are out on the streets already, not appre-
hended yet, but idle, substance abusing, and another homicide waiting to
happen. Why not engage them?"[36] In Richmond, objections to doing just
that have been largely overcome, even if the resources allocated to ONS
hardly meet the scale of need. Locally, far more young people need to find
jobs, return to school, or otherwise turn their lives around before they
end up dead or in the street-to-prison pipeline. ONS interventions, like
Richmond's broader implementation of community policing, can make
the community safer but not economically more secure for a population
still predominantly poor and working class.

FOUR

TUESDAY NIGHT CAGE FIGHTS

IN THE NOT SO DISTANT PAST, a snobby neighbor like the mayor of El Cerrito could dismiss Richmond as the "arm pit of the East Bay."[1] Now the
city was being hailed as a "progressive utopia." Richmond's policy innovation, including its exemplary crime-reduction efforts, landed Gayle Mc-
Laughlin and her city on the front page of the *New York Times*. Richmond
was feted in both the mainstream media and numerous left-liberal journals, and when our city council passed an ordinance better protecting the
formerly incarcerated against job discrimination, even Fox News hosted
a Richmond-inspired debate on the merits of "ban the box" legislation.

But beneath the warm glow of such favorable publicity, a more disturbing local reality was unspooling at Tuesday night meetings of the city
council. Politics in Richmond has long been a brutal, stressful contact
sport. In 2013–2014, election-year rancor became a permanent fixture of
civic life. Whether the proceedings were viewed in real time by the council's live audience or later via public access cable, the content was shocking.
The council chambers were filled with bitter, escalating clashes between
old and new political forces. Each faction commanded its own devoted
following. So when the verbal jousting started during "public comment"
periods, anyone seated on the dais—who was disliked or distrusted by one
side or the other—could become a target. The resulting public spectacle
was described by local author David Helvarg as the equivalent of "watching cage fighting on TV."

At these Tuesday night tussles, Mayor McLaughlin and her vice mayor, Jovanka Beckles, were the RPA leaders who saw the most action. At fifty-one, Beckles is youthful in appearance and exuberant in manner. She sometimes ends her political speeches with a Black Panther flourish. Thrusting her right fist high above her head, she signs off with a sixties catchphrase: "All power to the people!" She radiates such relentless good humor and palpable sincerity that she can deliver this line without coming off as hopelessly retro.

McLaughlin and Beckles were regularly pitted against fellow councilors Nat Bates and Courtland "Corky" Booze, whose last name is pronounced "Boo-zay." Bates was first elected to the council in 1967. His new sixty-nine-year-old sidekick, Corky, was a first-termer, elected in 2010 and previously dismissed by Bates and other black community leaders as "a noisy gadfly."[2] A former stock-car racer who became the owner of a gas station and auto shop, Booze has a flamboyant gift for gab that beguiled some in the press and attracted a core of devoted followers in the African American community. His personal life and business history were both marked by controversy, sometimes arising from physical scuffles with men and women much smaller than him (Booze is about six foot three, 230 pounds).

For two decades, Corky balked at cleaning up the accumulation of junk on his Richmond commercial property that the city deemed a public nuisance and fire hazard. Contra Costa County court records listed him as a defendant in more than thirty civil cases, mainly involving unpaid debts. With similar financial acumen he also failed to handle political campaign funds properly, triggering investigations and sanctions by the California Fair Political Practices Commission, involving some of his ten council races (only one of which was successful). Corky's personal narcissism and rhetorical bullying rivaled that of Donald Trump. Like "The Donald," he often referred to himself in the third person.

During Gayle McLaughlin's first term as mayor, she nevertheless recognized Booze's better side on several occasions. In 2007 he was among seventeen activists who received Richmond's Martin Luther King Jr. Leadership Award; three years later, Booze was among a smaller group of African Americans honored by the mayor during Black History Month.[3]

While running for reelection in 2010 on a platform calling for greater "fairness and civility in the exercise of government," McLaughlin endorsed Booze's own council campaign, as did her colleague Tom Butt.

Butt acknowledged that Booze was not always "politically correct," but touted him anyway, as someone "in tune with a large segment of the community that routinely goes unrepresented because they do not have money, power, and influence." According to Butt, "Everyone deserves a voice in Richmond. Corky has been that voice." These were endorsements both Butt and McLaughlin would later regret making. Neither had any idea at the time just how politically incorrect—not to mention uncivil—Booze's voice would later become, after he and his followers parted company with their 2010 campaign allies. As a new member of the council, Booze soon bonded with Bates, and the two began marching in lockstep with Chevron and other local business interests.

Both opposed the soda tax and the Richmond Cares program. Booze questioned the effectiveness of the city's Office of Neighborhood Safety and the money Richmond was spending on it. Both Bates and Booze opposed the Marin Clean Energy option, promoted by Butt as a way of making Richmond utility users less dependent on fossil fuel generation of electricity. Neither Bates nor Booze favored issuing a municipal ID card to undocumented immigrants in Richmond, and they also opposed curtailment of RPD traffic stops that had in the past targeted undocumented immigrants.

Both stances were much resented by the city's growing Latino community. But Booze's nearly overnight transformation from man of (some of) the people to Chevron's new best friend was well rewarded in the usual Big Oil fashion. YouthBuild, a local workforce development project that he favored, received back-to-back annual grants of $100,000 from Chevron. As Tom Butt noted, Corky took full credit for this funding, which "burnished his reputation and gave him the bragging rights to go with it."

In their pursuit of political advantage, Bates and Booze helped manufacture a city hall controversy over official recognition of gay rights, and Booze would not let up. Council clashes escalated after a rainbow flag was hoisted over Richmond city hall in June 2013 to celebrate Pride Month. The flag-raising was requested by Beckles, and McLaughlin agreed to it, leaving the official announcement to her top assistant, Nicole Valentino, who is African American and Beckles's partner in marriage. In an e-mail to six hundred city staff members and officials, Valentino explained that Richmond was simply supporting "Lesbian, Gay, Bi-Sexual, Transgendered, Queer, and Questioning struggles and movements for recognition and equality."

Bates and Booze demanded to know why gay pride colors had been raised without prior city council approval. They seized upon a handful of complaints from city workers who opposed this gesture of solidarity. One such e-mail expressed the fear that Richmond was becoming like San Francisco's Castro District, a predominantly gay neighborhood. Council meeting attendees aligned with Bates and Booze accused McLaughlin of simultaneously slighting Juneteenth, Richmond's annual celebration of the end of slavery. "Why was *our* flag not flown?" one speaker demanded to know.

Beckles insisted that it was her responsibility as the only openly LGBT person on the council "to represent that segment of the community which is still being discriminated against." Although her emerging chorus of critics tried to depict her otherwise, Beckles had always been responsive to victims of bias in any form.

"The mayor determined to fly the flag, but that is something that should be determined by the council," Bates insisted. "Now we have a big stink. We have to be more sensitive to all the people in our diverse community." Among the displays of sensitivity that followed was a hostile crowd reaction to the reading of a city council resolution honoring gay and lesbian teens involved with the work of the RYSE Center. During the public comment section of council meetings, Booze incited and condoned repeated verbal assaults on Beckles's own sexual orientation. Making clear that he disapproved of her "lifestyle," Booze also criticized his Panamanian-born colleague for not really being African American, due to her country of origin. "She says she's a black Latina," he complained "Well, you're either African American or you're not."[4]

Booze's unrestrained filibustering, accompanied by jeers, cheers, chanting, marching around, and heckling by his fans in the audience finally forced the exasperated mayor to respond like any good progressive parent.

Constrained by law from ejecting a disruptive fellow elected official, Mc-Laughlin was reduced to calling time-outs to help restore order among her fractious colleagues. Booze, in turn, denounced her meeting chairing as a racist violation of his free speech rights and those of his supporters when they were removed from the room.

In fact, Bates and Booze were engaged in a concerted effort to demonstrate that the mayor could no longer chair an effective meeting. Despite being a frequent target of personal attacks, from RPA opponents and media outlets amplifying their criticism, McLaughlin had always maintained her placid composure and air of cherubic earnestness. Passionate on the stump when delivering a Richmond rally speech or pep talk at an RPA meeting, she presided over council sessions with the patient sing-song voice of a kindergarten teacher. As she tried to rein in the unruly around her, the stress and strain of incessant verbal conflict and public disrespect began to mount, and the physical and emotional toll was increasingly visible.

Even a daylong retreat for council members and senior city staff failed to change the behavior of those baiting McLaughlin and Beckles. The facilitator for this event was selected by City Manager Lindsay. He hoped city council members would find common ground on routine procedural matters at least. Bates, who had pressed for the retreat, only stayed for half of it. Neither he nor Booze would join their five colleagues in a joint pledge of mutual respect. (Booze declined on the grounds that it might prevent him from staying true to his principles.) Meanwhile, some in the community continued to show Booze undeserved respect. At an annual fund-raiser cosponsored by Chevron, the Richmond NAACP made him its guest of honor in 2013. At this dinner Booze was pleased to accept the Martin Luther King Jr. Peace and Freedom Award.[5] McLaughlin and Beckles, a fellow NAACP member, boycotted the event in somewhat truer MLK fashion.

As the verbal sparring escalated, council meeting interruptions led to frequent agenda delays, which made it harder for city employees to do their jobs. "The atmosphere makes it challenging to get work done," Lindsay said. "It can be demoralizing to a staff person who goes to a meeting to give a presentation on an item and waits hours only for the item to be held over to a later meeting."[6] Chris Magnus was forced to expand his Tuesday night police detail because, as he wryly put it, "we certainly have an engaged community when it comes to council meetings." The RPD's role there was not to make disorderly conduct arrests, he explained. Officers were instructed to act only "in a civil capacity," functioning as sergeants at arms, which meant they needed to be responsive to the mayor, as the meeting chair.

Some Richmond cops got their signals crossed about who was in charge of such ejections. At one particularly raucous session in September 2013, Booze made a demeaning comment about his fellow councilor, Jael Myrick. In response, RPA cofounder Juan Reardon, a member of the audience, reacted with disgust, drawing Booze's attention. The latter demanded that Reardon be removed from the room. According to the responding officer's later report, Reardon had been "raising his arms in the air and flailing them around." When Reardon was asked to leave, he allegedly told the officer: "You are not the governing body, the mayor is the governing body, and I don't have to listen to you!" In the next day's *Contra Costa Times*, the RPA leader was criticized for having a double standard on council meeting decorum. At prior sessions, according to the paper, Reardon himself had "used the public speaker's microphone to lecture residents, who had been disruptive." In short, the "cage fights" made everyone look bad, sooner or later. Those creating a circus-like atmosphere in the council chamber clearly hoped to reap electoral benefit from this. In 2014 both Beckles and McLaughlin faced campaigns for reelection; voters fed up with city council "dysfunction" (but not following matters too closely) might blame them for it rather than those actually responsible.

Beckles's demanding day job, as a child protection worker for the county, put her in close touch with the needs of low-income families. Many struggle with drug use, domestic abuse, teen pregnancy, joblessness, and lack of affordable housing and child care. As the personal attacks on her increased, Beckles's second job, her part-time work on the council, became even more stressful, tiring, and time consuming. Even under more normal circumstances, when council sessions were not so acrimonious and didn't last until 11 p.m. or later, the official workload was great and public expectations high.

"I'm expected to keep on top of thousands of pages of documents every week," Beckles notes. "I'm expected to dig deep into issues to understand them. I'm expected to appear at dozens of events every week. I'm expected to counter the dozens of paid lobbyists and experts that corporations hire. I don't have a personal staff. All the Richmond city council members get to share one paid staffer. The only way that we can carry out a progressive agenda, once elected, is if we keep organizing." Yet several years into her career as a municipal official Beckles still encountered voters who "think that politics is about electing some savior."

The mounting attacks on Beckles worried RPA leaders because, as one confided, "The homophobic baiting had legs in the African American community. It was the nut cases who did it, but they had broader support." What the "nut cases" had to say was hard to justify under the rubric of free speech unless you were Nat Bates, also a strong believer in the First Amendment rights of corporate "persons" like Chevron. When Richmond resident Mark Wassberg and others were accused of using "hate speech," Bates defended them. "You're filth. You're dirt," a wild-haired Wassberg told Beckles during one council meeting, with no rebuke from Bates. "I'm going to keep coming up here and telling you how gays have no morality, because I have the constitutional right to say it."

Beckles's fellow councilor Jim Rogers was no profile in courage during such confrontations. While serving previously as a county supervisor, Rogers had marketed himself throughout the Bay Area as "the People's Lawyer," a stand-up guy for clients with small but important legal claims.[7] On Tuesday nights, amid the weekly crossfire at council meetings in Richmond, Rogers tended to keep his head down. In an interview, he explained why he rarely objected to Booze's constant disruptions and audience incitement. "Corky was so clever and good at getting inside people's heads and bringing them down to his level," Rogers said. "One of the things I'm most proud of is that Corky has not gotten me down to his level."

Rogers believed that city councilors, up for reelection in 2014, including himself, would not suffer from any voter backlash. He planned to run as a lonely "voice of reason" on the council, a thoughtful, results-oriented defender of the RPD, local public schools, consumers, and the environment. "I think that people who are incumbents are in good position," he told me. "The public ultimately judges us on how things are going on the ground, not based on what goes on at council meetings."

In contrast, Rogers's senior colleague Tom Butt didn't shy away from connecting the dots between the behavior of Bates and Booze and their main corporate benefactor. In a message to his constituents, Butt noted, "Virtually all the local organizations that routinely and repeatedly legitimize what Booze and Bates do are beneficiaries of Chevron, as are Bates and Booze themselves, both directly and indirectly. What all of these individuals who disrupt city council meetings and spew homophobic and xenophobic hate have in common is that they routinely criticize the RPA, the mayor, and Jovanka Beckles while extolling the virtues of Chevron."[8]

Chevron's public affairs manager for Richmond, Heather Kulp, found Butt's accusation to be not only "troubling" but also so "entirely false" that she demanded a public retraction. According to Kulp, no one in Richmond supported "the return of respect, civility, and good government" more than her employer. Chevron was, she asserted, a well-known foe of "hate speech in any form" and even boasted an in-house "PRIDE employee network that represents the company's core belief in diversity and inclusion." In Richmond, that network had hosted Beckles as a keynote speaker at a workplace Pride celebration. In addition, Kulp noted, the Human Rights Campaign, a national LGBT rights advocacy group, had rated the company one of the best places to work.

While Chevron distanced itself from the fray with its usual smooth dissembling, respected city figures, other local politicians, and Bay Area media outlets began to weigh in disapprovingly. In August 2014, the *San Francisco Chronicle* ran a front-page story detailing the "taunts, rants and ridicule about her sexual orientation and race" that Beckles had faced throughout her first council term. Two days later, the *Chronicle* ran a strong editorial condemning the use of "personal insults," involving "racial and sexual orientation slurs," at Richmond council meetings. "Re-establishing meaningful public debate is long overdue," the newspaper said. On her personal blog, park ranger Betty Reid Soskin argued that "the 23% of the Richmond population that is African-American was not well served [by city council misbehavior]." Soskin worried that there was "a growing racial barrier being reconstructed by the studied animosity being generated by the antics [of Booze and his followers]."[9]

As Richmond filmmaker Brenda Williams vividly captured in her 2015 documentary *Against Hate*, two of Beckles's most eloquent defenders were the Reverend Phil Lawson and the Reverend Kamal Hassan. These African American ministers spoke out at a packed city council meeting on September 15, 2014, attended by local gay activists and out-of-town supporters. Eighty-two-year-old Lawson, who participated in the 1965 civil rights march in Selma, reminded everyone present that "hate language hurts and kills and must never be accepted by the public." Hassan, pastor of Richmond's Sojourner Truth Presbyterian Church, argued that "African Americans, who have suffered oppression in all of its forms, must be against it in all of its forms." He condemned any misguided "use of the Bible to justify condemnation, rejection, and abusive speech and behavior towards same gender loving people." He joined other speakers in urging the council "to have zero tolerance for homophobic expression."

That big meeting turnout for Beckles, seven weeks before the council election, threw her usual foes on the defensive. It also helped build public support for a new code of conduct and city harassment policy to curb disruptions and limit hate speech at Richmond council meetings. Both guidelines are now in effect, with the first trying to balance the requirements of "robust debate" and a "public forum [that] provides an open, safe atmosphere" with a minimum of "physical disturbance." The updated policy against harassment is designed to discourage "public comment and critique" of city officials and employees that strays from their job performance or policymaking role to topics such as their race, ethnicity, sexual orientation, gender identity, or any other personal condition irrelevant to city functioning

BIG OIL STRIKES BACK

Over the past fifty years, few Richmond politicians have paid more consistent fealty to Big Oil than Nat Bates, now eighty-five years old. Bates is a veteran of the Korean War, a retired parole officer, and long-time pillar of the African American community. As a small boy he moved to Richmond from Texas and lived in wartime public housing with his mother, who cleaned railroad cars to support her family. Bates has always been a firm believer in the city's largest taxpayer and employer. What's good for

Chevron is, in his view, good for the community. Local refinery management reciprocated with generous financial backing for Bates's many successful campaigns for city council since 1967. Along the way he also got regular election year help from Darrell Reese, even after the Richmond firefighters' union leader and lobbyist for local developers pled guilty to felony income tax evasion.[10]

Getting Bates elected mayor in 2014 would definitely require the deep pockets of Chevron, with campaign spending unhindered by our local $2,500 cap on individual donations to municipal candidates. In 2010 the company had bankrolled Bates's failed attempt to prevent Gayle McLaughlin from winning a second term as mayor. Two years later, Bates bounced back strongly as the top city council vote getter, thanks to further industry spending on his behalf and stronger black turnout during a presidential election year. Although Richmond races are officially nonpartisan, Bates plastered the city with hundreds of campaign posters featuring twinned headshots of him and Barack Obama. These made it look like Obama had dropped Joe Biden in favor of Bates as his vice presidential candidate in 2012.

When I first met Bates, at a neighborhood party more than a year later, Richmond's senior city council member was still basking in the refracted glow of the Obama administration. He had just returned from a White House party hosted by the president and first lady (an event that included two hundred other guests). This event, I noticed later, had furnished Bates with a valuable photo-op. His picture with Obama was reproduced in full color on one side of a "Nat Bates for Mayor" fan, meant for use by Richmond churchgoers lacking air conditioning. On the other side of the fan Bates stood shoulder-to-shoulder with future presidential candidate Hillary Clinton, California attorney general Kamala Harris, and former San Francisco mayor Willie Brown, his past comrade in arms against the Richmond soda tax.

My first conversation with Bates was pretty much a one-way tutorial by him on the importance of knowing the right people in politics. At the Point Richmond holiday party where we met, he was surrounded by old friends and neighbors, past political patrons, and a few perennial adversaries. His genial hosts—ninety-year-old former California Assembly speaker

John Knox and his wife, Jean—welcomed such guests as US congressman George Miller, fellow Richmond city council member Tom Butt, and even two leading figures in the Richmond Progressive Alliance—Mike Parker and Margaret Jordan, who are neighbors of the Knoxes. By November 2014, three of these party guests—Bates, Butt, and Parker—would launch competing bids to become Richmond's next mayor.

At the time, only my new friend Nat was expressing much interest in the job or confidence in his ability to win it. In Bates's view, Richmond had become a magnet for political "nuts" with a "radical agenda." Under McLaughlin, city hall was "anti-business with tons of regulations, insensitive elected officials, and staff." Local progressives were out of touch with the real needs and concerns of longtime residents, regardless of their race, income, or neighborhood. But, Bates believed, the RPA had overplayed its hand. In 2014 the group was ripe for defeat because McLaughlin, its best-known standard-bearer, would be termed out, barred by state law from seeking a third term as mayor.

Bates regularly accused the RPA of practicing what he called "plantation-style politics." One example of this, in his mind, was McLaughlin's suggestion that Richmond consider renaming Macdonald Avenue, its main thoroughfare, for Nelson Mandela. Bates favored naming a street in Richmond after President Obama instead. McLaughlin was just trying to "generate African American votes for RPA candidates in November," he claimed. But that effort would fail because "they do not know the African American community as I know them."[11]

Meanwhile, the RPA's leading critic had no problem with the plantation-like feel of Big Oil's advertisements for itself in Richmond. In fact, he expressed full support for any and all Chevron media buys that made the company—and then him, as its favored candidate—look good to the electorate. "Chevron has been under attack by the RPA," he told me. "And they're going to protect their turf. . . . You better bet Chevron is going to favor someone with more sensitivity and compassion for what they're trying to do."

By the time Bates and I first talked, Chevron was already spending tens of millions of dollars on a multifaceted public relations campaign called Richmond Proud, which showcased the community-mindedness of his major benefactor. "For much of 2012 and even into 2013, all the billboards of Richmond's main streets were dominated by Chevron ads for its preferred city council candidates," Tom Butt observed. "Then they were replaced with the visages of smiling Chevron employees touting the company's dubious safety record. . . . Chevron appears constantly on TV and radio. There is nowhere you can go to escape the Chevron logo."

As the *Nation* reported, Chevron maintains a permanent "infrastructure of influence" in Richmond based on targeted philanthropy, as well as its outsize spending on local politics. After the 2012 fire, the company created a new vehicle for its charitable giving, called 4Richmond. Either through this 501(c)(4) organization or directly, Chevron began doling out $15.5 million in grants. In 2012, for example, "$37,000 went to the Richmond Chamber of Commerce, $10,000 to the Richmond Police Officers Association, nearly $450,000 to the local school district, and $15,000 to a local Latino merchants association."[12] Other lucky beneficiaries included Richmond neighborhood councils, local churches, ethnic festivals, the NAACP, YMCA, and Teach for America. Of course, worthy recipients of Chevron largesse, like the Police Activities League or the Familias Unidas, were happy to have their executive directors appear in Richmond Proud ads and billboards as a small token of their appreciation.

"They just infiltrate everything that is going on in the community," Butt said. "They spread around a lot of money to non-profits and most non-profits have community leaders on their boards, so they influence the community through co-opting community leaders."[13] While acknowledging, in his E-Forum, that Richmond's cash-strapped nonprofits need more resources, Butt objected to corporate philanthropy that has such "an ostentatious air about it" and just "reinforces the perception of Richmond as a company town." For Nat Bates, Chevron's post-fire charm offensive just added wind to his sails. If it succeeded, there would be no stopping his forthcoming run for mayor.

When I queried Melissa Ritchie, a local Chevron manager for external communications, about the connection between the company's political and charitable giving, she insisted that the "Richmond Proud Campaign has nothing to do with elections." She declined to provide any details about its budget, arguing that the more relevant figure was Chevron's larger financial commitment to making "our great community even better." Said Ritchie: "From 2009 to 2012, we spent over $500 million in this community, which includes our procurement spending with local businesses, the taxes the company pays, and its investments with nonprofits."

"Our participation in elections is focused on our independent expenditures campaign," she explained. "We generally don't provide direct contributions to candidates, including Nat Bates. And there are clear limits on what money can be given to candidates directly. . . . Our goal is to educate people about the qualifications of the candidates and allow voters to make their decision through their vote. All the monies we spend on elections are fully reported in accordance with government regulations."

Chevron's impending drive to retake city hall made finding a strong mayoral candidate a top priority of the RPA. During the winter of 2013–14, McLaughlin met privately with Butt to persuade him to run. Butt could not expect an official RPA endorsement, she explained, because he accepted donations from business. But, in McLaughlin's scenario, Butt and three RPA candidates, including herself running for her old council seat, would cross-endorse each other and run complementary 2014 campaigns. This left-liberal united front would increase everyone's chances of winning.

Within the RPA leadership, Butt was respected for his past civic leadership and willingness to criticize Chevron and work productively with RPA-backed city councilors on many issues. Progressive activists admired his savvy as an online communicator. For years Butt had been posting insightful political commentaries on his E-Forum, a list-serv with several thousand Richmond subscribers (an e-mail list rivaling the RPA's own). He was a deft and experienced handler of the mainstream press, always making himself available to Bay Area reporters and columnists covering Richmond issues.

Nevertheless, RPA's overture to Butt was made with some trepidation. Tom Butt is not a "movement person," as McLaughlin and others in the RPA think of themselves. He's an old-fashioned, good-government liberal, proud of his political independence. He was a lonely beacon of integrity during past politically troubled periods in Richmond. After RPA members joined the Richmond council, he became their frequent ally. But even then the founder of Interactive Resources, a local architecture firm, remained a political entrepreneur. He was not part of any collective organizational structure, whether the RPA or the local Democratic Party. Among Butt's RPA suitors in early 2014, there was some concern about how he would function as mayor, despite his forty years of experience managing a successful business. As one journalistic observer noted to me: "Tom, for all his pragmatism, is very intolerant of disagreement and other points of view. He's a take-my-toys-and-go-home kind of guy if he doesn't get his way."

Because of his background, Butt was sympathetic to small business concerns and wary of labor union agendas. For example, in 2014 he parted company with RPA council members over their attempt to fast-track city approval of a minimum wage hike. Butt believed that more time was needed to solicit Richmond business owner opinion about the impact of the increase. By the time a final measure was adopted—providing incremental increases to thirteen dollars per hour by 2018—Butt and fellow councilor Jim Rogers had succeeded in carving out exceptions for several categories of local business. RPA councilors grudgingly went along with the changes.

When Butt met with McLaughlin about the mayor's race, he expressed support for fellow Democrat Charles Ramsey, president of the West Contra Costa Unified School District Board. To Butt at the time, Ramsey seemed to have the best chance of beating Bates. He was a fifty-two-year-old African American attorney with close ties to contractors and building trades unions that valued his support for "project labor agreements" covering school construction and renovation. (These backers helped him quickly amass a $100,000 campaign treasury.) In the early stages of his mayoral campaign, Ramsey stressed that he, unlike McLaughlin, was a "consensus builder" who understood that "being adversarial and strident doesn't necessarily move the agenda forward."

Several months after the RPA's failed effort to recruit him, I interviewed Butt. In the lounge of the Hotel Mac, a century-old Point Richmond landmark that he helped restore and reopen, Butt seemed weary of recent city hall feuding. He displayed little enthusiasm for serving as mayor, recalling a previous run for the job in 2001, when he placed second in a field of four. Now, he said, "it takes a lot of money to get elected, races are excruciating and punishing." Those who win find themselves saddled with official duties that include "a lot of fluff stuff."

Sounding a bit like Ramsey, Butt yearned for more sensible centrism on the Richmond council. "It's really almost a shame that we don't have any moderate, smart, capable people willing to run," he told me. "Everybody out there is either on the progressive/socialist lunatic fringe or the Chevron, chamber of commerce, do-whatever-business-wants fringe." He expressed admiration for the RPA's field campaign and fund-raising capacity in the past. He was less bullish about how RPA standard-bearers, new and old, would fare in November 2014. "They've got a small bench," he said.

COMING OFF THE BENCH

After approaching Butt and learning of his choice for mayor, the RPA interviewed Ramsey too. Not surprisingly, the school board president was rejected as an alternative to Bates because of his "closeness to developers, unwillingness to reject major corporate contributions, and his lack of support for progressive struggles in Richmond," as Mike Parker later reported.[14] Next, the RPA sounded out Richmond native Doria Robinson about running for mayor. Robinson's work as director of Urban Tilth, Richmond's network of thirteen school and community gardens, gave her high visibility and lots of favorable publicity.

In fact, nothing symbolized the greening of Richmond more than the success of her privately funded but city hall–encouraged project. A graduate of Hampshire College in Massachusetts, Robinson had returned home to develop an urban agriculture venture that has trained and employed young people, conducted public education about the importance of healthy food, and provided greater access to it via its vegetable distribution. Founded when Richmond was fast becoming a "food desert," due to chain supermarket closures, Urban Tilth is now a widely acclaimed model for creating "a more sustainable, healthy, and just food system."

While considering the RPA's overture, Robinson sought advice from Butt. He suggested that she run for city council first, since no one had ever been elected mayor of Richmond without prior council experience. Ultimately, Robinson decided against running for any office, swayed by family considerations and some of the factors that initially deterred Butt from entering the mayor's race: the inevitability of facing a costly, grueling, and time-consuming campaign.

After Robinson demurred, a key member of the RPA's own candidate search committee, Mike Parker, decided to run for mayor himself, ultimately proving that the RPA bench was deeper than some people thought. During his six years in Richmond, Parker had become well known among local activists as a smart and articulate speaker at city council meetings. But his role in the RPA had mainly been behind the scenes, as an organizer and campaign coordinator. Parker had retired to Richmond after thirty-two years in Detroit, where he had been a skilled tradesman in the auto industry, a shop-floor socialist, and an advocate of union reform in the pages of *Labor Notes*, a national rank-and-file newsletter.

Before getting a job at Chrysler, Parker had studied political science at UC-Berkeley. Earlier in the 1960s he had belonged to the Young People's Socialist League at the University of Chicago, where he first met a fellow undergraduate named Bernie Sanders, who was also involved in the civil rights movement. Sanders went on to run for mayor of Burlington, Vermont, in 1981, when he was forty. Parker waited another thirty-three years to make his electoral debut at age seventy-three. Despite his background in the rough-and-tumble world of union politics, Mike was not a natural politician. The experience of being red-baited within the United Auto Workers, as a union dissident, would pale in comparison to what he would face after Chevron propagandists got hold of his radical resume.

So Parker reintroduced himself to the community with a substantive mayoral campaign website. It showcased his impressive grasp of local public policy details and his service as a McLaughlin appointee to Richmond's Workforce Investment Board. Parker also stressed his post-Chrysler work experience as a community college instructor, helping young people in Contra Costa County become industrial electricians and technicians. As mayor, he pledged, he would expand opportunities for similar job training so more of Richmond young people could qualify for better-paying private sector jobs. Parker's framing of the mayoral race stakes was simple and stark: "Chevron wants to retake the city council," he warned. "They want to sit down and negotiate with people they have already bought and paid for. That will be the main issue in this election."

Parker began his personal canvassing effort long before the normal election-year time frame for knocking on voters' doors. All spring and summer in 2014 he went door-to-door in various Richmond neighborhoods, while the RPA recruited an expanding pool of volunteers to do the same. Parker argued that "what we do in March and April is more important than September and October," and he was proven right, for several reasons. One was the increased use of mail ballots, which ended up being the way 50 percent of Richmond voters voted in 2014. Under California law, ballots can now be cast a month before an election, making traditional, last-minute turnout appeals less effective.

Parker developed the small donor based necessary for his campaign to seek local public matching funds (capped at $25,000). He also racked up helpful labor endorsements from Service Employees Local 1021 (which represents city hall employees), the California Nurses Association, National Union of Healthcare Workers, Amalgamated Transit Union, Communications Workers Local 9119, and others with members in Richmond. When a foreign labor organization, the Maritime Union of Australia (MUA), sought US allies for a global campaign against Chevron, Parker helped organize local solidarity. MUA's dispute with Chevron involved a $54 billion project to construct and maintain platforms for natural gas production. In an echo of its Richmond past, the oil company wanted to import contract laborers for this offshore work rather than employ MUA members known to make workplace safety demands.

Parker's labor activism, past or present, did not impress Big Oil's usual union allies in Richmond, who couldn't have been more unlike the militant MUA. In 2014, building trades leaders favored their old friend Nat Bates for mayor. When the Contra Costa County Central Labor Council met to endorse municipal candidates, Jim Payne, the financial secretary of USW Local 5 spoke on Parker's behalf. Payne reminded his fellow delegates that "Bates may have a building trades bug on his ass but his Chevron logo is bigger." The labor council ended up making no endorsement in the Richmond mayoral race, a partial victory for Parker supporters.

Parker's mayoral campaign overlapped fortuitously with Chevron's push to win city approval for a $1 billion refinery modernization plan, the major reason for its Richmond Proud campaign. At every stage of the permit approval process the RPA mayoral candidate was a forceful and persuasive critic of the company's blueprint for making its 112-year-old facility safer and cleaner. During the protracted local debate about refinery modernization, he spoke frequently at public hearings attended by hundreds of Chevron employees, building trades workers mobilized by their unions, local environmental activists, and concerned members of the community.

"The proposed way that Chevron wants to run its plant is unacceptable," Parker told the Richmond Planning Commission on one such occasion. He called for changes in refinery operating methods that would reduce "both local toxic emissions that damage our health and greenhouse gas emissions that damage our planet."

Modernization at Chevron had its own backstory. In 2005, the company had initiated a three-year push for city approval on a huge expansion project. There was strong community opposition then, based on fears that Chevron's not-so-hidden agenda was retooling so that it could process heavier and more environmentally hazardous crude oil. Nevertheless, a majority of Richmond city councilors voted to approve the state-required environmental impact report (EIR) necessary for the project to proceed. Communities for a Better Environment (CBE), the Asian Pacific Environmental Network, and others successfully challenged the project in court, based on shortcomings in the environmental impact study. Instead of filing a revised EIR, Chevron abruptly halted construction work, leading to twelve hundred layoffs. That management decision was no doubt influenced by the 2008 economic crash, which rendered refinery capacity sufficient for the time being. Per usual, the building trades blamed the resulting job loss on environmentalists linked to the RPA.

In 2013–14, Chevron revived its modernization plan, in scaled-back form, and initiated a new EIR review process. As details of its revised plan became clear, CBE, RPA, and others began organizing against it again. In their view, Chevron was still trying to reengineer the refinery so it could process dirtier and cheaper oil, boosting its profits but adding to local toxic emissions and greenhouse gas releases. With a promised one thousand jobs at stake, building trades unions favored quick approval by the city, with few questions asked and no conditions attached. Only about 10 percent of Chevron's several thousand workers actually live in

Richmond. Yet the company's most visible lobbying arm was hundreds of building trades workers, employed by Chevron contractors or even non–oil industry employers. They were mobilized repeatedly by their union business agents to attend Richmond community meetings and hearings about the refinery upgrade.

Refinery neighbors were a primary audience for Chevron's multimillion-dollar sales pitch. As part of its "commitment to transparency and accountability," and because "talking to our neighbors is important to us," the company conducted a series of "telephone town halls." These "open dialogues" drew up to four thousand participants. Chevron managers and safety engineers, air quality monitoring team members, and public affairs staff fielded questions on all aspects of refinery operations, employment opportunities, and product innovations (such as the invention of Techron, a fuel cleansing additive developed in Richmond).

After suspending its annual public tour of the refinery in 2012, due to fire-related damage repair, Chevron invited the neighbors over again the following year and just prior to the 2014 election. The event I attended had the air of family day at a factory anywhere. Many visitors were employees and their relatives. In white tents set up like a small farmers' market, kids could pick up a goody bag with a plastic "Chevron Fire Department" hat or a coloring book titled "See How Our Refinery Works!" Actual firefighters displayed their equipment and answered questions about on-site firefighting readiness. The requirements of plant security dictated that all our viewing of Chevron's 5,200 miles of pipe, threaded like strands of industrial spaghetti over 2,900 acres, be done through the windows of sleek, black, air-conditioned buses.

On my bus, our affable, well-informed tour guide was a Chevron environmental engineer who just wanted to "demystify what goes on in the plant" and assure us that the Bay Area has tough restrictions on "refinery flaring." He patiently explained the highly automated functioning of furnaces, reactors, exchangers, cracking and cooling towers, and storage tanks and spheres we passed on the tour. We learned about lubricant operations, distillation and reforming, "hydroprocessing," blending and shipping, and water recycling. As we passed the company's on-site Technology Center, the birthplace of Techron, our guide proudly noted that this was the first patented fuel additive ever developed for engines operating with unleaded gas. (With a staff that now includes 170 PhD scientists, Chevron in Richmond now files for about 125 new patents every year.) We also saw where "control center" crews spend twelve-hour shifts in bunker-like structures and where "outside operators" search for leaks and problems "to insure safe and reliable operation." We discovered that the refinery has its own "shelter in place building" if anything goes wrong.

Chevron neighbors who missed the tour got a knock on the door from a paid canvasser. Dozens fanned out to enlist ten thousand Richmond residents to sign a public statement of support for the company. When one of these signature gatherers came to our house, he simply asked: "Do you favor modernizing the refinery to make it safer?" Who was going to say no to that? The names collected were added to a giant list of modernization backers shown at public meetings. Positioning himself for his mayoral run, Nat Bates applauded this display of common sense. He accused Mayor McLaughlin and her environmental movement allies of thwarting much-needed job creation. Their demands for EIR changes and related financial commitments were "irresponsible" and "ridiculous," in his view. "They treat Chevron like a sugar daddy ATM machine with unlimited withdrawals," he grumbled.

Bates made his run for mayor official in May 2014. In an e-mail blast announcing his intentions, he urged voters to watch a short video so they could personally "witness the discord and lack of leadership in a dysfunctional city council." For six years, the parties responsible had milked the city's "welfare gift of taxpayer funds to all candidates," he said—a practice he would end. This characterization misrepresented how Richmond's public matching fund system actually works, since local office-seekers, with little support, frequently fail to raise enough private donations to qualify.[15] And, of course, when Bates held his own campaign kickoff at Salute, an upscale Italian restaurant on Richmond's waterfront, there was no pitch for personal donations at all, because he had relatively little need for them.

Bates's "People United for a Better Richmond" event was packed with representatives of his campaign's institutional investors—Chevron, the local business community, and building trades and public safety unions.

They were joined by members of the business-backed Black Men and Women (BMW) of Richmond and our local branch of the Black American Political Action Committee (BAPAC). Nattily dressed as always, Bates looked out at his admiring multiracial crowd and disclosed that his first order of business as Richmond's new mayor would be to impose a city council dress code. "Appearance is paramount," he declared, promising that his colleagues would soon be turning up in "decent attire." News of this important policy initiative was greeted with enthusiastic applause. The candidate then responded to the rumor, spread by his enemies in Richmond, that "Nat Bates is Chevron's boy."

Bates rightly objected to the racial connotation of this accusation, which I had never heard expressed in this fashion by any of his left-wing critics. "If I'm going to jump for anyone," he told the crowd, "it will be you!" (Given who was in the crowd, this was hardly a declaration of political independence.) Bates then noted how much Chevron contributed to the city's treasury as its largest taxpayer. "Any elected official who does not respect a large business corporation in your city doesn't deserve to be in office," he said. "Any candidate running for public office who would refuse Chevron's support is a damn fool!"

By the time of this event, Chevron's independent expenditure committee, called Moving Forward, had already lined up de facto running mates for Bates—three city council candidates who were not "damn fools" either. Whitehurst/Mosher, Chevron's trusted political consulting firm and winner of Richmond's soda wars in 2012, was already busy packaging them all as saviors of the city. In addition to planning huge media buys on Bates's behalf, Whitehurst/Mosher worked in tandem with Singer Associates, a San Francisco PR firm, to create two online vehicles for Chevron-friendly messaging.

One outlet was dubbed the *Richmond Standard*, while the other proclaimed itself to be *Radio Free Richmond (RFR)*. Before *RFR*'s unveiling, few residents realized that Richmond had become such a one-party state that we, like eastern Europeans during the Cold War, needed our own local version of Radio Free Europe to pierce the fog of official propaganda. Both the *Standard* and *RFR* were designed to look like independent sources of information about municipal affairs. They mixed coverage of

controversial political topics with helpful community service announce-
ments, profiles of local people, sports and crime reports, and publicity
about worthwhile volunteer projects.

The *Standard* was, in fact, a clever modern-day successor to the Hollywood newsreels that discredited Upton Sinclair's campaign for governor
in 1934. Those "California Election News" reports eighty years earlier
were similarly "anchored by a supposedly objective 'inquiring reporter.'"[16]
Playing that role locally in 2014 was *Standard* editor Mike Aldax. Like the
anti-Sinclair PR consultants Clem Whitaker and Leone Baxter, Aldax
had prior daily journalism experience. In his case, that included reporting
stints at the *San Francisco Examiner* and other newspapers from Hawaii to
New York City.

The *Standard*'s credibility as a real news organization was immediately
challenged by media watchdogs. As Joe Strupp from *Media Matters* reported, Aldax is a senior account manager at Singer Associates. His boss,
Sam Singer, is a legendary San Francisco flack and corporate damage control expert. The *Standard* was also panned in the *Los Angeles Times*, *San
Francisco Chronicle*, and even the *Guardian* and *Financial Times* in the United
Kingdom. Critics, including local journalism professors, described the site
as "an audacious attempt to disguise propaganda as news and manipu-
late public opinion."[17] Pulitzer Prize–winning columnist Michael Hiltzik
denounced Aldax for disseminating "bogus" news and making "readers
doubt that any news site exists without ulterior motives."[18]

Despite its poor reception in professional journalism circles, the *Standard* at least acknowledged its company backing, via a posted caveat: "This
news website is brought to you by Chevron. We aim to provide Richmond
residents with important information about what's going on in the community, and to provide a voice for Chevron Richmond on civic issues."
The same candor was not initially forthcoming from *Radio Free Richmond*.
RFR cofounders Don Gosney and Felix Hunziker announced that its "citizen journalists" would "help tell Richmond's story without fear or favor."
Their website would be "middle of the road" and focused "more on facts
and less on political ideology." Contradicting that claim right out of the
box was *RFR*'s choice of leading op-ed contributors. During its first few
months of publication, Nat Bates, Chevron-backed candidate for mayor,

and Bea Roberson, who lost her Chevron-financed run for city council in 2012, published nearly twenty times on the site.

An enterprising young UC-Berkeley journalism student, Jimmy Tobias, questioned the independence of *RFR* in the *Richmond Confidential*. He found that Chevron consultants John Whitehurst, Mark Mosher, and their associates who own Barnes Mosher Whitehurst Lauter & Partners (BMWL) were acting as the website's administrators. Plus BMWL supplied ghostwritten content for *RFR*. One sample of that was an article criticizing Mayor McLaughlin—a piece posted under the name of Antwon Cloird, a Nat Bates supporter and founder of a local nonprofit called Men and Women of Purpose.[19]

Both *RFR* and the *Standard* were strong defenders of Chevron's modernization plan. After attending a public hearing on that matter, *Standard* contributor Marilynne Mellander wrote to complain about an "abusive Richmond bureaucracy" that was engaged in "nothing more than a shakedown of Chevron—Pay to Play!" According to Mellander, RPA members on the city council and the Richmond Planning Commission would not be "be satisfied until Chevron is shut down completely."[20] Identified only as "Richmond resident," this particular citizen journalist spent twenty years as a research scientist for Chevron.[21]

ANYTHING LEFT ON THE TABLE?

After listening to lots of testimony, pro and con, in hearings attended by hundreds of people, the Richmond Planning Commission erected a final speed bump before the city council's vote on modernization. A predictably apoplectic *Richmond Standard* complained that its proposals would force Chevron to spend an additional $250 million over thirty-five years on community investments and replace all piping in the refinery installed prior to 1990.

Other changes and improvements in the company's plan were sought by California attorney general Kamala Harris and even the *Contra Costa Times*. Harris's helpful intervention led to management acceptance of a tighter cap on Richmond refinery emissions. The *Times* recalled how poor pipe maintenance practices had led to the fire and explosion in 2012, calling into question management claims that safety-related amendments to the EIR were now unnecessary and burdensome. "When Chevron officials say, 'trust us,' they forget that we once did," the newspaper editorialized.

In response, Chevron tweaked its plan further and proposed to double its community investment to $60 million for the "good of the company and the community," Chevron refinery manager Kory Judd explained. At a public hearing, Alex Smith, one of many Laborers Local 324 members pressing for a deal, praised these concessions for moving "labor, Chevron, and the community in the right direction." Among those urging city acceptance now was Henry Clark, once Richmond's leading community critic of Chevron. Clark was joined by the head of the Bay Area Air Quality Management District and the Richmond NAACP.[22]

Yet by Tuesday night, July 29, Chevron management was still facing pressure to sweeten the pot. After negotiations with city councilors Tom Butt, Jim Rogers, and Jael Myrick, the company agreed to upgrade all carbon steel piping in the refinery's crude unit and install more sensors and air monitors. It increased its proposed ten-year funding of the Environmental and Community Investment Agreement (ECIA) to $90 million. More than one-third of that sum would be allocated to a scholarship program benefiting college-bound Richmond high school seniors. As Butt reported, the rest "will fund greenhouse gas reduction and sustainability projects in Richmond, creating a lot of jobs and attracting perhaps additional millions in matching grants. Job training will move hundreds of Richmond residents into employment."

Before the city council's vote, Congressman Miller personally lobbied its members on Chevron's behalf. ("First time George Miller called me in 30 years," Butt reported in a Facebook post.)[23] Judd continued to complain about modernization plan alterations that imposed "significant constraints on our operations" but acknowledged in the *Contra Costa Times* that it had "[become] clear that we would need to do this."

Butt thanked all those "holding out for more stringent conditions and mitigations" because that "helped raised the ante for what we eventually achieved." Noting that RPA, CBE, and other groups wanted more, Butt himself wondered whether his negotiating team had left anything on the table. He argued on his E-Forum, "We will never really know. There is a limit that you can push anyone, even an insanely rich multinational corporation. Chevron has threatened before to sue the City for overreaching, close or downsize the refinery or go to the legislature for a CEQA [California Environmental Quality Act] exemption. All are possible."

From the RPA standpoint, the biggest item left on the table, or never making it there, was the demand that Chevron bail out Doctors Medical Center, the financially troubled public hospital in neighboring San Pablo. DMC operated the biggest emergency room in the Richmond area, handling most of the people who sought treatment after the 2012 Chevron fire. Without additional tax dollars from Contra Costa County or private financing, it faced downsizing or closure.

Jennifer Hernandez, the consultant hired by Richmond to assess the EIR, backed Chevron's claim that there was insufficient "legal nexus" between refinery safety and the fate of the DMC to require hospital funding as part of the community benefits agreement. Before the council voted on that, McLaughlin and Beckles tried to earmark nearly a third of the $90 million settlement for the hospital and held out for the Planning Commission's more stringent modernization conditions. They got no other votes in favor of either stand, so they ended up abstaining when a council majority approved the terms, as negotiated.

Beckles described the outcome for DMC as "horrible." By April 2015 hundreds of members of the California Nurses Association and the National Union of Healthcare Workers were all laid off at the facility. A public hospital that had served 250,000 area residents was closed, leaving the poor and elderly of West Contra Costa County "struggling to find new ways to get care."[24]

FIVE

AN ELECTION NOT FOR SALE

IN 2014, SEVENTY-TWO-YEAR-OLD Tom Butt became a late-in-the-game candidate for mayor against Nat Bates, his old council adversary. A Vietnam veteran, architect, avid environmentalist, and folk music lover, Butt is a native of Fayetteville, Arkansas, with a lingering hill-country drawl to prove it. During his forty years as a Richmond resident Butt had dealt with myriad issues arising from the working port, major highway, sewage treatment plant, Burlington Northern Santa Fe rail yard, and sprawling Chevron refinery that are all part of the sweeping non-bay view from his property. He and his wife, Shirley, have at times kept a mixed flock of sheep and goats grazing behind their house, on the steep hillside that also overlooks downtown Point Richmond. His annual "Refinery Town" barbecue and bluegrass party—attended by hundreds—is one of the liveliest open houses in the city.

As a city council member for two decades, Butt had led the fight to preserve historic buildings in the city, including the East Brother Island Lighthouse, Richmond's old Ford Motor Company assembly plant, and other buildings on or near the old Kaiser shipyard site. He had lobbied Congress to create the Rosie the Riveter WWII Home Front National Historical Park, where Betty Reid Soskin holds forth today. Butt's tireless work promoting community choice aggregation, through Marin Clean Energy, has greatly expanded local utility user access to renewable energy, saving Richmond ratepayers $2 million since 2014. In his early years on the council, he was a lonely foe of Darrell Reese, the Richmond Fire Department influence peddler and city hall string puller.

Butt helped hire Bill Lindsay, who restored competence to the city manager's office and backed Chris Magnus as police chief. During McLaughlin's two terms as mayor, Butt was often a key ally of hers and the two RPA councilors, Jeff Ritterman and Jovanka Beckles, whose first terms overlapped in 2010–12. When Corky Booze began his disruptive hectoring of Mayor McLaughlin and gay-baiting of Beckles, Butt defended both. And for many years he was one of Richmond's leading critics of Chevron's self-serving, overweening role in local politics and philanthropy.

As the filing deadline for the 2014 mayoral race neared in late August, Butt began to have second thoughts about not running. Charles Ramsey had dropped out of the race over the summer, announcing his candidacy for city council instead. This narrowed the field to Parker, Bates, and political newcomer Uche Uwahemu. A Nigerian immigrant, lawyer, and business consultant, Uwahemu was not expected to be a major factor in the race because he lacked Parker's grassroots campaign structure and the corporate funding, incumbency, and name recognition of Bates. Butt feared that Parker, despite his energetic campaigning, couldn't beat Bates, even in the kind of three-way race that McLaughlin had won twice with a plurality of the vote.

For Butt, the prospect of his old council adversary becoming mayor, undoing many years of work and putting Chevron's already ubiquitous logo back on city hall, was more than he could bear. His eleventh-hour decision to join the race put Parker in a difficult spot, personally, politically, and financially. During his six months of increasingly successful canvassing, Parker had loaned money to his own campaign to cover some expenses, but if he withdrew he would not receive any public matching funds, despite raising enough in small donations to qualify. At a hurriedly convened meeting at the RPA office, Parker consulted with sixty of his closest supporters. They expressed varying degrees of shock and resentment over Butt's last-minute move. After a difficult discussion, a straw poll showed that a third of those present believed that Parker should remain in the race, despite the risk of splitting the left-liberal vote to the benefit of Bates. Two-thirds agreed with Parker that he should withdraw in Butt's favor to avoid the appearance of being a spoiler, which might jeopardize the rest of Team Richmond, as the RPA called its four-member slate.

Before dropping out, Parker conferred with Butt to secure his commitment to campaign coordination, cross-endorsement of McLaughlin, Beckles, and Eduardo Martinez, and what he hoped would be future cooperation with them on the council. In his withdrawal statement, Parker pledged "to work very hard to continue the progress we have made in Richmond" by electing candidates "who represent a different kind of politics, based on organized people-power—not on corporate power." He also reminded some in his own camp, who were wary and resentful of Butt, about the overriding "need to challenge Chevron-backed candidates and those unwilling to stand up against Chevron when representing the community."

Butt graciously praised Parker's decision to bow out. Echoing a favorite RPA campaign theme in 2014, he declared that "Richmond is better off in every way—safer, cleaner, healthier, quieter, and greener. . . . We need to keep up this drive for excellence." He also bemoaned the fact that Richmond's "huge process" of civic improvement was now "in danger of being undermined by contention between the extremes, both on the council and in the community." Butt's attempt to plant himself in the moderate middle may have been helpful to his own campaign. But his political framing was neither accurate nor particularly supportive of the RPA. Its candidates had made their own substantial contributions to Richmond's progress, in addition to supporting him. Yet they were about to be tarred by Chevron as extremists of the most dangerous and contentious sort.

Within days of Butt joining the race, Chevron began a new wave of campaign spending. Most of it sluiced through Moving Forward—the Chevron-backed political action committee it labeled a "Coalition of Labor Unions, Small Businesses, Public Safety and Firefighters Associations." A smaller amount was spent in the name of Richmond Working Families for Jobs, which received all of its funding from Moving Forward. Overall, Big Oil put $3.1 million to work in its campaign against RPA candidates and for their main opponents, according to Moving Forward's post-election filings.

The most noticeable change in our local scenery was the addition of the benign visage of Nat Bates gazing down from countless billboards, like the ever-present Big Brother in George Orwell's *1984*. Bates's advertising popped up on the Internet, on local TV and radio stations, and in newspapers. Richmond voters got e-mails with links to YouTube videos featuring his homilies. Bates's glossy campaign literature showcased his traditional base by listing more than fifty local ministers as supporters, along with Senator Dianne Feinstein, former San Francisco mayor Willie Brown, Contra Costa County building trades leaders, Richmond police and firefighters' unions, and the chamber of commerce. An impressive number of Richmond residents displayed "Bates for Mayor" signs on their lawn.

The negative advertising and direct-mail blitz targeting Team Richmond, which included McLaughlin, Beckles, and Eduardo Martinez, never cited any actual policy disagreements with Chevron, such as the RPA attempt to impose more costly conditions on its refinery modernization plan. Instead Moving Forward fingered McLaughlin as the ringleader of an "extreme left-wing group." According to Big Oil's hit pieces, the Green mayor had for the previous eight years paid little attention to fixing potholes, creating jobs, or improving public housing. Why? Because she was always too busy promoting radical causes irrelevant to Richmond residents.

In Washington, DC, McLaughlin had lobbied to free five Cubans convicted of espionage in 2001. (The Obama administration eventually released them as a part of its bid to improve Cuban-American relations.) She had conferred, at Ecuadoran government expense, with an elected South American president now described by Moving Forward as "anti-American" and an "accused dictator." On this slim basis, Chevron-funded TV and radio spots, mailings, and billboards depicted the mayor as perpetually MIA. Each prominently displayed billboard included an unflattering picture of her and the accompanying message "IF YOU SEE GAYLE MCLAUGHLIN, TELL HER TO CALL RICHMOND."

This multimedia flaying of McLaughlin for alleged absenteeism left an impression on some residents. Leaving the RPA office one afternoon, I encountered a Richmond teenager who had just parked his bicycle on the sidewalk so he could more closely inspect Team Richmond posters in the window. He was staring at a familiar face beaming down at him from one of them when the light of recognition went on. "That's the lady who's always away!" he said, pointing at McLaughlin and then wheeling away on his bike before I could offer the briefest of rebuttals.

Two enterprising young journalism students from the *Richmond Confidential* did help set the record straight. They documented that between 2010 and 2014, McLaughlin had in fact "traveled less, missed fewer meetings, and spent less money on trips" than city councilor Nat Bates. His expenditure of city funds for forty-three days' worth of trips amounted to more than three times McLaughlin's city-paid travel. Bates had the worst council meeting attendance of any incumbent, missing eleven meetings, more than twice as many as any other member. (McLaughlin had missed one.) When questioned about this disparity, Bates explained that "you can't accomplish things staying at home and not engaging with the global community." A spokeswoman for Moving Forward, Alex Doniach, denied that its rendition of McLaughlin's record was flawed in any way. "We put out 100 percent accurate information about the candidates in order to provide voters with facts," she said.[1]

Multiple Moving Forward mailers claimed that Jovanka Beckles had the travel bug too. In her day job, Beckles may have been a dedicated child protection specialist for the county, earning a base salary of $65,000 a year. But according to Moving Forward, she was actually a big feeder at the public trough who mimicked "the lifestyle of the rich and shameless" on her out-of-town trips. Chevron's "100 percent accurate information" on this topic—gleaned from Beckles's own expense reports—dwelt heavily on several dinner menu selections, including a lamb chop ordered in a convention hotel restaurant. In Moving Forward literature, Beckles was thus simultaneously blasted as a threat to the city treasury whether she stayed home to advance the RPA agenda or left town and ate a meal. Either way, we were told, she was just too radical for Richmond.

In mailer after mailer, Moving Forward also informed voters that it was Beckles, not her harassers, who started "arguments and fights at the city council." The Chevron-funded Black American Political Action Committee made this same claim in a widely distributed door hanger accusing her of the same "abrasive, abusive, and combative behavior she blames on her colleagues and the public." BAPAC, of course, called for the reelection of Beckles's always well-behaved colleagues, Bates and Booze.

In 2014, the most memorable hit pieces were reserved for Eduardo Martinez. They illustrated the creative synergy between multiple forms of negative advertising employed by Whitehurst/Mosher, at Chevron expense, to defeat the RPA. Attack ads work, explains psychologist Drew Weston, because "our brains are highly reactive to threat—especially when, as in an ad, the threat isn't immediately countered or refuted. . . . [T]here's nothing like a sinister portrayal of a greedy, self-centered villain, replete with grainy images and menacing music, to stir up our unconscious minds."[2]

In real life, Martinez is no such villainous character. He's a sixty-five-year-old retired elementary school teacher who belongs to Richmond's Mexican American Political Association. He's silver-haired, soft-spoken, neatly dressed, and sports a distinguished-looking goatee. For years he has devoted himself to worthwhile local causes, like helping to organize "March 4 Education," a ninety-mile protest procession from Richmond to Sacramento, held in 2004, to seek more public school funding. On the Richmond Planning Commission, Martinez voted to impose additional air-quality and safety requirements on Chevron in return for city approval of its long-delayed $1 billion refinery modernization plan.

In 2012, backed by the RPA, he received eleven thousand votes for city council, which then lacked a single Latino community representative; Martinez was first runner-up after the three winners in that race. Two years later, to neutralize his growing name recognition, Moving Forward manufactured the candidacy of Al Martinez, a former Richmond police officer and postmaster. Since ballot confusion alone might not be sufficient to keep Eduardo off the council again, Chevron spent heavily on messaging that distinguished "the good Martinez" from his RPA namesake. The latter, we learned, was not really a community-minded liberal Democrat but actually a dangerous "anarchist."

This warning first took the form of a lurid four-color mailer with Black Bloc demonstrators pictured on the cover, wearing dark masks and brandishing shields on behalf of the 99 percent in Oakland in 2011. Inside, Eduardo was identified as an "Occupy Oakland member, who believes that anarchy is the highest form of government." In a brochure arriving several days later, Moving Forward claimed that, after enlisting in

Occupy, Martinez had urged others to join the group, "which has been blamed for violent protests that cost Oakland more than $5 million, hurt local business, and drove away new business."

Just as these glossy warnings arrived in the mail, our home phone started ringing. It was Research America, a Sacramento-based pollster, calling to discuss local politics. Who was paying for this opinion survey, I asked. Oh, we can't disclose that, my would-be interviewer said, but you can talk to my supervisor. Her supervisor didn't know or wouldn't say who was behind the call either, disclosing only that Research America had been retained by EMC Research, a firm based in Oakland, which was acting on behalf of some third party whose identity could not be revealed in order to "maintain as much impartiality as possible in the polling."

I objected to this policy of client anonymity but asked the supervisor to put her subordinate back on the line. "Okay," I said, "what do you want to know?" Actually she had some things that Research America or EMC wanted me to know first. Was I aware that Eduardo Martinez and Gayle McLaughlin were part of "an extreme left-wing group called the Richmond Progressive Alliance"? "It's a group of radicals out of touch with Richmond voters," I was told.

My Research America interlocutor gamely plowed through the rest of her survey script, reading and then asking my reaction to a long series of questions or statements, almost all of which distorted the political views, personal behavior, or public record of Martinez, McLaughlin, and Beckles.

Eager to confirm the identity of those polling with such "impartiality," I called and e-mailed Research America in Sacramento, EMC Research in Oakland, Chevron in Richmond, Moving Forward in San Rafael, and Whitehurst/Mosher in San Francisco, the "campaign consultant" listed on Moving Forward's initial financial disclosure forms. On its website, Whitehurst/Mosher cited Richmond city council races as a prime example of the firm's "expertise and experience in managing specialized, highly complex . . . independent expenditure campaigns."

Neither Research America nor EMC were listed yet by Moving Forward as additional "payees" for campaign services rendered. Only EMC responded in any form to my requests for information about how much they were being paid or who they worked for. Reached by phone, EMC president and founder Alex Evans told me that he has been a pollster since 1984 but would neither confirm nor deny that Chevron (Moving Forward) was currently his client. A Richmond city councilor in the late 1990s, Evans also wouldn't acknowledge any past work for the oil company, before, during, or after his council service. "We have no disclosure obligations, no professional obligation to disclose unless directed by our client," he said.

Just a few months before this informative conversation, Evans published an article in *Richmond Today*, the Chevron newsletter for refinery neighbors. In it he touted the results of polling that demonstrated widespread community support for refinery modernization. Evans was identified as a pollster who "works for Chevron and other businesses and political candidates in Richmond."[3]

As Evans correctly noted, however, there is no state-mandated disclosure of who is financing phone polling, no matter how misleading and propagandistic it may be. In California, corporations or unions bankrolling "independent expenditure" committees, like Chevron's Moving Forward, have to put their names on the direct mail brochures they send out to sway the electorate, and they must report their funding to the Fair Political Practices Commission (FPPC). But their hired public opinion surveyors are free to engage in push polling with complete funder anonymity—unless or until these vendors' names happen to show up in the sponsoring committee's later disclosures to the FPPC.

As registered Democrats under attack by a corporate behemoth, both Martinez and Beckles tried to get endorsed by the West Contra Costa County Democrats. When this political club met, Martinez argued that Chevron's massive display of post–*Citizens United* political spending represented a threat not just to Richmond progressives but candidates anywhere who might be critical of Big Oil. Martinez suggested that his personal refusal to accept business donations made him particularly worthy of a West County Democrats endorsement. When a vote was taken, neither RPA candidate received the two-thirds margin majority necessary for the party endorsement. Even Tom Butt, a lifelong Democrat himself and less controversial than the two RPA activists, couldn't win the backing of the

West County Democrats or the Contra Costa Democratic Party, according to his miffed campaign manager, Alex Knox.

Meanwhile, the other Martinez—Al—had little need for money or more organizational endorsements. Almost all the costs of his first run for office were covered by Moving Forward, which never coordinated with his own barely visible campaign apparatus. Al's anointment by Moving Forward gave him the ready-made backing of Richmond's two public safety unions, the building trades, and the city's largest employer. Thanks to Chevron's "independent" packaging and promotion, a candidate otherwise starting out with a very low profile gained high visibility, virtually overnight.

On my way home from an Eduardo Martinez fund-raiser, I encountered a canvasser for Moving Forward, part of the paid crews deployed in neighborhoods throughout the city. She was a young Latina trudging up and down our street with door hangers demonizing a candidate with an obviously Hispanic name and appearance. She could easily have been one of Eduardo's former elementary school students. When I gently questioned her about how the campaign was going, she seemed embarrassed by her role. "I just need the work," she said with a resigned shrug. Then off she went to warn other neighbors about Occupy Oakland's Manchurian candidate for Richmond city council.

FEELING THE BERN

By mid-October 2014, the main issue had become Chevron's increasingly blatant attempt to buy the election. Adding to the national press this was attracting, a not-yet-announced candidate for president came barnstorming into town. Bernie Sanders, the independent US senator and socialist from Vermont, was invited to Richmond by Mayor McLaughlin and Mike Parker. Sanders's solid record of accomplishment as mayor of Burlington, Vermont, had paved the way for his later career as an eight-term US congressman, twice-elected senator, and, not long after his Richmond visit, contender for the White House.

In Burlington's city hall, Sanders was initially dismissed, like McLaughlin locally, as a fluke, but he proceeded to confound all critics. Under his administration, Vermont's largest city backed worker co-ops, affordable housing, new cultural and youth programs, and development of the city's Lake Champlain waterfront in a way that preserved public access and use. Like other left-leaning mayors in the 1980s (and Richmond two decades later), Sanders saw "no magic line separating local, state, national, and international issues." As mayor, he protested Reagan administration tax cuts and military spending that left Burlington and other US cities without desperately needed funding for affordable housing and economic development.[4] His success in municipal government and support for like-minded city council members helped foster the Vermont Progressive Party, the nation's most successful and effective third party.[5]

In Richmond, Sanders helped the RPA raise thousands of dollars for its council candidates and organizational expenses. After a storefront reception with local donors, he spoke to a cheering crowd of five hundred in our municipal auditorium a few blocks away. He was introduced there by McLaughlin, Beckles, and Martinez, plus Tom Butt, who praised Sanders's record as a leading senatorial defender of veterans' health care. Gripping the lectern with both hands, slightly hunched over it, his crown of white hair not yet carefully groomed for prime time, Sanders launched into an hour-long speech that is now familiar to hundreds of thousands of people around the country. He began by recounting business-backed efforts to thwart progressive reform in Burlington. To succeed in the 1980s, his administration had been forced to "take on the Democratic Party, the Republican Party, the utilities, the restaurant industry, the entire chamber of commerce, and other big money interests," he said.

Expanded citizen participation was the key to winning. "We doubled voter turnout," Sanders reported, "Low-income people and working-class people came out in huge numbers, demonstrating that if you're willing to stand up to the powers that be and keep your word, people will stand with you." He denounced corporate domination of US politics today and accused Chevron of trying to teach Richmond a lesson about "who owns this community, who controls this community." Sanders proclaimed our city to be ground zero in the struggle against *Citizens United*, which he called "one of the worst decisions ever made by the Supreme Court in American history." In its wake, he said, "you're seeing right here, in this small city, unlimited sums of money from one of the biggest corporations in America, who says, 'How dare you ordinary people—working-class people, people of color, young people—how dare you think you have the right to run your city government.'

"If Chevron can roll over you, they and their buddies will roll over every community in America," he predicted. "If you stand up and beat them with all their money, you're going to give hope to people all over America that we can control our destinies." Amid a standing ovation and thunderous chants of "Run, Bernie, Run," Sanders expressed confidence that Richmond progressives would prevail "if we do our job and knock on doors and talk to our neighbors."

RPA candidates were already relying on just that kind of ground game, ten years in the making, to offset Big Oil's air war. Door-to-door canvassing by RPA volunteers got underway six months before Richmond was deluged with robocalls, push-polling, paid canvassing, and near daily mass mailings. Most mainstream political campaigns use canvassers to identify already convinced and likely voters who can be contacted again later with reminders to vote. The RPA, according to Mike Parker, "urged canvassers to take the time to talk to voters, providing information and having discussions that would go well beyond any script." As a result, he believes, "voters could easily tell the difference between our canvassers and those working for the Chevron candidates."[6]

The RPA's voter registration, identification, and later get-out-the-vote drive used four hundred volunteers who contributed an estimated twenty thousand hours of their time. Some just did phone banking. Others hosted house parties, made videos, maintained databases, and held signs or banners at events. In its voter outreach, the RPA stressed more strongly than ever that electing individual candidates was not good enough. Richmond needed a city council majority committed to working together and implementing a common program that would keep the city on its current positive path.

RPA campaign strategists debated the merits of going negative, too. The RPA's overall media budget was minuscule compared to Moving Forward's. So stressing the positive record of Team Richmond and stoking voter discontent over Chevron's election role remained a higher priority than debunking their business-backed opponents. Both the *Richmond Sun*, an eight-page RPA campaign newspaper, and *La Voz*, a bilingual paper for Spanish speakers, edited by Juan Reardon, did inform voters about the council voting record of Bates, Booze, and Jim Rogers (who opposed Richmond Cares and stronger minimum wage reform). The volunteer staff of *La Voz* printed and distributed twelve thousand copies of each issue. One pre-election edition stressed the "heavy responsibility" of eligible voters with Hispanic roots. "They will need to vote on behalf of the entire community because only one in three adult Latinos is registered to vote," noted Reardon. "Most cannot register because they are not citizens."

Before the 2014 campaign was over, Team Richmond and its allies were aided by some independent spending far smaller than Moving Forward's. This financial and organizational help came from Richmond Working Families, a coalition created, its organizers said, to help "stand up against the corporate money flowing freely into our election." Working Families was bankrolled by SEIU Local 1021 and the California Nurses Association. Each union had already maxed out with $2,500 contributions to individual Richmond candidates.[7] Other Working Families sponsors included the political action arms of two community organizing groups often allied with the RPA—the Alliance of Californians for Community Empowerment (ACCE) and the Asian Pacific Environmental Network (APEN).

According to Local 1021 staffer Millie Cleveland, also a leader of the RPA, Working Families canvassers knocked on ten thousand doors and called five thousand voters. They reached 1,900 people, identifying 1,222 as supporters of the five-member team they also branded, in a single mass mailing, Team Richmond. Working Families affiliates were not bound by any RPA-like rules about not backing candidates who accept business donations. So Butt and twenty-nine-year-old Jael Myrick, an African American Democrat serving on the council as an appointee, became part of their preferred ticket to "keep Richmond moving forward."

On the campaign trail, as exhausted candidates dragged themselves from one neighborhood forum to another, the differences between those responsible in some way for Richmond's renaissance and those denying its existence became more apparent. Nat Bates repeatedly stressed that his post-election priority as mayor would be to make things right with Chevron. As he told Rachel Maddow in one pre-election interview, "The first thing I will do is sit down with the CEO of Chevron and see what Chevron wants."

In contrast, Butt questioned the mind-set of politicians like Bates, whose first priority is always "to take care of Chevron and developers and the industrial community." This approach, he told *Chronicle* columnist Chip Johnson, was "Richmond's version of the trickle-down theory." He criticized Bates for his past lack of interest in keeping Richmond's shoreline accessible to the public, citing his opponent's memorable, almost Reaganesque claim that "Richmond has too many parks."

Friends of Bates in BAPAC, the Richmond Business PAC, and Black Men and Women (BMW) added their own hit pieces to Moving Forward's mounting pile. One of BAPAC's mailers race-baited the RPA just as Bates had done in the past when he accused white progressives in Richmond of collectively acting like "a slave master." BAPAC urged voter rejection of Team Richmond, plus Butt and Myrick, because all were part of a "Richmond Plantation Alliance" hostile to people of color. Oddly enough, BAPAC's own head shots revealed that three of these candidates *were* people of color. BAPAC's preferred ticket included only "independent thinkers"—candidates like Bates, Booze, and Al (not to be confused with Eduardo) Martinez.

The bad blood between Butt and BMW (which Bates helped found) had a long history. As Butt informed his E-Forum readers, Bates hosts "an annual golf tournament to replenish the BMW war chest. The donors are a rogue's gallery of city contractors, developers, industries, city fire and police unions, and, of course, Chevron." In the 2014 election cycle, one of BMW's biggest financial contributors was Veolia, the private contractor in charge of Richmond's sewage system and wastewater plant. Veolia's $7,500 donation was redistributed, along with others like it, to Bates, Booze, Al Martinez, and Donna Powers, a former city council member backed by Moving Forward.

BMW's pièce de résistance against Butt was a glossy brochure with a coiled snake on the cover. In big black letters it said: "Beware of this Arkansas Rattlesnake!" BMW urged all "good and decent Richmond voters, especially the African American, Latino, and Asian communities," to reject the menacing reptile in question (aka the Arkansas-born Butt).

Pre-election website postings by BAPAC similarly implied that Butt was a white racist, indifferent to poor people, and caring only about himself and "his elitist, wealthy friends." That accusation seemed a bit incongruous coming from well-financed local allies of John Watson, the white, Richmond-born CEO of Chevron.

In 2013 Watson's total compensation of $23 million suggested that his own social circle, out in wealthy San Ramon, where Chevron is headquartered, might be more elitist than Butt's friends in Point Richmond. By this point in his mayoral campaign, Butt had raised just $60,000 in relatively small individual donations. Even with an additional $25,000 in public matching money, his total campaign budget equaled one-thirtieth of what Chevron was spending on its favored candidates, including Bates.

At candidate nights, voter forums, and debates, Corky Booze rambled, ranted, and showboated his way to the campaign finish line. Before some audiences, Booze could still draw a few laughs. Outside his hard-core fan base, Corky's steady stream of Trump-like personal jibes proved less entertaining over time. He took every opportunity to bash Point Richmond, Butt's neighborhood, which he claimed wielded undue influence in city politics while "my people in other neighborhoods barely have any voice." Left unmentioned was the fact that Nat Bates, his council ally and preferred mayoral candidate, lived in Point Richmond too—in an upscale condo development facing San Francisco Bay.

Although several pro-Booze mailers were funded by the National Association of Realtors Fund, an industry PAC based in Chicago, Corky tried to position himself as the city's only true defender of public housing tenants (whose conditions in a project called the Hacienda were indeed not a credit to Richmond or the US Department of Housing and Urban Development). The realtors backed Booze because he opposed Richmond's anti-foreclosure initiative.

Booze's opponent for a two-year council seat was twenty-eight-year-old Jael Myrick, who had joined the council, as an appointee, after losing his first election bid, in 2012. Myrick became part of the council negotiations that produced Richmond Promise, the Chevron-funded scholarship program for graduates of Kennedy High, his alma mater, and other area schools. He worked as a field rep for state assembly member Nancy

Skinner, a leading liberal Democrat in the East Bay, and he credited the RPA with doing a "good job moving the political center to the left in Richmond."[8]

In his campaign, Myrick was equally willing to accept donations from the business community and RPA turnout help against Booze. While voting regularly with the council's left-liberal majority, he found the RPA's approach to be "too confrontational, too ideologically driven" for someone who was just a "kid from Richmond," more focused on the day-to-day concerns of his friends and neighbors. As election day neared, one good sign for Myrick was a last-minute mailing from Booze assuring everyone that he wasn't homophobic. As proof of this claim, he displayed a picture of himself arm-in-arm with his ex-wife, who now has a female partner.

As media scrutiny of Moving Forward's role in the election increased, not all of its anointed candidates fared well in the spotlight. Two of the three—Donna Power and Charles Ramsey—had to move to Richmond shortly before their campaigns began to be eligible to run. Power and Ramsey had at least both been elected to something before. Power had served on the city council in the 1990s before moving away from Richmond for fifteen years after marrying a Chevron consultant whom she later divorced. Ramsey had served on the Contra Costa County School Board for twenty years and practiced law in the East Bay, where his father was a prominent state court judge, law professor, and former Berkeley city council member.

Al Martinez was the shakiest member of their de facto slate. He had the swagger and self-assurance of an ex-cop but not much familiarity with local issues, including the fact that there was a sales tax measure on the 2014 ballot. At candidate forums, his bland generalizations about every conceivable topic except his own biography were embarrassing. One night he concluded the story of his charmed life with the revelation that now, "apparently, I am running for city council."

A few weeks before the election, the *East Bay Express* did some fact-checking on Martinez's work history. Reporter John Geluardi discovered that his career as a Richmond police officer had ended badly. In 1983 the RPD arrested and charged Martinez with nine felony counts after he broke into an evidence locker and took cocaine being held for evidence, a sawed-off rifle, and a handgun belonging to a fellow officer. Because the arresting officers mishandled drug evidence involved in the case, Martinez was acquitted after a twenty-three-day trial.

Moving Forward had already invested more than $60,000 in Al Martinez's candidacy and $262,000 on its campaign to discredit Eduardo Martinez from the RPA. But the newspaper's report on the former's criminal case and his refusal to discuss it led Chevron to sever all ties with him. The campaign websites of Moving Forward and Richmond Working Families for Jobs deleted him from their list of endorsed candidates on the eve of the election. In its exposé of Martinez, the *East Bay Express* also took voters down memory lane regarding Donna Powers's work history. During her first two years on the Richmond council, in the early 1990s, Powers "received national media attention" for keeping her day job of many years, "working as the topless mermaid at Bimbo's 365 Club in San Francisco."

During her Chevron-financed political comeback in 2014, Powers did not make much of a splash. As Geluardi reported, she "was somewhat aloof and attended only a few of the twenty candidate forums," perhaps assuming that Big Oil's expenditure of $330,000 on her behalf made showing up and answering questions unnecessary. At one appearance, before the League of Women Voters, Powers seemed out of touch with changes in the city during the decade and a half she had lived elsewhere. She claimed that Richmond's crime situation was still so bad that "many of my friends refuse to come here." Both Richmond public safety unions still had her back, though. Their Chevron-funded mailers on her behalf claimed she had "made our community safer" in the 1990s and would "keep our community safe now" if returned to the city council.[9]

ELECTION DAY AND NIGHT

On November 4, 2015, Donna Powers didn't have to persuade any out-of-town friends to brave Richmond conditions to serve as her poll watchers. Chevron-backed candidates had plenty of paid helpers performing such civic duties. Moving Forward deployed them as part of an election-day operation that provided free rides to the polls and, reportedly, free pizza vouchers for anyone who voted.[10]

On the RPA side, there were hundreds of volunteers holding signs, handing out slate cards, and distributing other literature at twenty-nine

voting places, including the Nevins Community Center in Richmond's
Iron Triangle neighborhood. There I found Jessica Montiel, a Richmond
resident for thirty years who was taking a day off from her school district
job in Berkeley. Montiel has been a campaign volunteer for the RPA since
Gayle McLaughlin's first run for mayor in 2006. She described RPA cofounder Juan Reardon as a personal hero who first got her involved in
local politics. Before that she didn't care much about voting, but with
Reardon's encouragement she became a California Green and got so active in the RPA that she even considered running for city council herself.
Richmond might be a working-class city, Montiel told me, but there are
"great minds here." Its last decade of progress should be "a total model for
other cities," she said.

On the street corner opposite of where I spoke with Montiel, I met
forty-eight-year-old Byron Miller, who was earning a day's pay by taking
the field against Team Richmond. A player of basketball, baseball, and
flag football until "the streets and drugs" led him away from sports, Miller
had dropped out of Richmond High in the ninth grade. The intervening
years had not been easy for him. His most recent job had been at Home
Depot in San Rafael. Now he was laid off and unemployed. "That's why
I'm doing this," he explained, brandishing his Nat Bates sign. Miller had
voted for Nat too and thought highly of Corky Booze because he "gets his
points across" and "work[s] for the betterment of the people."

When asked about changes in the city, Miller, unlike his candidate,
saw many positive improvements. "Chief Magnus has done a lot," he told
me. "He's made a difference with crime, violence, and all that shooting.
He came in with a plan and he utilized all the resources to make it happen." What Richmond needed now, Miller believed, was "jobs and more
programs for kids like the Police Athletic League." Without better things
for them to do, local youths will be "sitting inside playing video games,
which make it easy for kids to pick up guns, do acts of violence." His own
election-day choices notwithstanding, Miller wondered whether "it's time
for new blood" in Richmond because "lots of politicians say they'll do this
or that—and then it don't happen."

Three Richmond politicians who have tried to make things happen
returned to the RPA office after a final, wearying day of campaigning.

When McLaughlin, Beckles, and Martinez arrived, their campaign headquarters was packed with supporters. In the absence of any early returns, Team Richmond's own nervousness and uncertainty was palpable. McLaughlin thanked the assembled volunteers for insuring that "grassroots democracy is alive and well in Richmond today."

About a mile away, in his storefront headquarters on Macdonald Avenue, Nat Bates had every reason to expect better early returns than the numbers his son was posting on the wall. As preliminary totals went up, the small crowd of supporters was no longer in a confident mood. The big box cake with white icing and lettering proclaiming Bates "Our Mayor" went untouched. Bates and Booze were both facing defeat, by growing margins, in their respective races. Jim Rogers, who had never called them out on their misbehavior, was losing too. By 10:30 p.m., with half of Richmond's precincts reporting, the council candidates backed by Big Oil were far behind Team Richmond. As the mounting totals for McLaughlin, Beckles, and Martinez were announced, there were groans and gasps of dismay at Bates headquarters.

A middle-aged man in a 49ers jersey tried to rally spirits in the room by declaring: "It's just half time. We're going to come on back in the third quarter!" But Corky Booze, a new arrival to the celebration-turned-wake, didn't foresee any second-half rally by Team Bates. Its eighty-two-year-old quarterback was now slumped wearily in a plastic chair a few feet away. Wearing a gray suit jacket over a white campaign T-shirt with his own picture on it, Nat looked deflated in the harsh fluorescent lighting. Booze, meanwhile, turned to the nearest pair of ears in the room, which happened to be mine. Like a voluble commentator on pro football, he began a post-game analysis of the RPA's unexpected success. "I truly believe that the amount of money Chevron spent made them beneficiaries of a sympathy vote," he told me. "Chevron did not play this game right. When you attack people, they get a sympathy vote."

Booze did credit the RPA with a strong ground campaign, although he claimed that many of its election-day volunteers had been imported from Berkeley and Oakland. "The progressive group started campaigning a year and a half ago," he observed. "The RPA was very serious. . . . They played very dirty with me and Nat. They had eight or nine people at every polling place, handing out slate cards, with a special emphasis on people who couldn't speak English." (In a city where half the population speaks a language other than English at home, this wasn't a bad idea!)

According to Booze, the election results confirmed that Richmond "has turned into Berkeley 100 percent due to this progressive movement." Richmond politics no longer had any place for someone like him because he was just "too outspoken." As for his own voter base, he was bitter about its failure to support him over his younger black opponent and make Bates the next mayor. "We cannot save the African American community if they don't want to save themselves," he declared.

At Tom Butt's election-night bash, the mood was jubilant. There was, of course, good news to celebrate, not bad news to gradually absorb. Just after midnight, unofficial tallies showed Butt winning, with 51 percent of the roughly eleven thousand ballots counted so far. Bates had placed second with about 35 percent of the vote. Uche Uwahemu, the young lawyer, management consultant, and immigrant from Nigeria, who tried to straddle the pro- and anti-Chevron divide, received the other 14 percent.

In a message to supporters the next day, Butt professed to be genuinely surprised at his victory. Two years after trailing Bates by two thousand votes in the city council race that was such a total blowout for the RPA, Butt came away with a bigger mandate than Gayle McLaughlin had received in her two mayoral races. In both of her three-way contests she won with a plurality of the vote. Of the eighteen thousand ballots cast in person and by mail in 2014, Butt received an actual majority. The mayor-elect credited his success to a collaborative effort with the RPA that mobilized voters who were turned off by Chevron, impressed with the remarkable progress Richmond had made in recent years, and tired of city council meeting disruptions. Chevron's roster of close friends on the council was reduced to one—Nat Bates, who had two years remaining in his term.

Chevron's $3.1 million expenditure on a single municipal election was so jaw-dropping that it drew widespread media attention. On MSNBC, Rachel Maddow—who displayed a giggly second grader's fascination with the sound and double meaning of the mayor elect's last name—did a series of reports on Richmond's oil-stained politics. Post-election she had an "astounding" victory to hail. On his show, Bill Moyers discussed

Richmond developments with Bernie Sanders, after his visit to the city. A few weeks later, Moyers welcomed a victorious Gayle McLaughlin and Harriet Rowan, an enterprising young investigative reporter who described *Richmond Confidential* scoops on Chevron spending. "Not only is it a big story because it's so much money," Rowan explained. "It's a big story because it's an example of the real-life implications of the Supreme Court's *Citizens United* decision."[11]

Locally *San Francisco Chronicle* editors hailed "the rising spirit of independence" displayed by the Richmond electorate. The more conservative *Contra Costa Times* urged Chevron to "apologize for its horrible slate of candidates" and "excessive, abusive campaign," saying that the company had "lost its credibility with the community—again." Chevron ignored this suggestion. Instead the company defended its expenditure of $140 per voter as a League of Women Voters–type of service to the public. Big Oil's goal, it said, was merely "to fund direct communication with voters so they could make informed decisions about which candidates are best to lead Richmond."

Chevron spending in Richmond equaled the total amount it devoted to congressional races in 2012 and 2014 throughout the entire country. In those election cycles, the company similarly sidestepped the cap on donations to individual candidates by running its cash through a super PAC aligned with GOP House Majority Leader John Boehner (R–Ohio). In mid-term elections for the House, in 2014, higher-spending candidates from either party won 94 percent of the time, often with the help of negative advertising that buried opponents with fewer resources. In the context of Richmond, the result was different, in part because of the smaller scale of the electorate. Enough voters had personal contact with RPA candidates or their well-organized supporters to realize that the picture being painted of them was a "lie factory" production.

In Richmond even beneficiaries of Big Oil's extraordinary largesse had post-election regrets. "There was so much mail from Moving Forward that when I scraped together to put my own pieces out, no one paid attention," Donna Powers complained. "People were throwing everything in the garbage because they were so fed up with it." During her campaign, of course, Powers never objected to promotional mailings on her behalf or

Moving Forward hit pieces directed at her competitors. Yet post-election even she was exasperated by their content. "How many times do we have to hear that Jovanka ate lamb chops?" she asked.[12]

Charles Ramsey did acknowledge that Moving Forward's mountain of mailers "might have got my profile out more." But, in his post-election view, the company's spending just hurt his own fund-raising efforts. "I had a hard time raising money for my campaign because it looked like Chevron was supporting me," Ramsey said. "People thought, 'We don't need to support you.'"[13] During the campaign, Ramsey had in fact confided to Eduardo Martinez that his real challenge was finding ways to spend the $100,000 he'd had no trouble raising from contractors and building trades unions. Many normal campaign expenses didn't have to be covered by them, thanks to the quarter of a million dollars spent by Moving Forward on Ramsey's behalf.

Ramsey also regretted not doing more RPA-style precinct walking and other forms of neighborhood campaigning "If I had to redo the election, I'd tell all the groups that I didn't need any more money or support. I'd have been fully independent and done my own campaign completely," he told a reporter.[14]

Among those taking note of how Chevron's blitzkrieg backfired were representatives of labor, the African American community, and local business. "The fact that they're getting less bang for their buck is pretty amazing," one USW Local 5 leader told me after the election. If Big Oil's political critics in Richmond could survive its retaliatory propaganda barrage, perhaps Chevron's largest union could take a bolder public stand as well? Just three months later, refinery workers in Contra Costa County proceeded to do just that as part of their first industry-wide strike in thirty years.

Other political activists, public officials, and community leaders condemned the election tactics of Chevron and its allies. A victorious Jael Myrick noted that Black Men and Women (BMW) and the Black American Political Action Committee (BAPAC) "tried to use ugly politics in my race and the mayoral race. That is why they are becoming irrelevant. They tried to play these dumb games and they don't work with my generation."[15] Kathleen Sullivan, leader of Black Women Organized for Political Action (BWOPA) agreed that "folks in Richmond just want something different."

When interviewed on election day outside a neighborhood polling station, Sullivan complained that Bates supporters had chastised her for "dividing the black vote" in the 2014 mayoral race. After interviewing all three mayoral candidates, BWOPA members had endorsed Uwahemu instead of Bates. As Sullivan talked with voters and handed out flyers for Uwahemu, she expressed exasperation with "people trying to run the race card all the time."

In a post-election interview for this book, Alvin Bernstine, pastor of the Bethlehem Missionary Baptist Church, faulted BMW and BAPAC for their "lost focus" and attempt to turn "black against white," in a contest where the real difference between candidates "was not ever around race, it was around principles." County supervisor John Gioia, who backed Beckles and Butt, agreed with Bernstine and echoed Myrick's assessment of the 2014 electorate. "Richmond voters have changed and evolved," he told me. "Whether you're black, Latino, or Asian, you're less responsive to racial politics today."

Vernon Whitmore, the former publisher of a black community newspaper who was about to become CEO of the Richmond Chamber of Commerce, told me he wanted to distance that organization from the biggest employer in town. "I'd like to get the Richmond chamber, which has always been perceived as an arm of Chevron, away from that 100 percent," Whitmore said. After the election he extended a rare olive branch to the RPA. He invited Mike Parker, the socialist critic of Chevron, to speak at his inauguration as chamber CEO in January 2015, along with the city's newly elected mayor, Tom Butt, and former mayor Irma Anderson. It was the first chamber dinner since the RPA was formed to be attended by a table full of local progressive activists.

In contrast, Chevron was not inclined to change its approach to Richmond politics or reconcile with longtime critics. Post-election, its spending habits—now more widely scrutinized and chastised than ever before—were challenged on several fronts. Advocates for corporate responsibility sought more disclosure via rule making by the Federal Election Commission (FEC) or Securities Exchange Commission (SEC) and, in the case of individual firms, corrective action by their own shareholders.

In a petition to the FEC, Ralph Nader's Public Citizen organization asked why the most "politicized of polluters, Chevron"—the recipient of $1 billion a year in federal contracts to fuel military vehicles and provide other services—should be allowed to buy elections via "super PAC spending" when federal contractors have been barred from direct contributions to candidates and parties for seventy years.[16] Editors of the *New York Times* appealed to President Obama to sign an executive order at least requiring federal contractors (including Chevron) to "disclose their donations to political candidates."[17] Pressure was also mounting on the SEC to impose a similar requirement, two years in the making, on all publicly traded companies.[18]

Shareholding activists, including those from public-employee pension funds, achieved some success curbing the anonymity of unlimited corporate contributions unleashed by *Citizens United*. After the New York State Common Retirement Fund began pressing the issue in 2010, "twenty-eight major public companies like Comcast and Delta Air Lines—adopted or agreed to adopt political spending disclosure procedures." Impressed by this trend, one business journalist predicted that "forcing executives to justify political activities on the corporate dime, and allowing shareholders to object, could limit political spending altogether."[19]

In regard to Chevron, that was pretty wishful thinking, as the company's 2015 annual meeting confirmed. When shareholders and protestors from around the world gathered at corporate headquarters in San Ramon six months after the Richmond election, money in politics had plenty of competition as a contentious issue. During the question-and-answer period, critics "raised questions about Chevron's track record regarding oil pollution in the rain forest of Ecuador, a gas explosion off the coast of Nigeria, hydro-fracking in the United States, cost overruns in its liquefied natural gas field in Western Australia, its ties to a dictatorship in Myanmar and its connections to the Taliban in the Middle East."[20] In short, a lot to answer for all around the world.

The Sierra Club, through Green Century Funds, had submitted a proxy proposal calling for "cessation of the use of corporate funds for political purposes." CEO John Watson was already dealing with "the toughest year for the American oil industry in more than a decade, due to the worldwide decline in crude oil prices." So he was in no mood for too much shareholder democracy.[21] Nor was he willing to change political course, based on a single Richmond election—or even a series of them.

In a bit of verbal sparring from the floor, Andrew Behar, head of a corporate social responsibility group called As You Sow, tried to engage Watson in a discussion of our planetary future. He urged Chevron to reduce its carbon footprint to help avert further global warming and resulting human catastrophe. "If Chevron does business as usual," he pointed out, "its actions will create tens of millions, perhaps hundreds of millions, of energy refugees."

Watson responded that "the pathway to prosperity is through affordable energy"—generated by oil, gas, and coal. When the topic of Richmond finally came up, Watson was bullish about the future of our local refinery because of its continued profitability and operational flexibility. After a billion dollars' worth of modernization, Chevron Richmond would be even "more efficient and reliable," he predicted.

But then there was the matter of another local investment in 2014 that particularly rankled one speaker at the meeting. Richmond's own allegedly Occupy-inspired "anarchist," Eduardo Martinez, now a Richmond city councilor, took the microphone. He confronted Watson about the unsuccessful attacks on him by Moving Forward, pointing out that "the three million dollars spent by Chevron in the Richmond city council elections produced nothing other than ill will."

"The election was six months ago," Watson informed him. "And we have moved on." The proposed curb on Chevron's future political spending was then defeated, as expected, by the shareholders.

SIX

CELEBRATING OUR DIFFERENCES?

RICHMOND'S FOUR SUCCESSFUL COUNCIL candidates and its new mayor were officially sworn in on January 13, 2015. Swooping down from Sacramento to do the honors for two of them was Gavin Newsom, California's Hollywood-handsome lieutenant governor. Newsom praised Richmond for its diversity and for demonstrating "that it's possible to live together and prosper together across every conceivable and imaginable difference." Newsom offered to assist the new city hall administration in any way he could because, he said, "the state's vision can only be realized on the local level." Since Governor Jerry Brown's own administration had reduced Newsom to near irrelevance, it was unclear what help he could actually provide before replacing Brown, if elected as his successor in 2018.

Interviewed by the *Richmond Pulse*, RPA cofounder Juan Reardon offered a diplomatic assessment of the city hall transition. "Each mayor has their own strengths and weakness," he said. "I'm sure that they will come into play. We will get some good things from Tom Butt being mayor and perhaps we will miss a few things that Gayle had. But I'm confident that the strong presence of Gayle and the progressives on the city council will help the new mayor reaffirm the direction that we want this city to realize." Richmond park ranger Betty Reid Soskin, who in a private capacity campaigned for Jovanka Beckles, was another witness to the swearing in.

She was equally satisfied with our election results: "I think the city has found its direction, and that direction is going to need more discipline. This mayor is going to provide that. I think it's all good."

It was not long, however, before the new mayor's preferred direction—described by the *Pulse* as "pro-development centrist"—and the RPA's own priorities began to diverge, testing the limits of an electoral coalition born out of Chevron-inspired necessity. At one of his first public speeches after being inaugurated, a first-ever address to the Richmond Chamber of Commerce, Butt briefly laid out an ambitious agenda. In a State of the City report to the city council several days later, he provided additional detail. The content of each presentation was impressive, but his upbeat, forward-looking message was certainly not delivered in the language of the "movement mayor" he replaced.

Despite four decades spent building a successful Point Richmond architecture and engineering firm, Butt noted that he had long "been considered an outsider or even an adversary" by organizations, like the chamber, that represent the local business community. Now, he said, various people hoped he would become "the environmental mayor, the solar mayor, the education mayor, the history mayor, or even the farming mayor, rattlesnake mayor, or hillbilly mayor." He promised he would "be a bit of each," while suggesting that his professional training and entrepreneurial experience made him "uniquely qualified to be the business mayor."

"What architects do is make order out of chaos," he said. "Even though everyone wants something different, you have to end up with one building that works for all. Government has to do the same thing."

Butt's policy blueprint placed a high priority on continuing to attract new businesses like Nutiva, a food products firm, and Alta Vista, a construction services company, that are now among the Bay Area's hundred fastest-growing companies. By the end of the year, as things turned out, the market for Richmond manufacturing space reached an all-time-low vacancy rate, down 50 percent from the year before. Plus, local unemployment was headed toward 5.1 percent by the end of Butt's first year in office, one of the lowest local rates of joblessness since the end of World War II.

To encourage further job creation, the new mayor planned to host a series of business roundtables, where local firms would discuss their plant or office relocation decision and offer feedback on city programs and services that might attract more small and medium-sized businesses to join them in Richmond. Butt launched a campaign to raise private funds for "rebranding" and marketing the city better. "The old Richmond that many people around the Bay Area continue to perceive as a dangerous industrial city no longer exists," he declared, in a bit of overstatement. "We need to get out and sell the new Richmond." Among the city improvements he wanted to accelerate was the resumption of ferry service between Richmond and San Francisco, to discourage commuting by car on the East Bay's already clogged bridges and freeways.

Butt also put his young and energetic staff of three—Terrance Cheung, David Gray, and Alex Knox—to work on long-standing city challenges such as the incorporation of crime-ridden, poverty-stricken North Richmond into the city. He also pledged to find a "successful future for the Hilltop Mall," which had "sucked the life out of downtown Richmond" only to become, forty years later, "an out-of-date retail model" itself and a bank foreclosure target.[1] Along Macdonald Avenue, the business district that Hilltop had helped devastate, Butt foresaw a retail comeback supported by the private-public partnership known as the Richmond Main Street Initiative.

The warm glow of left-liberal victory wore off fairly soon, with the onset of political jockeying over who should fill the city council vacancy created by Butt's election as mayor. At a post-election debriefing attended by about thirty people in the RPA office, two of the RPA's three elected council members, Beckles and Martinez, viewed this as an opportunity to add another person of color to the council, preferably someone younger, Asian, or Latina. Tarnel Abbott, a founding member of the RPA, disagreed and called for the appointment of Marilyn Langlois. After privately interviewing an undisclosed list of candidates, the RPA steering committee agreed that Langlois was indeed "the best qualified and best prepared person for the job."

Unfortunately, as a sixty-five-year-old white woman, Langlois did not fit the profile initially favored by Beckles and Martinez. Nor was she likely to be embraced by Butt or Myrick. She was a founder of the RPA with five years of valuable city hall experience under McLaughlin, dedicated service on the Richmond Planning Commission, and a 2012 council race under her belt. But her council campaign had suffered from her online speculation about US government involvement in the 9/11 attacks on New York City and Washington. Langlois is also a federal war tax resister whose $15,000 worth of past IRS tax liens made her additionally vulnerable to Chevron-funded smears.

When the RPA leadership unveiled its "informal consensus" in favor of Langlois at a big RPA general meeting in January 2015, there was no membership discussion or vote. Members were simply exhorted to bombard Butt and councilor Jael Myrick with phone calls and e-mail messages demanding that they back Langlois. As Beckles, now a Langlois supporter, told a reporter later, after the battle lines had hardened, "The mayor and Jael . . . would not be there if the people hadn't supported them, and now they are going against the people."[2]

This RPA lobbying for Langlois did not succeed on the council, in the press, or even among some of "the people." Unfairly or not, Marilyn's past role as McLaughlin's mayoral assistant seemed to count for less, in the minds of some, than her alleged connection to "9/11 Trutherism." Even a leading African American supporter of Beckles disagreed with the RPA's pick. "Marilyn's such an ideologue," she told me, with distaste, indicating her preference for a non-RPA candidate instead. By the filing deadline, Butt's vacant council seat had eighteen seekers. Among the contenders were former Richmond mayor Rosemary Corbin, recently defeated city council member Jim Rogers, and former mayoral candidate Uche Uwahemu. If the new council could not agree on a replacement, Richmond would have to wait eight months and spend $500,000 to hold a special election to fill the job. Meanwhile, votes might easily be deadlocked, 3–3, on any number of issues, as long as the council was short one member.

Of the two targets of the RPA's pressure campaign, Butt was the first to invoke the specter of "bloc voting" if progressives gained a four-person majority on the council via the appointment process rather than voter mandate. In one press interview, Butt threatened to resign if the RPA gained a majority that rendered him irrelevant. "I have better things to do than be a figurehead," he said. At a council meeting during the controversy, Myrick echoed Butt's concern. "If so much power is going to be concentrated in one organization," he said. "I think it needs to be done through an election."

John Geluardi of the *East Bay Express*, a reporter usually sympathetic to the RPA, accused it of making "an awkward power grab" and thought its "attempts to demonize Butt and Myrick" were ill-advised. *San Francisco Chronicle* columnist Chip Johnson, a past critic of McLaughlin, penned a distinctly unflattering and inaccurate account of how RPA members function on the city council. According to Johnson: "[They] carry forward decisions made by a steering committee and don't have the authority to compromise on proposals without checking with their membership first. . . . If [the RPA] gained a majority, there would be nothing to stop it from deciding public policy from behind the doors of their offices on Macdonald Avenue, taking it to the council and simply dictating city policy."[3]

The most compelling outside defense of the RPA, amid accusations that it was an undemocratic political machine, bent on making Butt its fifth wheel, came from Tim Redmond, a Bay Area political consultant and former columnist for the *San Francisco Bay Guardian*. On his online local news outlet, *48Hills*, Redmond argued that the real question posed by Richmond's appointment controversy was this: "What's the proper role for an active community group that becomes the equivalent of a political party in a city where, of course, all elections are non-partisan?"[4]

In Redmond's view, "the concept of a grassroots organization electing candidates to local office and then holding them accountable" was quite constructive and much needed elsewhere. The alternative model, as he pointed out, was "the Democratic Party, which elects people who turn out to be far more centrist than they promised, and then fails to hold them accountable . . . to the progressive agenda. . . . As long as the community group is open, elects officers freely, holds regular meetings, and represents a legitimate grassroots base (and not some big-money interests)," its efforts to develop and maintain a principled, programmatic voting bloc should be encouraged, Redmond argued.[5]

Mike Parker, Team Richmond campaign coordinator in 2014, denied that the RPA sought to function as a "shadow government." He also publicly addressed several of Redmond's concerns about organizational transparency and internal democracy. Parker explained that, as the RPA grew, "we set up a steering committee of the most active people. We added to it as more people became active." Now, he said, "We have decided to be a membership organization, and we've set up a committee to figure out how to restructure."[6]

This announcement struck some RPA dues-payers (including me) as a little odd. After all, when we paid twelve dollars a year, what were we joining—and encouraging others to join—if not a membership organization? In several post-election presentations, Parker seemed less concerned about member recruitment than training and developing "cadre," as he called them. By this he meant the RPA's most active members—those who had become part of its inner circle. In his view, there were "problems with the current cadre due to the aging of the RPA's core."

Particularly during nonelection years, Parker explained, the "people who have the most time are the most active." Thus, RPA's hardest-working volunteers tended to be older, white, retired, or semiretired. They included past or present teachers, public employees and nonprofit organization staffers, health-care workers, former union activists, and several retirees with private sector management experience. The racial and ethnic composition of the RPA's activist core was not reflective of the demographics of an 80 percent nonwhite city, a perennial source of embarrassment to the veteran antiracists in its predominantly white leadership.

In addition, as Parker reported at a conference in Chicago on left and independent political action, key RPA activists are mostly registered Greens, while "the membership is overwhelmingly registered Democrats." To maintain unity and avoid divisive ideological squabbles (of the sort that often plague left groups), the RPA "fudges over questions about the nature of the system, focusing on local issues instead."

Parker also acknowledged the challenge the RPA faced in maintaining a "relationship between Richmond's local elected officials and the activists who elected them." Progressive city councilors—such as Jeff Ritterman during his single term—do not always agree with each other or the leadership of their de facto political party. When Ritterman favored a controversial waterfront development project, he was reproached by some RPA steering committee members who opposed it. In her forthcoming book, *Against All Odds: A Decade of Progress in Richmond*, McLaughlin also chides

Ritterman for being insufficiently collaborative with her during negotiations settling Chevron's tax disputes with the city.

"No one expects them to vote together on every question," Parker said, about RPA representatives on the council. "But we expect them to vote in accord with our basic principles. Where the RPA has adopted a position, our expectation is that the elected officials will pay close attention to what the RPA has to say. . . . But there are a lot of gray areas. One person's tactical issue is another person's principle."

Eduardo Martinez provided an example of non-bloc voting early in his first term. After several council meetings, where no one got enough votes, Martinez broke the political deadlock over filling Tom Butt's vacant seat by throwing his support to Vinay Pimple. Forty-seven-year-old Pimple (pronounced "Pim-play") certainly added diversity to the council. He is blind, a person of color, and a South Asian immigrant, with multiple professional degrees and job experience in the telecom industry. However, as Butt noted, "Pimple seldom, if ever, sided with the RPA on anything controversial"—an outcome that could have been avoided, in his view, if RPA leaders "had not been so intransigent."[7]

By this point in the vacancy-filling process, the candidacy of Langlois had been dead and buried for several weeks due to Butt's and Myrick's refusal to support her. Claudia Jimenez, a thirty-six-year-old immigrant from Colombia and former organizer for the Contra Costa Interfaith Supporting Community Organization (CCISCO) emerged as the RPA's second unsuccessful choice for the job. In Tim Redmond's apt description, Jimenez was "friendly with RPA but not, ahem, a Card Carrying Member."[8] Fellow traveler or not, she proved to be no more acceptable as a compromise candidate than Langlois. Although Jimenez is, like Butt, an architect by training, and has a master's degree in environmental design from UC-Berkeley, Butt and Myrick considered her less qualified than several other self-nominated contenders with a longer history of community engagement.

Throughout the appointment dispute, Butt insisted that there were multiple candidates who met his criteria of having "held or run for office and endured the public scrutiny and rigors of campaigning for office or . . . have served with distinction on one or more city boards or commissions."

One person he found acceptable—and even nominated—was Ben Choi, a Richmond Planning Commission member appointed by McLaughlin who works for Marin Clean Energy. (Fifteen months later, Choi became a candidate for election to the council. Yet, in 2016, he no longer met Butt's approval because he had joined the RPA, secured its formal endorsement, and favored rent control.)

Meanwhile, Jimenez's success in rallying Richmond Latinos on her behalf raised her profile in case she sought public office in the future. She also played a valuable role, along with other younger activists, in a survey that queried Richmond community leaders about how the RPA might broaden its political base. Interviews conducted by Jimenez and others on the RPA's restructuring committee confirmed the need for organizational changes. Part of the feedback they got was that "young people do not feel welcome in [RPA] meetings" because "the majority of the members are old folks" and the whole "culture of the organization is not welcoming."

Despite the RPA's successful deployment of several hundred canvassers during the 2014 election, one respondent chided the group for not "using volunteers effectively" or having a good understanding of their strengths and weaknesses. According to this survey participant, members should be able "to contribute in a specific way without having to be part of everything the RPA is doing." According to another, the RPA's "framing of issues doesn't fit well with people of color." As a result, some respondents indicated, Richmond Latinos had little feeling of connection to the group.[9]

A REFINERY LABOR UPRISING

Meanwhile, Chevron's largest union in Richmond, United Steel Workers Local 5, was about to frame its own issues in a way that better resonated locally. Along with oil workers across the country, Local 5 members were preparing to strike, for the first time in three decades, over unsafe practices like the maintenance delays that led to our 2012 refinery fire.

The USW's stalled contract talks coincided with the Chemical Safety Board's return to Richmond for a public briefing on January 28, 2015. The board still lacked any statutory authority to compel safer operation by Chevron. But it did release timely recommendations based on its

Richmond investigation. Once again, the CSB faulted lax maintenance practices for "the catastrophic pipe rupture," hydrocarbon release, and resulting vapor cloud that engulfed nineteen Chevron employees and nearly killed them two and a half years earlier. The agency criticized a corporate "safety culture" that "encouraged continued operation of a unit despite hazardous leaks" and discouraged unionized refinery employees from asserting their contractual safety rights. Don Holmstrom, lead CSB investigator of the Richmond fire, cited evidence of "increased reluctance" among Chevron refinery operators "to use their 'stop work' authority despite being concerned about the results of maintenance deficiencies."[10]

Members of Local 5 turned out in force for this city hall event. They wore union jackets and held signs publicizing their safety-related contract demands. Not surprisingly, the USW's 2015 bargaining agenda tracked the CSB proposals. Local 5 Secretary-Treasurer Jim Payne welcomed government support for "stop work" protocols that would make workers feel more secure about bucking management in moments of imminent danger. Speaking as a newly reelected city councilor, Gayle McLaughlin endorsed the CSB/USW "call for workers' right to shut down operations when they feel it's unsafe."

Looking around the CSB briefing room, I noticed that McLaughlin's building trades opponents were not in attendance. As one USW leader explained: "They're silent on issues related to safety and anything outside of jobs." Labor adherence to the company line has its rewards, however. Greg Feere, who calls himself the "CEO" of the Contra Costa Construction Trades Council, is a welcome contributor to *Richmond Today*, the Chevron newsletter for Richmond residents. In this and other management-funded media outlets, Feere writes articles with titles like "Jobs, Jobs, Jobs," while applauding Chevron's use of outside contractors in its "safe and modern facility."

The union views or activism of seven hundred workers represented by Local 5 never gets equivalent mention. In fact, it took the first big oil strike in thirty-five years to better inform Richmond refinery neighbors about USW safety concerns. Nationwide, about thirty thousand workers were seeking a new master contract with Shell, Chevron, ExxonMobil, and other smaller firms Their complaints included "onerous overtime, unsafe staffing levels, the daily occurrences of fires, emissions, leaks and explosions that threaten local communities . . . and the flagrant contracting out that impacts health and safety on the job."[11]

In February 2015, four thousand walked out in a "selective strike" aimed at nine refineries. Among the strikers were Local 5 members in the city of Martinez, who were protesting safety hazards at Tesoro, an oil refiner with a Chevron-like history of them. Other USW members, including those employed at Chevron in Richmond, remained on strike alert.

In anticipation of USW picket lines, Chevron covered its main gate signs so its corporate logo wouldn't appear in any protest-related TV coverage. Inside the facility, Local 5 president B. K. White accused management of trying "to quell the voices of workers with the fear of the refinery's closing, whether it is from regulatory agencies or community activists."[12] The resulting eight-week work stoppage at other refineries exposed historic rifts between USW leaders and their counterparts in the conservative building trades.

Locally and nationally, the latter perceived USW demands for less contracting out as a threat to *their* "union jurisdiction." At a February 2015 meeting of the Contra Costa Central Labor Council (CLC), construction union delegates acted accordingly. They blocked any expression of solidarity with workers picketing at Tesoro just a few miles away. Among the nay-sayers was Tom Baca, a national vice president of the Boilermakers. At a Richmond banquet honoring Betty Reid Soskin just a few months earlier, he had publicly apologized for the Boilermakers' lack of solidarity with its own nonwhite dues payers during World War II.

Now, nearly eight decades later, building trades officials like Baca threatened to quit the CLC if struggling members of another union were not wronged as well. Despite this modern-day betrayal, many Bay Area trade unionists turned out for Tesoro strike rallies. The strikers themselves did a lot of fraternizing with environmental activists long maligned by employers in their own industry. In fact, it could be said that members of Communities for a Better Environment, the Sunflower Alliance, the Sierra Club, and Movement Generation displayed more picket-line enthusiasm than the politically divided AFL-CIO body housed in Local 5's own union hall.[13]

The strike proved to be a galvanizing experience for a new generation of refinery workers who had never before engaged in such a major work stoppage. The results were hailed as a victory for labor.[14] But, like contract settlements in other industries where workers' power has been eroded, the steel workers' deal with Big Oil fell short of some announced union goals. In Richmond, refinery operators emerged from the negotiations with their hard-earned base pay intact and increased.[15] They did not get broad "stop work authority" written into their local contract because management strongly rejected this proposal, according to Local 5 representative Mike Smith. "The company doesn't mind if you stop a single job," Smith points out. "They do mind if you shut down a whole unit that is making them hundreds of thousands of dollars."

Ironically, just a few months later, Richmond residents received a reassuring, if misleading, safety update from Chevron general manager Kory Judd. In a "Chevron Speaks" column for the *Richmond Standard*, Judd announced that he had issued a "Stop Work Authority" card, with his personal signature on it, to everyone on the payroll. With this card in their pocket, all workers were now empowered "to stop any work if they believe that it is not being done safely."[16] Judd noted that very few companies "encourage employees to stop or pause work in other workplaces." But Chevron was not like them. Its own "internal surveys, audits, and other feedback mechanisms" confirmed that Richmond refinery "employees and contractors feel supported in their use of Stop Work Authority and credit Chevron's strong safety culture."

Judd didn't mention Local 5's attempt to make "stop work authority" part of a legally binding labor-management accord. Nor was Chevron's long-time industrial union nemesis credited for anything else of note during its recent negotiations. (An employee named Mike Smith was rewarded, behind the scenes, for his role in local USW-Chevron talks when the company canceled his union leave shortly thereafter.)[17] Any Chevron labor organization lobbying for workplace safety rules, engaging in strike activity, or consorting with environmental groups could count on being Photoshopped out of all official portraits. Like recipients of Chevron's election year propaganda, readers of the *Richmond Standard* had to read between the lines to discern who was really making Big Oil safer, for workers and the community.

RICHMOND PRIDE (WITH LESS CONTROVERSY)

In June 2015, on the second anniversary of our city hall fracas over the Gay Pride flag raising, Richmond celebrated its growing diversity, in new and old fashion, with no controversy at all. Duane Chapman, a cofounder of Richmond Rainbow Pride, had long encouraged local African American participation in San Francisco's annual Pride parade, just across the bay and one of the biggest in the nation. But whenever he had sounded out friends in Richmond about the advisability of sponsoring a local event like it, they'd counseled him that the time wasn't right yet. In June 2014 Chapman was among two hundred people of all ages gathered in Marina Bay Park for Richmond's first Pride Family Day picnic, an opportunity for the local LGBTQ community to come together publicly. That such a day had finally arrived in Richmond brought tears to his eyes, Chapman confessed.[18]

Juneteenth—Richmond's annual festival commemorating the end of slavery—drew thousands of spectators along its downtown parade route. Cosponsored and partially funded by Chevron, Juneteenth is increasingly a public demonstration of local ethnic diversity as well as black pride. Its participants, in June 2014, included African American cowboys, members of the Road Runners Motorcycle Club, local sports teams, church-sponsored floats, dancers and musicians, and two contingents of classic cars. The first fleet included many shiny, perfectly maintained Corvettes, while the second featured lowriders, whose vehicles were fewer in number but all capable of sudden one-sided elevation.

Richmond's senior city councilor and most wily political survivor, Nat Bates, rode in the parade. He was waving as grandly as if he had been elected mayor eight months before, instead of losing to Tom Butt. Other participants in the procession included his longtime RPA foes on the council and various other public office holders. Members of the Black Women Organized for Political Action (BWOPA) marched with the group's main organizer, Kathleen Sullivan. BWOPA supporters brandished signs calling for more black female leaders.

Among municipal officials, none seemed to be more engaged with the crowd gathered on sidewalks along the parade route than Chris Magnus. Some of the time he was marching just few steps away from his husband, mayoral assistant Terrance Cheung. Magnus spent the entire march detouring from the middle of the street to the sidewalks on either side of Cutting Boulevard so he could say hello, shake hands, or deliver hugs to people he recognized. The large number of Latino parade watchers was indicative of the city's ongoing demographic shift in their direction.

When Magnus completed the Juneteenth parade route, he waited near the reviewing stand, in front of Nicholl Park, where organizational booths and a stage were set up for the rest of the day's festivities. One newly arrived group of marchers was the Richmond Steelers, a peewee football team with plenty of energy. Encouraged by the parade MC, this nearly all-black squad broke ranks and mobbed Magnus like he was a much-larger white quarterback on an opposing team. In other cities, where public confidence in cops has dropped to its lowest level in several decades, police chiefs are more likely to be surrounded by protestors than youthful fans.[19] The Steelers grabbed for the RPD "Junior Officer" stickers that Magnus was handing out and proudly affixed them to their black-and-gold football jerseys.

Yet, even in Richmond, people doing public safety work could not rest on their laurels for long. In his usual straightforward style, Chief Magnus reported not long after Juneteenth that the city was "experiencing a troubling upswing in both violent and property crime"—a 16 percent increase overall in 2015 over the previous midyear rate, with armed robberies going up 26 percent.[20] More alarming was a 9 percent increase in January-to-June calls to the RPD about shootings—nearly 750 "calls for service" in all. Gunfire claimed ten lives during this period, just one less than Richmond's homicide total for the whole previous year. By the end of 2015, homicides had doubled in number compared to 2014.

The year 2015 got off to a bad start when twenty-three-year-old Sirmonte Bernstine was killed on January 13 in Crescent Park, a federally subsidized apartment complex. Retaliatory shootings followed, as Bernstine's gang, the Lils, targeted the Manor Boys, based in Monterey Pines, part of Melvin Willis's ACCE canvassing turf and previously known as Kennedy Manor. Gun violence there on July 14 took the life of Fontino

Hardy Jr., a graduate of Tennessee State University with a degree in criminal justice. Hardy was known for his pep talks encouraging other young
people to enroll in college and learn a trade, before he was drawn back
into illicit activity himself.[21]

What police were seeing, Mark Gagen reported in the *Richmond Standard*, was an uptick of "young people being manipulated and encouraged
to involve themselves in street-level gunplay and violence at the pressure
of older gang members."[22] "Richmond is still sucking people back in,"
agreed Malcolm Marshall, editor of the *Pulse*. "As my father used to say,
you can take the boy out of the hood but not the hood out of the boy. It's
hard to escape family, friends, and the lifestyle. The root cause is poverty
and long-standing issues of violence, drugs, and guns that are not resolved."

Like Marshall, Magnus cited the continuing lack of economic and
educational opportunities and "a vacuum not necessarily being filled by
great things" in Richmond.[23] "Our resources, including staffing, [are] reduced—so community partnerships are more important than ever," he
wrote in an open letter to Richmond citizens. "We can reverse this recent trend, but we must take it seriously and respond now by working
together." Magnus reminded residents of the city that they needed to look
out for each other. Sounding very much like a Richmond community organizer, he recommended a two-step approach: "Get to know your neighbors, then get organized!"[24]

Six months later Magnus was getting to know new neighbors—in Arizona. Looking for fresh career challenges, he left Richmond to become
police chief in Tucson, which has a public safety department five times
larger than Richmond's. Awaiting him there was a not-very-warm welcome from the local police union. Its leaders had opposed his appointment
and preferred a candidate from Dallas. During the hiring process, Brad
Pelton, vice president of the union, came to Richmond with a fellow
officer to interview Magnus. He noticed a framed political cartoon of
Magnus, depicting his role in the post-Ferguson vigil on Macdonald Avenue. "That it was hanging prominently on his wall spoke volumes to me,"
Pelton reported.[25]

On the Arizona union's scorecard of his record in Richmond, Magnus was credited with "reduced crime, increased police staffing, increased officer compensation, and improved community relations." But that didn't outweigh his negatives, which included the fact that he had "participated in a 'Black Lives Matter' protest and brought in a civilian to replace the commander in the internal affairs division." Members of Tucson's Citizen Police Chief Appointment Advisory Committee viewed his record more favorably. They voted in favor of hiring Magnus by a margin of 11 to 3; the city council agreed, and Richmond's loss became Tucson's gain.

SEVEN

GENTRIFICATION AND ITS DISCONTENTS

TO DEFEATED CITY COUNCILOR Corky Booze, the 2014 election results were proof that Richmond had become another Berkeley, one of the earliest converts to rent control in California. In reality, the more worrisome model for the future lay just south of Berkeley—in Oakland. There recent housing market changes and demographic shifts provided a case study in wholesale dislocation of poor and working-class people.[1]

As one housing analyst reported, "During the foreclosure tsunami, Oaklanders lost their homes and their family nest eggs. In East Oakland, home ownership declined by 25 percent between 2006 and 2013. Over 11,000 homes were foreclosed. . . . There continues to be a steady decline of the city's African American population, 24 percent or 33,502 residents, between 2000 and 2010. Since 1990, the city has lost more than 50,000 black residents." Further accelerating the city's "loss of racial, age, economic, cultural, and social diversity" and its increase in income inequality (now thirteenth highest in the nation), Oakland experienced "rent increases ranked first or second highest in the nation for multiple consecutive quarters."[2]

A longtime community organizer and lawyer named Randy Shaw was one of the first critics of gentrification to warn that Richmond might be engulfed by similar trends. By 2014 some Oakland neighborhoods were reaching San Francisco levels of housing unaffordability. So Shaw, director of San Francisco's Tenderloin Housing Clinic, predicted that "Bay Area urban pioneers" might eventually "need a new city to call home." What better place than Richmond, "a city with a working-class multi-racial population and a direct BART line to San Francisco. A city with a Green Party mayor, a progressive grassroots political organization, and an already burgeoning arts scene."[3]

According to Shaw, "those seeking affordable housing along with a diverse culture will not find a better Bay Area locale." In Shaw's assessment Richmond was already "where Oakland was 15 years ago." While that much bigger city went from being poor, crime-ridden, and economically stagnant "to hip seemingly overnight," the same process might take a bit longer in the shadow of Chevron. Nevertheless, Shaw was convinced: sooner or later the *New York Times* would be hailing our refinery town as the Bay Area's next hipster haven.

Locally this scenario seemed fanciful to some. But Shaw's projected time frame for Oaklandization became far more plausible after Richmond won a five-city competition to provide additional space for the University of California's Lawrence Berkeley National Laboratory (LBNL). Lobbyists for Richmond, including then city council member Jeff Ritterman, Mayor McLaughlin, and City Manager Lindsay, steered UC toward a Richmond site it already owned several miles south of Point Molate. Unfortunately LBNL then lost the federal funding necessary to pay for its relocation, but UC-Berkeley's powerful chancellor, Nicholas Dirks, reconceived the project on a far grander scale. He announced plans to build in Richmond a new educational and research complex that would be the school's biggest expansion in 147 years, adding 40 percent to its existing campus infrastructure and creating a student and staff population there of ten thousand.

According to Dirks, this Berkeley Global Campus (BGC) would function as an "international hub where some of the world's leading universities and high-tech companies will work side-by-side in a campus setting . . . advancing knowledge in bioscience, health, energy development, and data studies"—all funded by hundreds of millions of dollars' worth of private investment. If sufficient private capital was raised, the BGC would have a bigger Richmond workforce than the Chevron refinery and Kaiser's downtown medical center. Describing its local impact, Dirks likened his planned new campus to the Kaiser shipyards during World War II. It would be a major "catalyst for developing the city's shoreline into a vibrant mixture of high-intensity light industrial, commercial, and residential uses."[4]

During the 2014 municipal election, incumbent city council members from Bates to Butt to Team Richmond all claimed credit for luring LBNL to Richmond. Yet Dirks's change in plan raised concerns about one likely consequence of university expansion—namely, an influx of upscale, white-collar young people fleeing the gentrification of San Francisco and Oakland but contributing to it in Richmond. As BGC development manager Terezia Nemeth told the *San Francisco Business Times*, one of the key "benefits of the Richmond location is that there is housing available . . . probably the most reasonably priced housing in the Bay Area at this point."[5]

What remains reasonably priced—and for how long—depends on the size of your pocketbook. "The Richmond real estate market is exploding," reported Joe Eskenazi for *San Francisco Magazine* after finding that a Richmond home selling for $225,000 in 2013 was going for $375,000 two years later. "You cannot underprice your home," real estate agent Luther Martin told him. "You will get multiple offers. The market dictates price."[6] This sellers' market was good news for older homeowners able to cash in and move out. It was not promising for residents generally because, except for neighboring San Pablo, Richmond still has the lowest median household income of 101 cities in the nine-county Bay Area. Among Richmond Latinos, annual family income is about five thousand dollars less than the median, making their search for affordable rental units or homes to buy even more challenging.

Two East Bay organizations—Local 3299 of the American Federation of State, County, and Municipal Employees (AFSCME) and the Haas Institute for a Fair and Inclusive Society—helped shape the emerging debate about housing, employment, and the BGC's impact on both. Their partners in the campaign to "Raise Up Richmond" included the Contra Costa Interfaith Supporting Community Organization (CCISCO), the ACCE, and the RPA. Researchers at the Haas Institute produced a glossy fifty-page study entitled "Anchor Richmond." It weighed the potential costs and benefits of UC expansion in a place with "a concentration of low-wage jobs, an education system unable to prepare students to access opportunity, a heavy environmental health burden, and housing costs that outpace income." A companion report, "Belonging and Community in Richmond," warned that the risk of displacement was greatest among sixty-seven hundred tenants who earn less than $35,000 annually and already spend more than 30 percent of their income on housing.

Local 3299 based its BGC strategy advice on many years of collective bargaining for twenty-two thousand UC-system workers. These include several hundred Richmond residents, largely black and Latino, who are employed as janitors, groundskeepers, and service workers at UC-Berkeley. According to AFSCME, their labor has been so undervalued in the past that some could even qualify for public assistance. In 2014, Local 3299 won a new collective bargaining agreement, improving pay, benefits, and conditions, but only after statewide strike activity. One unresolved issue was subcontracting. The union's warning to Richmond reflected that experience: "When the university plans a major expansion in your midst, get all its promises in writing!"

LOCAL 3299 CAREFULLY DOCUMENTED the university's growing reliance on private contractors. This trend has adversely affected immigrants and people of color by relegating them to the bottom tier of a two-tier workforce. The union unearthed nearly forty-five contracts covering thousands of workers providing custodial services, groundskeeping, building maintenance, food services, parking lot work, and related services. Some of these long-term contingent laborers earn half the pay of their union-represented counterparts. According to AFSCME, many have been hired during the same time that direct employment of UC service workers has shrunk despite enrollment growth and facility expansion.[7]

With good reason, AFSCME members in Richmond feared that the university itself or its private sector BGC partners would opt for further outsourcing. Contracting out would leave BGC employees doing the same job as career UC workers, just a few miles away in Berkeley, with less pay, few benefits, and no job rights. At Richmond church briefings about the BGC, in campus meetings with students, and in rally speeches, AFSCME members made a strong case for the City of Richmond being proactive

vis-à-vis their employer. "UC likes to staff with temporary contract workers," warned Luster Howard, a husky, bearded Local 3299 leader who
earns sixty thousand dollars a year as a driver for LBNL. "I have friends
and family who need job opportunities. We already have plenty of McJobs
in Richmond. We need better ones."

Local 3299 also includes Latino immigrants who live in Richmond and
landed union jobs on the Berkeley campus after years of personal struggle.
One frequent public speaker on their behalf was Maricruz Manzanarez,
formerly an undocumented worker but now a UC-Berkeley janitor, Richmond homeowner, and mother of three children. "I came up from nothing to make a life in this country that would be better for my kids," she
told her student and community allies. Based on her union experience, she
warned that it would take escalating pressure on UC to get a community
benefits deal that is legally enforceable. "We have to make it happen," she
said. "They're not going to do it out of goodwill."

Feeling pressure from the "Fight for $15" movement locally and na-
tionally, UC president Janet Napolitano did raise hourly wages to thirteen
dollars in October 2015 for lower-paid members of its direct workforce of
two hundred thousand and contract employees on ten campuses. By late
2017, further increases would bring them to fifteen dollars an hour. However, Napolitano still balked at changing UC contracting practices.[8] The
university continued to use private firms for permanent staffing needs,
leading AFSCME to file unfair labor practice charges over wage cuts and
management retaliation against workers who protested their employment
status. The union also organized a successful campaign to persuade invited speakers to boycott UC-Berkeley until one hundred subcontracted
custodians and parking attendants were offered direct employment with
the university.

In Sacramento, AFSCME got the Democratic majority in the state
legislature to pass a bill requiring that subcontracted workers receive equal
pay for equal work. But California's labor-backed governor Jerry Brown
vetoed it, so AFSCME members in Richmond had no recourse other than
future collective bargaining over the issue or securing a "community benefits agreement" (CBA). By a vote of 5 to 1, the Richmond City Council, including Mayor Butt, urged UC-Berkeley to sign such an agreement

with community stakeholders covering the BGC. According to the council, its terms should include local hiring and job training goals, living wage standards, use of unionized construction labor, respect for collective bargaining rights of campus workers, use of local businesses as vendors, and creation of an "anti-displacement fund" to subsidize the development of affordable housing units and protect low-income tenants from gentrification of adjoining neighborhoods.

After the council's resolution, a UC-appointed twenty-five-member working group held monthly meetings in Richmond, open to the public, to consider such proposals. The City of Richmond, local businesses, two local labor councils, faith-based and community organizations (including the ACCE and CCISCO), and neighborhood groups were all represented. The group's coordinator, UC-Berkeley community relations director Ruben Lizardo, pledged that this advisory body's mission would include "evaluating strategies to mitigate displacement of local residents." Working-group recommendations landed on Dirks's desk by the end of 2015. Seven months later, Dirks was still waffling on what commitments the university could make. While awaiting a more definitive response, AFSCME tried but failed to collect enough signatures in Richmond to put a measure before voters designed to give CBA campaigners more leverage in their dealings with UC-B. This ballot initiative would have required developers of a city-assisted project, like the Global Campus, to get voter approval for any related tax breaks or public borrowing.

While supporting the concept of community benefits, Mayor Butt predicted that the city council's proposed "displacement fund" would be a nonstarter with the university. According to Butt, "There are a lot creative ways UC and Richmond can collaborate to address affordable housing, but a cash transfer is probably not going to be one of them." He chided ACCE, whose political action committee had endorsed him for mayor, for failing to understand that "UC-Berkeley is not Chevron. It is a cash-strapped public agency with limited resources." In late August 2016, Chancellor Dirks cited lack of funding as his reason for indefinitely suspending the multibillion-dollar BGC project.[9]

The mayor also came to the defense of Guadalupe Campos, a Mexican immigrant who owns two Bissell Avenue apartment buildings in

Richmond and nine more in four other cities. ACCE members, including tenants of Campos, trekked to Millbrae, south of San Francisco, to picket his home over recent rent increases. With ACCE help, about thirty tenants also conducted a rent strike, protesting the same 20 percent hike. After Butt intervened, Campos and his son, who manages the buildings, scaled the increase back to 15 percent. This left most tenants still facing a $150 per month increase and ACCE organizer David Sharples questioning whether we could expect Mayor Butt "to swoop in and negotiate with every landlord every time they jack up the rent on a vulnerable tenant."[10]

In an e-mail exchange with Sharples, Butt said that he and the ACCE shared "a fundamental belief that the inequality gap in America is harming us all and that lifting people out of poverty in Richmond and the Bay Area is an objective that will make all of our lives better." Rather than rent control, which he called "a failed experiment" in other cities, Butt favored "supply side solutions" like setting up a community land trust to acquire properties for both rental and sale to low-income people and using social impact bonds to acquire vacant properties that could be rehabilitated and resold to them.

Above all, Richmond needed "increased economic vitality to create jobs and provide more housing." The policies advocated by ACCE will have the opposite effect, Butt argued. "They would destroy Richmond's economy in the name of mitigating poverty."

As for his old allies in the RPA, Butt urged them to "support the level of construction needed to increase Richmond's housing stock, particularly low-income housing." Butt noted that "no significant market rate housing has been built in Richmond for over a decade." Yet, in his view, RPA council members raised unreasonable objections to Shea Homes, a market rate, luxury condo project whose construction would generate $14 million worth of "in-lieu fees" to build affordable housing elsewhere in the city. He also accused progressives of being "opposed to a 155-unit affordable housing project because it was 'too dense.'" His bottom line: "You can't have it both ways: guaranteed low rents and no new housing or only low density projects."[11]

A PAINFUL PERSONAL ISSUE

Butt's arguments against rent control were not persuasive among Richmond reformers of more modest means. Local rent increases at rates far greater than inflation or average wage growth were a painful personal problem for some longtime activists. Even Gayle McLaughlin, Butt's city hall predecessor—now living on half her previous income as mayor—expressed personal anxiety over her future as a Richmond renter.

Andres Soto, the RPA member who ran with McLaughlin for city council in 2004, had rented a nice three-bedroom house in Richmond with a front yard, back yard, and fruit trees, for twenty-nine years. By 2010, when he was evicted, he was paying $1,100 a month. Soto's subsequent search for a similarly affordable rental place proved fruitless, so he ended up moving twenty miles away to a mobile home in Benicia, in Solano County.[12] Like Soto, Stephanie Hervey has roots in Richmond and wanted to stay. But she was evicted from her apartment in May 2014 after a dispute with the landlord over poor maintenance and unsafe conditions. A year later, the forty-two-year-old single mother of two teenagers who belongs to both Black Mobilization Organization Education Richmond (BMOER) and the RPA, was still living with friends. "For two bedrooms, there is no affordable housing in Richmond that we can find," she reported, "that does not have a one-year waiting list."[13]

Alma Rodriquez and Roberto Cortes were threatened with displacement and became rent control advocates when their landlord suddenly announced a four-hundred-dollar-a-month increase—from $850 to $1,250—effective August 1, 2015. Roberto earns eighteen dollars an hour doing construction, with little prospect of getting an equivalent 47 percent boost in his wages to cover his increased housing costs.

To drum up participation in city hall hearings and meetings of tenants like these, ACCE organizer Melvin Willis went door to door, day after day, in apartment complexes throughout the city. Willis is a veteran of soda-tax and anti-foreclosure campaigning who belongs to BMOER. A native of the city, he is funded by the Alliance of Californians for Community Empowerment, which carries on the work of ACORN. (The latter's national network of low-income community organization imploded in 2009 after external attacks and internal problems.)

Under the leadership of statewide campaign director Amy Schur and Contra Costa County coordinator David Sharples, ACCE became a key catalyst of local resistance to bank foreclosures and then rent hikes. Unlike the low-budget RPA, which receives no foundation funding and rarely has full-time campaign staff, ACCE has plenty of both. In Richmond alone it was able to field two part-time and two full-time organizers in addition to Willis. With a claimed membership of ten thousand in six cities, ACCE operated with a budget of $2.5 million a year, primarily funded by social change foundations and some unions.

The critical doorstep conversations that Willis and other ACCE organizers had with tenants in some of Richmond's toughest neighborhoods enabled them to identify people with landlord problems, then get them registered to vote and to sign pro–rent control petitions. In some cases, those canvassed were willing to attend a public meeting or session of the city council. Perhaps further on down the line they would even become dues-paying ACCE members or new local leaders. As a result of this issue-oriented outreach, ACCE boosted its local membership by several hundred.

GOING TOO FAST OR TOO SLOW?

On June 23, turnout efforts by the ACCE, the RPA, and other groups packed the city council chamber. The meeting got off to a grumpy start. Tom Butt objected to changing the agenda so that nearly forty signed-up speakers could weigh in on rent control earlier rather than later in the evening. A city hall staff presentation by City Manager Lindsay proposed a "go slow" approach that offered less immediate protection for tenants. The largely pro–rent control crowd was not sympathetic to gradualism.

"If we take strong action now," argued Richmond resident Rebecca Auerbach, "we are free to scale back, but if we do less, and we discover later that our actions were too weak, it will be too late. If rents skyrocket, we cannot lower them. If struggling families lose their homes, we cannot give their homes back to them. If our community is torn apart, we will have no way to put it back together. Please don't let this opportunity go by. There won't be another."

Gayle McLaughlin seemed reinvigorated by the ACCE-assisted surge in favor of rent control. Calling the council meeting audience "amazing," she confided that it brought "back memories of meetings related to the Chevron fire and the proposed, and now rejected, Point Molate casino." The former mayor reminded her council colleagues and constituents that "Richmond has gained prestige nationwide by showcasing itself as a city that cares for all our residents." It would be a mistake, she said, to "sacrifice that prestige now" based on "wishful thinking" that "market forces, apart from our involvement, will solve the problem of affordable housing."[14]

For his part, Butt began to see his latest disagreements with the RPA as "signaling an end to a long and productive working relationship." He reminded his E-Forum readers that "when the RPA came to town, they set themselves up as the antidote to corruption and old style power politics in Richmond." Now, he lamented, the "RPA has taken on many of the trappings of the power politics they once eschewed." Privately he was even more scathing, telling me that RPA leaders were "only interested in Richmond issues that fit their narrow interests."[15] Publicly Butt expressed resentment, and not for the first time, about his council colleagues' alleged unwillingness "to share credit for anything good that has happened in Richmond." In his sarcastic rendition of its publicity claims, the RPA "single-handedly saved Richmond, beat Chevron, won every election (including mine), and will go on the save the world."

In public McLaughlin remained diplomatic. She noted at one RPA meeting, in May 2015, that the mayor "has many, many good points but doesn't understand the importance of movement building to build a better society" or the importance of "protecting the most vulnerable." In a private message to the RPA steering committee—complaining about the role played by Butt and his lawyer son Daniel in Richmond's rent control debate—McLaughlin's tone was more critical, personal, and even plaintive. "I am soul sick," she wrote, "over how the Butts have battered us during this whole process and batter us still."[16]

On July 21, the city council was scheduled to consider two rent control options presented by city hall staff. One created a process for mediating landlord-tenant disputes and the other instituted full rent control with just-cause protection. In the run-up to the meeting, things were not looking good for the latter choice, known as Option D. It could not be adopted without Vice Mayor Jael Myrick joining forces with the three already committed RPA councilors. Myrick, on several occasions, called for a forty-five-day emergency moratorium on local rent increases (that was never enacted). However, shortly before the July 21 meeting and vote, he gave mixed signals to a local newspaper reporter. The resulting *Contra Costa Times* headline predicted "No Fourth Vote on Rent Control."

In response to Myrick's perceived waffling in the press, SEIU Local 1021 helped deluge his office with pro–rent control phone messages and e-mails. The RPA similarly urged its members to let Myrick "know that we do not consider an unenforceable 'rent mediation' procedure as a step toward rent stabilization." On a local radio station, Mike Parker made the same point in a lively debate with Jeffrey Wright, a Richmond realtor and former CEO of the West Contra Costa County Association of Realtors. Behind the scenes, Myrick's council colleague Gayle McLaughlin offered him compromises on the language of Option D. These changes tweaked the formula for permitted annual increases and created a separate rent control board, instead of having the council itself function in that capacity on an interim basis.

The proposed regulatory regime would cost the city between $1.5 million and $2.2 million annually, but that amount would be raised through a landlord-paid fee, averaging about $370 per unit. Landlords were allowed to pass along half that cost to their tenants. Rent hikes would be limited to 100 percent of the Consumer Price Index or, at the moment, about 2 percent a year. By late afternoon on July 21, Myrick was "comfortable with moving forward" because of such tweaks and the assurance that rent control "wasn't going to devastate the city's budget."[17]

Myrick called Tom Butt to let him know he would be supporting the stronger Option D, as amended. At the council meeting that evening, more than 135 residents signed up to speak during the public comment period, for or against city council action on rent control. Local property owners lined up to criticize its unfairness to them and warned that it would limit their ability to repair roofs, appliances, and building foundations. One rent control foe was eighty-year-old Mon Lee, a twenty-five-year Richmond resident who described the ups and downs of life as a landlord. He objected to a "punitive law" that would require him to "subsidize" his tenants. "I've worked all my life since I bought this property," he testified. "It has been in a negative cash flow and nobody helped me. Now that I'm retired and can't work, you change the law?"

Butt let exasperation with Myrick, his vice mayor at the time, and other irritants get the best of him. Just before the vote was taken, after a motion by McLaughlin to cut off debate, Butt threw up his hands and headed for the door. "I vote no, and I'm also leaving," he announced. "I can't deal with this." The mayor took Vinay Pimple, the council's one appointed member, by the arm and led him out too. This left only Nat Bates, Richmond's most reliable tribune for the business community, to cast the only vote against rent control at the close of the council's six-hour session.

It was a jubilant crowd of labor, community, and tenants' movement activists who left the council chambers near midnight on July 21. In addition to initial backers like the ACCE, CCISCO, the RPA, AFSCME Local 3299, SEIU Local 1021, and CNA, the pro–rent control coalition now included the Centro Latino Cuzcatlan, the Iron Triangle Neighborhood Council, Urban Habitat, Urban Tilth, and Saffron Strand, a group assisting the homeless in Richmond.

Richmond organizers—who had responded promptly and effectively to the landlord-tenant tensions already occurring over rent hikes and evictions—saw little downside to the council's action. State law restricts rent regulation to housing constructed before 1995. In Richmond, that would leave about nine thousand residential units covered, giving nearly thirty thousand people "real tenant protections," according to ACCE. The just cause for eviction requirement would apply to all landlord-tenant relationships in rental apartment buildings, condos, and single-family homes, new and old.

Randy Shaw, the San Francisco housing lawyer who had warned about the Oaklandization of Richmond, hailed the vote as a great rent control breakthrough, California's first in nearly thirty years. In Shaw's view, the "absence of massive new federal funding for housing" left affordable housing advocates with few other tools for "protecting economically diverse neighborhoods in urban America." By following in the footsteps of thirteen other California cities, Shaw wrote, "Richmond is saying that displacement and gentrification are not inevitable but instead can be limited through the political process."[18]

Even *Chronicle* columnist Chip Johnson declared that the city had made "the right call on rent control." The crusty Johnson is, like Butt, no fan of "lemming-like behavior among uber-liberals who jump on the band-wagon for any and all policies that carry the 'progressive' stamp of approval." He praised the new mayor for being "one of Richmond's most consistent politicians for years" but rebuked him for taking "a vacation from otherwise sound thinking" on the issue of rent control. "In a part of the country where market-rate housing is beyond the financial reach of a majority of the residents . . . rent control, while far from perfect, is one of the few ways middle-income residents in the Bay Area are able to hang on," Johnson wrote. According to the columnist, Richmond should not let "political ideology" (in this case, the mayor's) stand in the way of "a better public-policy idea."[19]

In the flush of victory, Jovanka Beckles weighed in with characteristic flourish. In a Facebook post she warned that some rent control foes might try "evict people to get back at the city" or hike rents before the new ordinance went into effect in early September. "The light will shine on those greedy, selfish, arrogant landlords," she predicted. Some landlords did contact the Richmond Housing Authority (RHA), seeking to opt out of the Section 8 federal voucher program, used by some of their tenants, due to the impending greater difficulty of evicting problematic ones. Under new just-cause protections, landlords would have to justify eviction notices, based on bad tenant behavior, with police reports or complaints from neighbors, some of whom might fear retaliation. Without proof of just cause, landlords could be on the hook for two months' worth of rent, plus relocation costs. According to RHA executive director Tim Jones—no friend of rent control—building owners "don't want the headache. They would rather get off the program, sell the unit, and go to another city where they don't have to deal with this."[20]

Just a month later, Richmond landlords won a rent control reprieve, thanks to the rapid response of their industry group, the California Apartment Association (CAA). In a replay of past corporate counterattacks in Richmond, the CAA retained a political consulting firm that in turn hired professional canvassers. These door knockers received up to $12.50 per signature, six times the normal rate, to secure the names of 7,000 Richmond voters. Only 4,100 valid signatures were needed to suspend rent regulation until reaffirmed in a citywide vote. The cost of overturning a majority decision by a democratically elected city council, estimated at $50,000 or more, was a small down payment on the CAA's anticipated spending against rent control as a Richmond ballot question.

Truthfulness is not always a strong suit of signature gatherers paid on a piece-rate basis. When some Richmond residents inquired about the purpose of the CAA's anti–rent control petition before signing, they were assured it was "to stop unfair evictions in Richmond!" On the petition itself, any indication of industry sponsorship was omitted. One CAA sub-contractor, interviewed by the *Contra Costa Times*, described a training session in which even canvassers like him were told that the Richmond petition drive "was *for* rent control."[21]

Based on questions he fielded from residents confused about the pe-tition's intent, RPA volunteer Zak Wear estimated that "up to half of the signatures obtained are from rent control supporters who have been fooled." (County officials later invalidated about 20 percent.) Of course, not all petition circulators made fraudulent or misleading claims, because doing so is a misdemeanor in California, although a rarely prosecuted one. California legislators have passed bills requiring disclosure of those pay-ing for the petitioning and making it an additional misdemeanor to pay signature gatherers based on the number they collect. Governor Brown vetoed both measures, along with other reforms of California's now corporate-dominated initiative process.

Vice mayor Jael Myrick opposed taking city council action to put the suspended measure before Richmond voters. So rent control advo-cates had to gather and submit more than 5,500 signatures on behalf of a revised "Fair Rent, Just Cause for Eviction, and Homeowner Protec-tion Ordinance." About a hundred volunteers participated in this petition drive, along with some Local 1021 members paid by the union to help out. In July 2016, county election officials certified that the initiative, sponsored by the Fair and Affordable Richmond Coalition, had won a spot on the November ballot. The California Apartment Association's "Vote No" campaign against it insured that big money, from at least one new source, would be flowing into Richmond in the fall of 2016. In ad-dition to deciding three council races, voters would have the final say on rent control.

MOVING FORWARD, RPA-STYLE

For a supposedly well-oiled and all-powerful political machine, the RPA seemed to be suffering from the summer doldrums a year before Richmond's next election cycle. On a Saturday afternoon in late July 2015, the crowd gathered for a report from Gayle McLaughlin about the city council's vote for rent control was modest in size. In fact, those filling the chairs at the Bobby Bowens Progressive Center were the same twenty-five to thirty dedicated members, predominantly white and older, who attend every monthly meeting. Quite a few belonged to the RPA steering committee, helped plan the agenda, or chaired subcommittees scheduled to make reports. Missing, as McLaughlin noted, were most of the hundred or so local activists who jammed the same Macdonald Avenue storefront eight months before in the flush of progressive victory over Chevron. "Right after the election," she said, "this room was so crowded you could hardly breathe."

A brief membership report confirmed that there was some internal organizing to do. During the 2014 election campaign, more than 80 new recruits had signed up, pushing RPA membership to an all-time high of 382. Not everyone who pays twelve dollars to join bothers to renew a year later or is asked to do so. So more than half of the total membership was by mid-2015 in arrears on its dues. The RPA counted 450 people—members and additional election-year helpers—on its "key list," and another 3,400 Richmond voters were part of its overall e-mail database. These supporters got regular organizational updates, with 500 to 700 recipients actually opening their messages from the RPA.

After McLaughlin spoke about rent control, she introduced a visitor to the Bay Area who had come all the way from Syracuse, New York, to check out the RPA. A frequent Green Party candidate in his home state—most recently running for governor—labor radical Howie Hawkins was duly impressed. He praised the RPA's singular dedication to maintaining a year-round, issue-oriented organization, with dues-paying members, rather than just fielding a pickup team of election-year volunteers. As Hawkins surveyed RPA headquarters, he could see plenty of evidence of past campaigning. The high-ceilinged, single-room office looked a bit like a theatrical company prop room, albeit one with chairs, desks, a conference table, and copy machine. Stacked in the back corners and posted on walls were handmade banners and printed signs accumulated during a decade of issue-oriented campaigns—from taxing sugary drinks to stopping crude-by-rail "bomb trains." For information and membership education purposes, there was a bulging bookshelf against one wall, crammed with old paperbacks on labor and black history, environmental issues, workers' rights, and community organizing.

Next to this community library was a radicals hall of fame—several dozen head shots (a few looking like mug shots) of an eclectic group of movement heroes, heroines, and martyrs ranging from Lucy Parsons, Emma Goldman, and Mother Jones to more contemporary political icons like Malcolm X, Martin Luther King Jr., Angela Davis, and Subcomandante Marcos. Also displayed were the portraits of three South American presidents, two of them dead (Salvador Allende and Hugo Chavez) and the other, Richmond's Ecuadoran comrade-in-arms, Rafael Correa, still alive and kicking. On the opposite wall, the late Bobby Bowens was memorialized. In 2013 the RPA renamed its office in his honor to recognize his long record of community service, beginning with his Black Panther years in Richmond. Next to Bowens's smiling face, a big, hand-painted blue and green RPA banner declared "A Better Richmond Is Possible."[22]

Members of the RPA were justifiably proud of their electoral success. During the ten-year period between 2004 and 2014, progressive candidates racked up a total of eight election wins (half of them by McLaughlin) versus only six losses (three by candidates who later won a city council seat after running a second or third time). Few similarly constituted electoral coalitions with a focus on city politics boasted a better win-loss record anywhere in the country during the same decade. Hawkins, for example, has run as a Green Party candidate twenty times but never successfully; he has done best in several campaigns for municipal office in Syracuse.

By the spring and summer of 2016, the RPA was gearing for another round of frenetic campaigning. Its goals were re-adoption of rent control, in a citywide vote, and securing more RPA seats on the council. In a presidential election year, senior city councilor Nat Bates seemed assured of reelection, running as a loyal Democrat on Hillary Clinton's coattails. His junior colleague, Jael Myrick, would also benefit from incumbency, if he ran for a second time. The council's appointed member, Vinay Pimple, seemed most vulnerable to defeat, due to his lower name recognition and opposition to rent control, police commission reform, and other progressive initiatives.

RPA members voted to back the council candidacy of forty-five-year-old Ben Choi, a Marin Clean Energy staffer and six-year member of the Richmond housing commission. Choi favored the rent regulation that Butt, Bates, and Pimple opposed and Myrick was ambivalent about because he feared retaliatory rent hikes by local landlords. Unlike these incumbents and the mayor, Choi refused to accept corporate contributions. In 2016, when landlord money (or Chevron largesse) started flowing in the form of maximum donations to individual candidates or much larger "independent expenditures" on their behalf, Choi would not be among the beneficiaries. Joining him on the RPA's "Team Richmond 2016" slate was Melvin Willis, now twenty-six years old and also a veteran of planning commission work. Without Willis's tireless door-knocking as an ACCE organizer, rent control might not have made it onto the November 2016 ballot.[23]

To succeed in 2016, the RPA first got its own house in order. As RPA activist Kathleen Wimer admitted, the group had too many "old, white, economically comfortable retired people of leisure running things." Despite fitting that description herself, Wimer was among the RPA leaders most actively trying to recruit a younger and more racially diverse membership, including "working people with kids at home and jobs." She and others on the RPA steering committee believed it should be member elected, not self-selecting. The latter method was not only politically embarrassing; it didn't reflect the democratic values that local progressives had long promoted in Richmond.

The RPA succeeded in reforming itself, by adopting most of the recommendations of its internal "restructuring committee." In late 2015 new draft by-laws were approved at a meeting of about fifty members. That was followed by a first-ever membership vote on a new steering committee that represented both individual dues payers and affiliated organizations. In January 2016 older activists like Wimer stepped aside, enabling others in the group to assume bigger roles. In her case, she handed membership recruitment duties to twenty-seven-year-old Zak Wear, a past canvasser for that purpose.

Other leaders elected included Choi and Willis, Janet Johnson from the Sunflower Alliance, ACCE organizer David Sharples, worker co-op advocate Najari Smith, CNA organizer Marie Walcek, immigration lawyer Sharron Williams, Friends of the Earth staffer Michelle Chan, and Latino activists like Claudia Jimenez, Tania Pulido, Sergio Solis, and Marcos Banales (who replaced Parker as co-coordinator of the RPA). Women and people of color constituted a majority of the RPA's new leadership body. The average age was much lower than ever before. Two RPA city councilors, Beckles and Martinez, remained on the steering committee; McLaughlin did not, hoping to find more time for writing about her mayoral years.

At his invitation, a delegation of RPA leaders, old and new, conferred with Mayor Butt about working more collaboratively on city problems, while continuing to disagree about rent control. As a New Year's resolution for 2016, Butt pledged to develop "a more productive relationship with the RPA." He praised its members as "critical allies" in past struggles over "hugely controversial issues" but questioned its current "aggressive social agenda" and affiliation with "special interest organizations" like ACCE, the California Nurses Association, and SEIU Local 1021.

Butt's belief that it was a "clear conflict of interest" for RPA city councilors to be aligned with Local 1021, the largest city employees union, did not bode well for future consensus on municipal labor relations issues involving its 360 members in Richmond. In fact, it wasn't long before differences flared up again over the city budget, Point Molate development decisions, and even subjects of past left-liberal agreement like public safety reform. During the debate about Police Commission changes, Butt accused RPA councilors of cop-bashing; he described Jael Myrick as "arrogant and self-righteous" for siding with the RPA. Myrick, in turn, urged all his council colleagues to "stop constantly questioning one another's motives when we have disagreements" due to conflicting "perspectives, ideals, and worldviews."[24]

Prior to launching its 2016 rent control and city council campaigns, the RPA held strategy sessions and discussions on the lessons of past election battles. At one such gathering, about forty RPA supporters met at Richmond's main library to consider how the city's changing political ecosystem might affect the outcome of voting in a presidential election year. For example, would there be defections among more affluent, home-owning voters, who shared RPA concerns about Chevron but agreed with Tom Butt's critique of rent control? Would any loss of support in that segment of the Richmond community be offset by an electoral surge by low-income tenants with the most to gain from this reform? Or would Richmond's disproportionately lower levels of Latino voter registration, turnout, and eligibility to vote (due to non-citizenship) make winning rent regulation via referendum too difficult? (Later polling by friends and foes of rent control confirmed strong support for the concept among likely voters.)

At a workshop to help Richmond immigrants apply for citizenship, new RPA cochair Marcos Banales acknowledged the barriers to political participation by Latinos and the cynicism of some who could already vote. "In one-on-one talks, they tell me, 'politicians always promise a lot of things but nothing changes, so why worry about it?'"[25] If that mentality can't be changed, Banales believed, the RPA should rely instead on young people inspired by Bernie Sanders's social justice message or alarmed by the xenophobia of Donald Trump.

At another public forum, this time at a church in Oakland, Gayle McLaughlin compared notes with a forty-three-year-old Indian immigrant named Kshama Sawant. She had become the US left's best-known local elected official by winning a Seattle city council seat in 2013. In her reelection battle two years later, Sawant got much support from young people newly enthused about local politics because of their Sanders campaign experience.

As a backer of rent control and other Richmond-style reforms, Sawant still had to overcome what she called "a tsunami of corporate cash." Top executives from Starbucks, Boeing, Alaska Airlines, local banks, and builders gave $100,000 to her opponent, the African American CEO of Seattle's Urban League. Six of Sawant's nine fellow city councilors backed this chamber of commerce effort to knock her off the council. She also faced attack ads and mailers funded by a super PAC formed to collect money from corporations across the country.

Sawant's own formidable fund-raising, aided by her membership in a national organization called Socialist Alternative, attracted 4,000 donors from Seattle and out of town. For a district election decided by less than 32,000 voters, her campaign raised $450,000 and recruited 600 volunteers. The latter knocked on 90,000 doors and made 170,000 voter-ID and get-out-the-vote calls. According to Sawant, her 56 to 44 percent victory showed "that it's possible to run a serious campaign entirely powered by donations from ordinary people inspired by a bold, pro-worker platform."[26]

McLaughlin argued that an influx of "more people of color and younger people" as "key leaders of the campaign" would produce similar success for the RPA in 2016. To pay for its expanded organizing, Richmond progressives made their first-ever national fund-raising appeal, via RootsAction, a vehicle for online activism and political crowdfunding cofounded by Norman Solomon, a Northern Californian neighbor who writes for the *Nation*.[27]

RootsAction hailed the RPA as "a model for progressive action" that was "rising up against corporate control of the democratic process." The pitch raised more than four thousand dollars to help pay the rent and revive the RPA's campaign newspaper, the *Richmond Sun*. In November 2016, RPA campaigners would face another test of their now much-practiced ground game. More than money, always in short supply, they counted on volunteer recruitment, voter identification and education, and systematic turnout. If the RPA succeeded, it would gain a council majority for the first time since the group was formed, an electoral outcome far from certain and definitely not welcomed by all.[28]

MAKING LOCAL PROGRESS

EARLY IN HIS FIRST TERM as mayor of New York City, Democrat Bill de Blasio was widely hailed for tackling local manifestations of national problems, like inequality, by harnessing the power of the social movements that helped get him elected. *Dissent* magazine described cities like New York, under de Blasio, as "lighthouses in the reactionary storm" that will only get worse if the "conservative movement gains total control of the federal government" in 2016.[1] In its own "Cities Rising" series, the *Nation* regularly applauded de Blasio's "new urban agenda" as a leading example of municipalities becoming "laboratories for progressive innovation," despite "widespread despair about national politics."

New York's municipal reformers have benefited greatly from the city's system of public matching funds, which encourages reliance on small donors and reduces municipal candidate dependence on wealthy individuals and local business interests.[2] After de Blasio was elected in 2013, he and his city council's nineteen-member Progressive Caucus racked up a series of victories. They were able to extend mandatory sick leave to an additional five hundred thousand workers, launch a universal pre-kindergarten program, issue municipal ID cards to undocumented immigrants, experiment with participatory budgeting, raise the minimum wage for city workers to fifteen dollars an hour, and secure rent increase relief for tenants. "Every time we succeed, it builds momentum for other cities," de Blasio told Gayle McLaughlin and other visiting members of Local Progress in

December 2014. Thanks to activist leadership in cities across the country, "change is coming," de Blasio said, "and working its way up—real, sustained, and lasting change."

Unfortunately, mayors do not rule the world, so their attempts to make change are frequently hobbled. Even in the Big Apple, renewing rent control, imposing new affordable-housing requirements on private developers, undertaking infrastructure repairs, and addressing public education problems all require help or approval from Albany. Want to impose a five-cent fee on disposable plastic shopping bags for waste-reduction purposes in NYC? It doesn't happen without state legislators threatening, in bipartisan fashion, to block any municipality from enacting such a surcharge, a move that forced city council member Brad Lauder, a Local Progress leader, to accept delayed implementation of the tax he proposed and got the council to approve.[3]

After only eighteen months of such experiences, Mayor de Blasio was venting fiercely about how much control his state's governor and legislature exercise over New York City affairs. The mayor's main source of upstate frustration was New York governor Andrew Cuomo, a fellow Democrat and favorite of Wall Street. His claimed successes have been capping property taxes, reducing corporate taxation, and creating tax-free zones for startup firms. During New York's 2014 elections, Cuomo openly reneged on a pledge, made personally to de Blasio, to help elect more Democrats to the GOP-controlled state senate. Instead, as *Nation* columnist Eric Alterman reports, the governor "worked to elect a Republican legislature, undermining candidates of his own party."

Post-election, Cuomo returned to Albany and personally "batted down every one of de Blasio's proposals, particularly those advancing affordable housing and early childhood education."[4] Even editorial writers at the *New York Times* were forced to conclude that their endorsed Democratic candidate for governor "had acted disgracefully toward the 8.5 million people of the city Mr. de Blasio leads."[5]

Amid continuing academic and journalistic celebration of municipal innovation and mayoral leadership, the Cuomo–de Blasio rift provides a good reality check on the constraints faced by elected leaders in cities large and small. De Blasio responded, of course, with a forceful defense of what he called "fundamental achievements with a very big reach."[6] They include a local rent freeze helping many New York City tenants, progress on affordable housing creation, and the rollout of his universal pre-kindergarten program (although Cuomo helped nix the tax on higher incomes that the mayor proposed to fund it). Yet thanks to ongoing upstate sabotage of his downstate agenda, the mayor could still wake up to front-page headlines like this one from mid-2015: "Messes Pile Up for de Blasio in 2nd Year."[7]

Richmond is one-eightieth the size of New York, but municipal officials there face multiple challenges of their own. Like their counterparts in New York, mayors and city councilors in California have far less influence over county, state, and federal policy than they would like and limited resources at their disposal. Even if local initiatives are far from utopian, their funding requires a shared commitment to social and economic problem solving at higher levels of government.[8] Not only is that too often absent, but powerful private interests (like plastic-bag manufacturers, developers, or landlords) can use their sway elsewhere to thwart regulation or revenue generation.

In Mayor de Blasio's city, state legislators are particularly reluctant to relinquish their current role in school administration, taxation, and mass transit operation. And the only long-term structural remedy for that would be rewriting the state constitution, via the complicated process of holding a constitutional convention. (Such a convention can only be convened by popular referendum, and its results must be confirmed the same way.)[9]

In Richmond, city government's ability to address local manifestations of national problems related to poverty, inequality, and health-care access is hampered by scarce financial resources and lack of local control. Richmond's troubled public schools are run by a "unified school district" encompassing other cities. Its board members are not elected by Richmond residents alone. Doctors Medical Center, the public hospital long used by low-income Richmond patients, was operated by the West Contra Costa Healthcare District, which has an elected board similarly composed of representatives from multiple communities. The DMC was closed—despite objections from the people most dependent on it—just as many other public hospitals in California have been shuttered in recent years.

Local finances are greatly affected by state and federal spending priorities, and in California, property taxation is imposed at the county level, not locally. The work of Richmond's downtown revival has been hampered by the state legislature's bipartisan "dissolution of local redevelopment agencies, a policy that hit cities like Oakland and Richmond extremely hard, taking away millions previously used for economic development programs and affordable housing."[10] The scope of any rent control approved by Richmond voters in November 2016 is limited to newer rental properties, per past landlord-friendly action by state legislators. And rent regulation by itself, as supporters and opponents agree, does not increase the city's supply of low-income housing through new construction.

"What we really need," argues Gayle McLaughlin, "is a major federal affordable housing program." Yet, in recent fiscal years, Richmond's own federal housing grants have steadily diminished in size due to sequestration-driven budget cuts and Housing and Urban Development funding that was inadequate to begin with. As a result, cities like Richmond, trying to expand their affordable housing stock, must continue to rely on collecting "in lieu" fees from builders of market-rate housing or persuade these developers to set aside some units for lower-income tenants. However, Governor Brown and powerful real estate interests favor a new quid pro quo for this private subsidization of greater housing affordability. They want development projects that designate a small percentage of units as affordable to be exempted from normal environmental review and community-approval processes, which are already under real estate industry attack.[11]

THE FISCAL SQUEEZE

During Tom Butt's first year in office, Richmond depended on new revenue from a sales-tax increase—approved by voters in 2014—to keep its annual budget of about $140 million in technical balance. In 2015 Richmond also had to use one-time revenue sources, such as Chevron's latest installment payment on its multiyear tax settlement, to eliminate a projected $9 million deficit. The alternative would have been cuts in public safety or library services and staff, although not on the scale of the cutbacks in 2003.

Future infusions of Chevron money, owed to the city under the terms of the refinery modernization deal, cannot be used in the same fashion. Those incremental payments are already earmarked for programs like Richmond Promise, the scholarship program open to graduates of local public and charter schools. As for closing future budget gaps with any Chevron damage payment for the 2012 fire, Tom Butt predicted that the city's lawsuit against the company "will take a couple of years to pay off." According to Butt, "It's going to get settled on the courthouse steps." But as this book went to press, in mid-2016, lawyers for both sides hadn't gotten that far yet.

In June 2015, Moody's Investors Service downgraded Richmond's bond rating to "medium risk," citing the city's "unhealthy dependence on Chevron for a large portion of property taxes and a history of borrowing from various funds to balance the budget." This action was vigorously contested by Butt, as was a related probe of the city's finances suddenly announced by the California comptroller's office and then just as abruptly canceled after city officials argued that it was not warranted. Striking a populist RPA-like note, Butt decried the role played by Moody's (and its two fellow ratings agencies) in holding "life and death decision-making authority over public agencies, with a handful of self-appointed 'experts' playing God with the fate of cities like Richmond."[12] Moody's downgrade proved costly because it forced Richmond to renegotiate terms of one ten-year-old bond. To avoid paying an immediate $30 million bond termination fee, the city agreed to pay the holders higher interest, amounting to $10 million, over the life of the bond.

"While the City of Richmond faces continuing fiscal challenges, it is in many ways no more challenged than most municipal governments," Butt insisted. "The city is not even close to any kind of financial failure." Unfortunately, balancing the budget became a continuing challenge for the new mayor, while creating an annual source of political tension with his predecessor and her RPA colleagues. As the deadline approached for adoption of the city's fiscal year 2016–2017 budget, Richmond faced a $3 million shortfall. The mayor, city manager, and their staffs were resigned to some combination of job cuts, city service curtailment, and/or health-care cost shifting to balance the budget. (The employee benefit changes required negotiation with city unions.)

McLaughlin, Beckles, and Martinez weighed in with an alternative plan, inspired by the practices of the Mondragon Cooperative, a famous worker-owned enterprise in Spain. They proposed to balance the budget with "graduated salary reductions"—temporary pay cuts that would not affect city workers making less than $60,000 annually and would fall most heavily on those making $80,000 or more. This creative attempt to minimize city-service cuts did not sit well with the mayor, the council majority, Richmond's management employees, or the unions representing its higher-paid public safety workers.

In Butt's view, the proposal was "irrational and delusional." It could not be implemented in time to balance the budget and would only trigger an exodus of city employees. "These kinds of measures may be possible in dictatorships," the mayor asserted. "But they are virtually impossible in our type of government." In the end, a new budget was approved unanimously, avoiding what Richmond's bond counsel, John Knox, called "a potentially damaging financial outcome." Said Knox: "Those of us who watch the position of the city in the financial markets can exhale for the time being." Usually a fierce critic of the RPA and its "radical socialist agenda," Knox thanked the progressive councilors for their "spirit of cooperation" and willingness to "put the good of the city above their own agenda."

As McLaughlin pointed out during this budget debate, Richmond will always be under fiscal duress without major tax reform.[13] For nearly four decades, property tax revenue in every California city has been adversely affected by Proposition 13. Prop. 13 was passed statewide in 1978 by voters seeking tax relief for themselves, as homeowners. It also created a giant loophole for businesses like Chevron, by sparing them tax payments based on the assessed current market value of their property. This has led to a huge shift in the property tax burden from corporations to homeowners.

In 1978, California businesses contributed about 44 percent of all property tax revenue, while homeowner payments produced the other 56 percent. Today the corporations' share is down to 28 percent and homeowners are responsible for 72 percent of the total property tax bill.[14] As tax reform advocate Michael Bornstein points out, "Because some large commercial property owners are paying deeply discounted taxes based on 1975 assessments, everyone else has to pay more—$9 billion more."[15] Chevron alone saves about $225 million statewide and $30 million locally, thanks to Prop. 13 tax breaks. If the company paid its fair share, Richmond would not be forced to reduce services, cut staff, or seek health-care concessions from its employees. Instead, the city could balance its budget without such measures—and spend more on infrastructure repair, its reserve fund, future pension liabilities, and retiree health care costs.

In 2012, to boost public school funding, California voters did pass Proposition 30, a tax hike for higher-income earners (some of whom tried to hide their heavy personal spending against it).[16] Unfortunately, Governor Brown pressured the California Federation of Teachers to withdraw its own stronger "millionaire's tax" as a competing referendum proposal. Later on, Brown balked at extending Proposition 30 beyond its scheduled 2019 expiration date, a question placed before voters in November 2016. The governor was similarly unwilling to undo Prop. 13 despite having once described it as "a fraud and a rip off." In a speech to a real estate industry audience, Brown claimed that taxing commercial property at current market value—the system in place everywhere in the country except California—would involve "a lot of complexity."[17]

Make It Fair, a coalition of twenty-five labor, community, and nonprofit organizations, strongly disagrees with Brown, and so did 55 percent of likely California voters when they were polled in May 2015 about closing commercial-property tax loopholes.[18] The tax reformers in this coalition nevertheless decided not to put the issue before voters in 2016. Make It Fair organizers plan to do so in the future when they have built even broader popular support and a war chest big enough "to withstand fierce industry opposition spending $50 to $100 million against us."[19]

STILL KING IN CALIFORNIA?

Amid raging forest fires and a four-year drought (at least partially attributable to climate change), some of the same business interests opposed to property tax reform also thwart action on global warming. In its 2015 session, the state senate voted to cut "petroleum use by cars and trucks in half over the next 15 years and reduce greenhouse gas emissions to 80 percent below 1990 levels over the next 35 years."[20] Governor Brown described this legislation as "absolutely necessary if we are to have any chance of stopping potentially catastrophic changes to our climate system."[21] He urged the state assembly to pass a companion bill to SB-350.

In a countermove familiar to Richmond voters, Chevron's regional trade organization, the Western States Petroleum Association (WSPA), created an "astroturf" group called the California Drivers Alliance. The alliance ran $10 million worth of ads warning that Sacramento was trying to "limit how often we can drive our own cars" and "penalize and fine us if we drive too much or use too much gas." This propaganda targeted assembly Democrats worried "that the measure would harm the low-income communities they represent."[22] To stoke that concern, Chevron doled out $235,000 in new campaign donations to key assembly members, mainly Democrats.[23] That corporate spending, plus $1.5 million paid to various lobbyists in Sacramento, helped derail the assembly version of the senate legislation.

On September 10, 2015, Brown abandoned his own administration's attempt at a 50 percent reduction in petroleum use by 2030. Senate president Kevin de León acknowledged environmental defeat at a press conference bemoaning the oil industry's "bottomless war chest." Said de León: "I don't think we've seen an amount of money spent like we have seen in the last four months—tens of millions of dollars to create this smokescreen."

The *Sacramento Bee* was even more blunt and scathing in its editorial page postmortem: "In the Capitol and in the campaign for public support, the oil industry and its lobbyists and consultants outmaneuvered and outmuscled the governor, Democratic leaders and environmentalists." With genuine alarm, its editors asserted that "global warming will consume us if we don't overcome our carbon dependence" and asked, "How long will this blue state let oil remain king?"[24]

How long indeed? Labor and community activists often ask the same question about the status of new rules designed to make refinery operations and crude-by-rail transport safer or less polluting. The acronyms of the various regional, state, or federal agencies involved in these efforts may be different. But all of them—the CSB, DOT, EPA, Cal-OSHA, and BAAQMD—proceed either at a snail's pace, with not enough clout and a thinly disguised industry orientation, or with an overdose of due process for those being regulated and inspected.

"Right after the Richmond fire, there was great momentum for real reform," said USW Local 5 leader Jim Payne. "Now some are forgetting that nineteen people almost died." When I met with Payne and his union coworker Mike Smith at their office in Martinez in August 2015, California's Interagency Refinery Task Force had just visited Richmond. Smith had attended its presentation, which focused on ways that state regulators could improve "process safety management" in California refineries, a concept promoted by the CSB. Much of what Smith heard was positive and headed in the right direction.

The long projected time line for adoption and implementation of new refinery safety rules was worrisome, however. "We've already seen draft language erode due to the industry strategy of attacking parts of it," Smith reported. Formal public comment on the proposed rules wasn't scheduled for another year. This led Payne to speculate, with a mix of realism and resignation, that "regulatory reform is not going to be what we hoped."

Despite these doubts, Local 5 continued to bird-dog the rule-making process. The union's advocacy got a boost eight months later when a RAND study confirmed "that new process safety management regulations would improve safety at California refineries" and "result in fewer releases of hazardous materials."[25] If stop-work/shut-down authority for refinery operators remained part of the new regulatory regime, when finalized by California in 2017, that would create an important precedent for other states and federal OSHA.

The changes would also strengthen Local 5's future bargaining with Chevron over job-safety issues and, in Richmond, be more "empowering" than Kory Judd's pocket-card. Of course, in the meantime, Chevron was still contesting, rather than just paying, the $963,200 in penalties originally assessed by Cal-OSHA for its August 2012 violations of the old rules. In response to the company's administrative appeals, some of those fines had already been reduced.

As the fourth anniversary of the Richmond fire approached, Local 5 joined environmental groups long toiling on a parallel regulatory track. Together, they pressed the Bay Area Air Quality Management District to adopt "an enforceable numeric cap on emissions that negatively impact our workplaces and the environment."[26] Industry opponents of the cap responded with a mass mailing from "Bay Area Refinery Workers" to elected officials and their constituents in the nine counties covered by the district. This largely nonunion front group described refineries in the region as "the cleanest in the world" and questioned whether "local government employees should decide what technology and equipment will best protect air quality."

By mid-June 2016, the BAAQMD was leaning the wrong way on the cap, even though it might prevent future importation of dirtier crude, from Canadian tar sands. In weaker or stronger form, the new emissions rule ultimately adopted by the district board faced a likely legal challenge. The oil industry was already suing over five other recent BAAQMD rule changes "that tightened controls on equipment and required refiners to disclose changes in the properties of crude oil they use."[27]

The encouraging display of "blue-green" cooperation at the BAAQMD was not evident around SB-350. In drafting that bill, Governor Brown and Democratic leaders failed to address the employment impact of California drivers reducing their petroleum use. Because of this serious omission, some USW strike allies, like the RPA and Sunflower Alliance, were themselves torn about endorsing SB-350. The bill's lack of any job security protections or displaced worker benefits led to pressure on Local 5, from USW headquarters in Washington, to join the industry lobbying that killed the legislation.

As Tony Mazzocchi, who died in 2002, often reminded us, trade unionists will not join "blue-green" alliances in large numbers unless they're assured of a "just transition" to nonpolluting employment. To facilitate that shift for refinery operators and others he represented, Mazzocchi proposed that a federal "superfund for workers" be created to pay for their retraining and job transitioning. Mazzocchi's visionary idea built on methods of environmental remediation still in use today, but its adoption is nowhere on the horizon, notwithstanding the best efforts of those who carry on his work.[28]

"It's going to be many years until we can actually transition workers—our members in the oil industry—to jobs with equivalent wages and benefits," one Local 5 leader concludes. In the meantime, as this leader knows better than anyone, embracing environmental concerns, while representing oil workers, is "like walking a tight-rope."

COP 21—TOO LITTLE, TOO LATE?

How much time we have left for remedial environmental action, whatever its job impact, was much debated at "COP 21"—the United Nations–sponsored talks on climate change in December 2015. Prior to that global negotiation in Paris, 350.org, cosponsor of the biggest environmental protest in Richmond history, was sounding the alarm about the latest sign of global warming, saying that 2015 was "on track to be the hottest year in recorded history."[29] With that, plus floods, fires, droughts, rising sea levels, and related catastrophes helpfully focusing their minds, world leaders met and agreed on common goals for reducing greenhouse gases.

At the invitation of Paris mayor Ann Hidalgo, Richmond's new mayor Tom Butt attended the simultaneous Climate Summit for Local Leaders. There Butt reported on community choice aggregation (CCA) and other green energy initiatives that have made Richmond a model for sustainability. He then returned home and discovered, much to his dismay, that the California Public Utilities Commission (CPUC), appointed by fellow Paris conferee Jerry Brown, was making it more costly for consumers to switch from investor-owned utilities like Pacific Gas & Electric to renewable energy suppliers like Marin Clean Energy, the option Butt has promoted in Richmond.

One part of the Paris deal that will be particularly hard to implement is curbing further exploitation of vast underground oil reserves owned and controlled by companies like Chevron. According to 350.org, what's required, sooner rather than later, is a multinational commitment "to keeping at least 80% of fossil fuels underground and financing a just transition to 100% renewables by 2050."[30] That's not the kind of energy solution Chevron has in mind in Richmond or anywhere else it operates. So, as Bill McKibben argues, environmental justice campaigners must still fight everywhere to insure "that the Paris agreement turns into a floor and not a ceiling for action."

On the US presidential campaign trail in 2016, there was only one candidate talking the same way. Like McKibben, he was from Vermont and a past visitor to Richmond. Bernie Sanders called for a tax on carbon emissions to cut the country's greenhouse gases 80 percent by 2050. In his challenge to Hillary Clinton for the Democratic Party nomination, Sanders also promoted legislation called the Keep It in the Ground Act. It would cut potential future global warming emissions in half by blocking extraction of oil, natural gas, and coal from public lands or offshore. When asked by environmental groups to refuse campaign contributions from fossil fuel companies, Sanders immediately took the pledge. Hillary Clinton and all Republican presidential candidates refused to follow suit. Greenpeace estimated that by April 2016 Clinton had collected $4.5 million from oil industry employees and registered lobbyists. The Clinton Foundation's solicitation of large donations from Chevron and other oil companies also drew fire from environmentalists like Naomi Klein.[31]

Sanders rose from near invisibility in national polls, as an undeclared candidate at the time of his 2014 town hall meeting in Richmond, to becoming Clinton's main rival for the nomination. By the following summer, Sanders was drawing rock concert–size crowds forty to fifty times bigger than his Richmond audience. One reason his message resonated so widely was growing public rejection of big money in politics. In a June 2015 poll, the *New York Times* found that a large majority of US citizens "reject the regime of untrammeled money in elections" and "favor a sweeping overhaul of how political campaigns are financed."

> More than four in five Americans say money plays too great a role in political campaigns . . . while two thirds say that the wealthy have more of a chance to influence the election process than other Americans. . . . Some expressed a profound alienation from their own government. They said they did not expect elected figures to listen to them. They described politics as a province of the wealthy. And, despite being inundated with political advertising—and being repulsed by the billions of dollars required to pay for it—they said they sometimes did not feel informed enough to come to an opinion about the candidates.[32]

Sanders introduced Senate legislation authorizing public funding with a formula far more favorable than Richmond's modest municipal election match.[33] Meanwhile, the fund-raising division of labor for business-backed presidential candidates looked familiar to any observer of our 2014 experience. A PAC controlled by close allies raised the bulk of their money and covered major paid-media costs. Any money given directly funded "a smaller campaign operation handling the candidate's travel, press relations, and strategy."[34] According to *Wall Street Journal* reporters using disclosure reports filed with the Federal Election Commission, "Super PACs backing 17 presidential candidates raised more than $250 million in the first six months of [2015], roughly doubling the $125 million raised by the candidates for their campaigns."[35]

Wealthy Democrats, including friends of Hillary Clinton on Wall Street, gave millions to Priorities USA Action, the Moving Forward of her campaign. To raise $112 million in 2015 alone, Clinton relied heavily on exclusive fund-raisers with a minimum ticket price of $2,700. Meanwhile, she argued "that the only way to overturn the *Citizens United* ruling and do away with super PACs is to elect a Democrat." Of course, she also said, "we can't unilaterally disarm"—a refrain common among Democrats, like Barack Obama, who promise election-law reform before they get elected but neglect that goal afterward.[36] When Clinton unveiled her own campaign-finance proposals, one of her advisors publicly acknowledged that "90 percent of those things aren't going to happen anytime soon."[37]

Sanders, on the other hand, declared that he was "not going to start a super PAC" or "go around the country talking to millionaires and billionaires, begging for contributions."[38] Those who did so, he implied, were not true critics of a legal decision that "undermines American democracy and moves us towards an oligarchy in which the economic and political life of the country is increasingly controlled by a handful of billionaire families."

Instead, the Vermont senator raised more than $220 million in 2015–16. His small donor base grew to an unprecedented size—reportedly 2.5 million people, who gave more than 8 million times. Even the *New York Times*—whose reporters often dissed and dismissed Sanders throughout his campaign—was forced to acknowledge that the "insurgent social democrat . . . has shown that it's possible to amass a war chest from ordinary people who are sick and tired of big money in politics."[39]

Wherever he could on the presidential campaign trail, Sanders linked up with local candidates like the Richmond progressives he aided in 2014. (And three of them—McLaughlin, Beckles, and Martinez—provided reciprocal support for Sanders two years later; Arkansas-born Tom Butt stuck with Hillary Clinton and her husband, who had a Richmond reunion with the mayor shortly before the California primary.) In Chicago Sanders helped Chicago Teachers Union (CTU) vice president Susan Sadlowski Garza defeat a longtime city council incumbent, who was backed by Mayor Rahm Emanuel. She became the first CTU member to serve on the city council, after running a very Richmond-style campaign that "focused on public health and workplace safety campaigns" and "brought together refinery workers with community environmental activists."[40]

A later Sanders-for-president rally in the Windy City featured Carlos Ramirez-Rosa, a twenty-six-year-old newly elected gay colleague of Sadlowski Garza's who was outspent 3 to 1 in his race for office.[41] In Sanders's home state, his presidential campaign inspired other young supporters to seek legislative office, either as Democrats or candidates of the Vermont Progressive Party, already the most successful third party in the nation.

At giant rallies, attended by an estimated 1.5 million people, Sanders made it clear how his supporters could overcome corporate opposition in cities and states across the country: "Real change only comes about when a large number of ordinary Americans speak, vote, and get involved in the democratic process. If we stand together, we will win. If we are divided, the big-money interests win."[42] However, as the RPA's experience in Richmond demonstrates, even successful electoral work conducted at the local level over many years does not by itself build year-round, multi-issue political organization. That takes an unconventional approach to politics, before, during, and after any election.

In Richmond, during its 2016 election, one thing remained unchanged: campaign spending by powerful business interests was still not subject to any curbs. A year before the voting, Chevron spokesperson Leah Casey would only confirm that her employer had not yet "defined how or if we will participate in the local Richmond elections"—a stance subject to change. In the same e-mail message, she did reassure me that the company's electoral participation, if any, would be "fully transparent."

In the 2015 session of the California legislature, concern about the growth of independent expenditure campaigns—which now account for 25 percent of all legislative election spending—did lead to increased "transparency." A bill signed by Governor Brown now requires "larger, bolder disclosures on campaign mail sent by independent groups, stating that the advertisement doesn't come from a candidate."[43] In Richmond, this means that readers of future Chevron mailers may no longer need magnifying glasses to locate the small-type disclosure of their funding source. As no less a fund-raising expert than Andrew Cuomo points out, *Citizens United* created a "fiction" that independent expenditure committees "would actually, truly act independently" of their favored candidates. Instead, what Cuomo calls "the collusion, the coordination, the subterfuge, the fraud in the current political system is rampant," from New York to Richmond, and requires bigger solutions than less fine print.[44]

THE CHEMISTRY OF COMMUNITY

When he visited Richmond in October 2014, Bernie Sanders—now well known for thinking big about national problems—stressed the importance of smaller-scale change too. "I love municipal government," he told his Richmond crowd. "I'll tell you why. Because at the end of the day, establishing community, bringing people together, creating a sense of place where people feel good about each other, that's the best that we can do. And that's what you can do at the local level."

Under a visionary mayor, city hall can definitely bring people together for all kinds of virtuous civic purposes, particularly in a human-scale polity of one hundred thousand or less. Mayors and their city council allies can promote much-needed public policy experiments, even if some stall or fail. They can throw roadblocks in the path of powerful private interests long used to getting their own way, the public be damned. They can try to address, with the limited resources at their disposal, some of the pressing social and economic needs left unmet by the failures of government at higher levels. Municipal reformers can also foster a stronger sense of community and place, making people feel better (at least some of the time) about where they live and who they live with.

Cronyism, corruption, corporate domination, and economic decline once made Richmond a poster child for doing city business the wrong way. "Divide and conquer" sometimes feels like it was invented here, despite much historical evidence to the contrary. Richmond's old political culture helped to reinforce America's best-known mantra of citizen frustration and resignation: "You can't fight city hall!" Even among local activists experienced in fighting for peace, justice, labor rights, racial equality, or revolution elsewhere, Richmond city hall was not initially viewed as something you could also fight *for*—and win.

Fifteen years of political organizing by RPA activists and other Richmond reformers before them has altered that calculus. Richmond's exemplary mix of electoral campaigning around issues and candidates, principled and persistent follow-up by elected officials, and some skilled professional city managing have made it a model for municipal action on behalf of people poorly served by local government in the past. Those responsible for Richmond's renaissance are not always on the same page politically. Personal spats and pet causes can be a source of distraction and, at times, embarrassment. But no process of change anywhere—much less in a place like Richmond—can occur without there being some community disagreements and divisions, personality conflicts, or racial and ethnic tensions.

Collectively, Richmond reformers have listened to city residents rather than downplaying or ignoring their concerns. They have not lined their own pockets or shilled for Big Oil, like some local "public servants" in the past. They have reduced popular estrangement from municipal government and fostered a high level of citizen engagement. Results of semiannual polling by the National Research Center, during the eight-year period between 2007 and 2015, show broad agreement about Richmond's "before" and "after." Residents surveyed believe that the city has improved, often dramatically, by each metric used: overall quality of life and image, community characteristics (whether it is a good place to work, live, or raise children), governance (including services like public safety and street repair), and, last but not least, sense of community.[45]

What the Richmond experience demonstrates are the continuing advantages of making change locally as part of a longer-term and eventually more sweeping progressive strategy. What activists have going for them at the city level—an advantage almost nonexistent in the big-money-dominated realms of state or national politics—is greater personal connection to voters. Forging what Gayle McLaughlin calls authentic relationships isn't a spontaneous process, however. It takes time, organization, and systematic outreach around issues that affect peoples' daily lives. It also demands a great deal of emotional energy, plus—for those in elected positions—a very thick skin. It is understandable why many who want to make Richmond a better place do so through various forms of community service rather than partisan political combat.

In all its local forms, civic engagement helps create personal connections and community solidarity. In successive electoral campaigns, these have become the great equalizer in Richmond. Dedicated political volunteering has facilitated face-to-face contact and one-on-one conversations with thousands of people. The conversations are not always pleasant; everyone does not always agree. But what former city hall reporter Robert Rogers calls "this noisy democracy we have now" is a big improvement on what existed in Richmond before. And, in most election years, the grassroots mobilization capacity of the local left has been able to neutralize the usual advantages enjoyed by corporate adversaries with overall campaign budgets fifteen or thirty times larger.

There is no single road map for social change in the United States, no one-size-fits-all organizing strategy for countering and containing corporate influence. Certainly Richmond's challenge to the power and prerogatives of a global energy giant points the way forward for other communities, frontline or not, where similar struggles for environmental justice and election law reform are underway. Counterintuitive as it may be, going local may be the most effective individual and collective response to economic challenges and environmental threats that are dauntingly national and global in scope.

If urban political insurgencies are going to succeed in more places, they will need models for civic engagement like Richmond provides. Our city's emergency response lesson is this: when we shelter in place together, we can change our communities for the better. If we remain frozen in a state of individual fear, apathy, alienation, or powerlessness, the world around us remains the same—until the next warning siren sounds, and all the ones after that, until there are too many fires to put out and not enough time left to reverse the damage they've done.

ACKNOWLEDGMENTS

REFINERY TOWN HAD MANY sources of inspiration. My primary muse is a very special California city, where getting to know a colorful cast of local characters was not just a book-writing exercise. It was also a valuable form of social and political networking for a newly arrived refugee from New England winters.

Back east, I was a union activist for forty years and employed for much of that time by the Communications Workers of America. On a freelance basis I also wrote for various organizational publications, national newspapers, monthly magazines, some academic journals, and online media outlets. As readers of my previous labor-related books know, much of that freelance journalism, book reviewing, and newspaper opinion piece writing addressed trends and issues related to the workplace. (For details, see steveearly.org.)

Embarking on this Richmond-related project, I had to familiarize myself with a broader range of subject matter. At the outset I was much inspired by reading Tracy Kidder's *Hometown*, Gordon Young's *Teardown*, and Charlie LeDuff's *Detroit: An American Autopsy*—insightful accounts of community life, politics, and policing in Northampton, Massachusetts; Flint, Michigan; and Detroit, respectively. In a fashion most similar to Young's work, *Refinery Town* is an exercise in participatory journalism, reflecting a personal perspective on citywide social, economic, and political problems in my new hometown.

In the interest of full disclosure, I should note that I'm not a neutral observer of Richmond politics. I've paid dues to the Richmond Progressive Alliance (RPA) since moving to the city in early 2012. I also joined the Alliance of Californians for Community Empowerment (ACCE) and Communities for a Better Environment (CBE), two other groups mentioned in this book. None of the views expressed herein should be mistaken as speaking on behalf of any of the above. All three groups have their own official spokespeople.

In various Richmond election years, I have donated money to the campaigns of Gayle McLaughlin, Jovanka Beckles, Eduardo Martinez, Tom Butt, Mike Parker, Marilyn Langlois, Melvin Willis, and Ben Choi. I've also done volunteer work for these candidates, and in 2016, four of them supported my mayoral appointment to the Richmond Personnel Board. In 2014 I helped organize several fund-raisers that benefited either the RPA or its endorsed candidates. During part of that year, my daughter Alexandra served as a canvassing coordinator for the RPA. I also helped bring an old comrade from Vermont (and later 2016 presidential candidate) Bernie Sanders to Richmond for RPA fund-raising and publicity purposes. Like several million other people "feeling the Bern" in 2015–16, I was a contributor to the Sanders for President campaign. I also assisted a national network called Labor for Bernie.

I have with mixed results tried to interview people on all sides of local and national controversies described in this book. In 2014, after sending Chevron a detailed information request related to an article I was writing for the *Nation*, the company's media relations department provided a rather generally phrased e-mail response. Two years after that piece appeared, I contacted the company again, with an updated set of book-related questions. I also sought a personal audience with its media relations people, who work just a ten-minute walk from my house. Again, they responded only by e-mail, in a fashion pithier than before. Two of the company's main outside mouthpieces, Singer Associates and Whitehurst/Mosher, were similarly tongue-tied, both in 2014 and since then, when I sought interviews about their lucrative work on behalf of Chevron.

In writing about the words and deeds, good or bad, of various public figures in Richmond, I've tried to meet the fairness standard set by radical sociologist C. Wright Mills. "I don't claim to be impartial," Mills once said, "but I do try to be objective." In that spirit, *Refinery Town* draws on a huge body of political work and insightful reporting by many others on various sides of the participant-observer divide in Richmond. The book also uses information and opinions shared, in multiple ways, by elected city officials and municipal employees, members of Richmond commissions and neighborhood councils, local ministers and lawyers, nonprofit organization leaders, and representatives of the business community.

Among them, I would like to thank Nat Bates, Jovanka Beckles, the Reverend Alvin Bernstine, Bruce Beyaert, Ron Blodgett, Devone Boggan, Corky Booze, Allwyn Brown, Andrew Butt, Dan Butt, Tom Butt, Leah Casey, Whitney Dodson, Vivian Feyer, Mark Gagen, David Gray, John Goia, Felix Hunziker, Margaret Jordan, Kory Judd, Donnel Jones, Alex Knox, John Knox, Heather Kulp, Marilyn Langlois, Ruben Lizardo, Chris Magnus, Gayle McLaughlin, Eduardo Martinez, Jael Myrick, Al Nero, Vinay Pimple, Melissa Ritchie, Jeff Ritterman, Joey Schlemmer, David Schoenthal, Jeff Shoji, Ben Therriault, Nicole Valentino, Vern Whitmore, and Kyra Worthy.

Among local political activists, the following were particularly helpful: Tarnel Abbott, Marcos Banales, Michael Beer, Patsy Byers, Miguel Cavalin, Gail Eierweiss, Diane Feeley, Daniel Goodwin, Stephanie Hervey, Janet Johnson, Margaret Jordan, Greg Karas, Jeff Kilbreth, Paul Kilkenny, the Reverend Earl Koteen, Tim Laidman, Jonathan Mayer, Byron Miller, David Moore, Jessica Monteil, Yvonne Nair, Edith Pastrano, Mike Parker, Jeff Parker, Richard Perez, Joe Puleo, Jamin Pursell, Juan Reardon, Eugene Ruyle, David Sharples, Jane Slaughter, Charles Smith, Gerald Smith, Andres Soto, Pam Stello, Kathleen Sullivan, Melvin Willis, Kathleen Wimer, and Zak Wear.

Among my fellow trade unionists who have helped out, special thanks go to Buck Bagot, Gail Bateson, Garrett Brown, David Campbell, Millie Cleveland, Brad Dodge, Tom Edminister, Carl Finamore, Chris Finn, Jon Flanders, Ryan Haney, Aram Hodess, Bill Hoyle, Craig Merrilees, Mike Miller, Junior Ortiz, Jim Payne, Sal Rosselli, Tracy Scott, Mike Smith, Robert Travis, Marie Walcek, Mary Virginia Watson, B. K. White, Jeff Wickham, and Michael Wilson.

On the local media front, as the footnotes to this volume indicate, I am greatly indebted to the dedicated reporters, community journalists, and journalism students who have written about Richmond. Among them, I want to thank Rebecca Rosen Lum and Robert Rogers, formerly of the *Contra Costa Times*, and Robert's successor on the Richmond beat, Katrina Ioffee; John Geluardi, for his many years of informative Richmond coverage at the *East Bay Express*; Malcolm Marshall and his talented staff at the "youth-led" *Richmond Pulse*; Harriet Rowan, Jimmy Tobias, and their fellow students, past and present, at the UC-Berkeley School of Journalism's *Richmond Confidential* project; Chip Johnson and Tom Barnidge, regular columnists for the *San Francisco Chronicle* and *East Bay Times*, respectively; and Joe Eskenazi, former investigative reporter for *SF Weekly* and a very incisive observer of Richmond.

Mike Parker's two long accounts of RPA activity in *Social Policy* (Summer 2013 and Winter 2016) should be consulted by progressives involved in local electoral politics anywhere in the United States. For historical detail missing in chapter 2 for space reasons, consult Parker. The story of Gayle McLaughlin's first mayoral election victory is also recounted in Mike Feinstein's contribution to Jonathan Martin's excellent collection, *Empowering Progressive Third Parties in the United States: Defeating Duopoly, Advancing Democracy* (2016). Gayle is writing about her own political work in a book tentatively titled *Against All Odds: A Decade of Progress in Richmond*. For publication details, when available, see the RPA website, http://richmondprogressivealliance.net/, where links to Parker's *Social Policy* articles can also be found.

The personal archive and written recollections of RPA cofounder Juan Reardon were extremely helpful and generously shared. Juan's attention to detail as a successful campaign manager is exceeded only by his meticulous collection and filing of material from two decades of Richmond political activism. His instructive history of the early years of the RPA can be found at http://richmondprogressivealliance.net/docs/RPA_Origins.pdf. Mayor Tom Butt offered similar access to his voluminous files, but who needed that when the archives of his E-Forum provided many years' worth of detailed commentaries on events described in this book. Tom is a prolific and felicitous Richmond wordsmith, whose un-ghosted blogging is a testament to his ability to get by on little sleep! His E-Forum entries may not always be politically correct but never fail to inform (or, on April 1, fool) in one fashion or another.

Professor Shirley Ann Wilson Moore's *To Place Our Deeds: The African American Community in Richmond, California, 1910–1963* and the Reverend Alvin Bernstine's *A Ministry That Saves Lives* were indispensable as source material. Betty Reid Soskin, US park ranger extraordinaire, cannot be thanked enough for her enormous contribution to living history in Richmond and chapter 1 of *Refinery Town*. She and her colleagues at the Rosie the Riveter Historical Park are National Park Service treasures. Bill Jennings, a former member of the Black Panther Party in Richmond and a wonderful BPP archivist, supplied much-needed background on local BPP activity.

Brenda Williams's documentary film *Against Hate* vividly recounts Richmond's struggle over homophobia and hate speech in 2013–14. I benefited greatly from information sharing related to our overlapping projects. *Against Hate* is available for use as a teaching tool; for ordering information, contact BK Williams Productions at againsthate2015@gmail.com. *Nat Bates for Mayor*, a ninety-minute video documentary by Eric Weiss and Bradley Berman, is another valuable resource. It is available online at www.natbatesformayormovie.com. Weiss and Berman provide important insight into the African American community resentments and insecurities that have been stoked by Richmond's changing demographics, gentrification pressures, and, of course, by our local dispensers of big money in politics (Big Oil, Big Soda, et al.).

The Golden Shore: California's Love Affair with the Sea, by Richmond journalist and environmental activist David Helvarg, provides a firsthand account of the campaign to save Point Molate. For further information about local, national, and international campaigns involving Chevron, readers should consult, as I did, the website and reports of the True Cost of Chevron Network, the largest coalition seeking to reform this company and the entire oil industry. (See http://truecostofchevron.com/.) Oil Change International also does valuable research and advocacy revealing the true costs of fossil fuel use and promoting clean energy alternatives. (See http://priceofoil.org/.)

In the San Francisco Bay Area, the Sunflower Alliance's Chevron Watch performs a similar watchdog function at http://www.sunflower-alliance.org/campaigns/chevron-watch. The Climate Justice Alliance's Our Power

Campaign promotes a "just transition" to green jobs in Richmond and other communities through the activities described at http://movement generation.org/our-work/movementbuilding-2/cjaourpower/. The defense of "frontline communities" by Communities for a Better Environment is described in several chapters of this book. Many thanks to CBE staffer and former city council candidate Andres Soto for his "toxic tour" of Richmond, always valuable local history lessons, and tireless efforts to protect refinery town residents.

Fred Glass's book, *From Mission to Microchip: A History of the California Labor Movement*, provided insight into Richmond teacher struggles in the past. Even though controversies over public education were, for space reasons, beyond the scope of this book, I also learned a great deal from Lillian B. Rubin's *Busing & Backlash: White Against White in an Urban School District.*

As noted in chapter 4, *Richmond Standard* and *Radio Free Richmond* believe their online commentaries provide a counterweight to the views expressed in Tom Butt's E-Forum and the *RPA Activist*, the e-newsletter skillfully edited by Patsy Byers. I agree more often with the Chevron-related postings of Butt and Byers but do want to thank *Standard* editor Mike Aldax and *RFR* cofounders Don Gosney and Felix Hunziker for material from their sites referenced in this book. Many thanks also to Doria Robinson and Najari Smith for creating the Real Rich Facebook page, with its lively (and often very quotable) exchanges about community affairs. I also learned much from the Richmond Historical Society, directed by Melinda McCrary, and the Point Richmond History Association.

Refinery Town draws on my own previously published work about Richmond. Little of this freelance reporting and commentary would have seen the light of day, in print or online, without the editorial patronage of Katrina van den Heuvel, Roane Carey, and Lizzy Ratner at the *Nation*; Joel Bleifuss, Micah Uetricht, and Jessica Stites at *In These Times*; Randy Shaw at *Beyond Chron*; Josh Frank and Jeffrey St. Clair at *CounterPunch*; Michael Albert at *Znet* and *teleSur*; Margaret Flowers and Kevin Zeese at *Popular Resistance*; Leslie Thatcher at *Truthout*; Sarah van Gelder and James Trimarco at *Yes*; Al Bradbury at *Labor Notes*; Wade Rathke at *Social Policy*; and the editorial team at *Huffington Post*.

Among fellow authors of books about neighborhood renewal or municipal reform efforts, I want to recognize the particularly helpful research and writing of Pierre Clavel, Peter Dreier, William Domhoff, Steve Herbert, Randy Shaw, and Mike Rotkin, former mayor of Santa Cruz. Clavel is professor of city planning at Cornell University and author of *The Progressive City* (1986) and *Activists in City Hall* (2010). His Progressive Cities and Neighborhood Planning website (http://progressivecities.org/) includes an essential bibliography.

Among current practitioners of progressive urban politics, some of the most promising are part of Local Progress, a network directed by Ady Barkan at the Center for Popular Democracy in New York. For information on Local Progress national meetings and resource materials, see http://localprogress.org/. One of the multistate groups that has helped Local Progress members in New York and nine other states get elected is the Working Families Party network, now recruiting and training more candidates for local office inspired by the Sanders presidential campaign. For details, consult http://workingfamilies.org/states/new-york/.

Left Elect provides similar networking opportunities for people involved in "left/progressive parties, coalitions, and organizations." Information on its "independent political action" work can be found at https://leftelect.net/.

Family members and friends with political campaign experience provided insights for this book as well. They include Alexandra Early, Jessica Early, Phil Fiermonte, Ellen David Friedman, Rand Wilson, Torie Osborn, Sal Rosselli, Dan Siegel, Dan Hodges, James Haslam, Liz Blum, Karen Smith, and Paul Kumar. On the subject of money in politics, former CWA president Larry Cohen offered key feedback based on his Sanders campaign volunteering as a senior labor advisor and his current service as chair of the Our Revolution board. (For more on OR's work, see https://ourrevolution.com.) Steve and Karen Kittle gave me a different perspective on Richmond—from the waters of the bay—and their warm welcome to the neighborhood represents Point Richmond at its best.

At Beacon Press, it has been a pleasure working with my editor, Joanna Green; Beacon's director, Helene Atwan; and their wonderful colleagues Tom Hallock, Pamela MacColl, Alyssa Hassan, Nicholas DiSabatino, Alyson

Chu, Susan Lumenello, Beth Collins, Morgan Tuff, Aseem Kulkarni, and Ayla Zuraw-Friedland. Freelance copy editor Chris Dodge caught and corrected many a manuscript error. Without Joanna's skillful sculpting of the manuscript, the resulting book would have been far longer and much less readable.

Many thanks to my agent, Anne Borchardt, for steering me in the right direction for *Refinery Town* and for taking me on ten years ago as a second Borchardt Agency author in the same household. Which brings me to my last (but never least) thank-you note. Suzanne Gordon was originally slated to be coauthor of this book. Then she bailed out to complete her own forthcoming study of veteran's health care in the United States. Her penance for that desertion was enduring my various stages of manuscript-related distress. My symptoms were always alleviated, if not completely cured, by her calm reassurance, reliable advice, and skilled editing help. Suzanne is the rare book doctor who makes house calls (it helps to share the same address with her). She is a prolific journalist, an author, and the non–tiger mother of our two daughters, Alexandra and Jessica. I hope that some future book will be a long overdue joint venture—the ultimate test of marital bonds nearly four decades old!

NOTES

MUCH INFORMATION IN THIS book comes from interviews that were conducted between 2013 and 2016 in person, by phone, or via e-mail with residents of Richmond or others involved in its affairs. Among them are Nat Bates, Jovanka Beckles, Lorie Fridell, John Goia, John Knox, Marilyn Langlois, Bill Lindsay, Chris Magnus, Malcolm Marshall, Eduardo Martinez, Gayle McLaughlin, Byron Miller, Jessica Monteil, Jael Myrick, Mike Parker, Jim Payne, Richard Perez, Charles Ramsey, Juan Reardon, Melissa Ritchie, Jeff Ritterman, Jim Rogers, Robert Rogers, Bernie Sanders, Marilaine Savard, Tracy Scott, David Sharples, Mike Smith, Betty Reid Soskin, Andres Soto, Kathleen Sullivan, Ben Therriault, Tamisha Walker, Mark Wassberg, Zak Wear, Vernon Whitmore, Kathleen Wimer, and Melvin Willis.

Unless otherwise noted below, any quotes from those individuals came from those personal interviews, their remarks at public events I attended, their e-mail or other written communication with me or other Richmond residents, or their recorded statements on local cable TV and/or in Richmond-related documentary films.

INTRODUCTION: FROM COMPANY TOWN TO PROGRESSIVE CITY

1. Former San Francisco supervisor Scott Wiener, as quoted in Claire Cain Miller, "Liberals Turn to Cities to Pass Laws Others Won't," *New York Times*, January 26, 2016.
2. James Fallows, "Why Cities Work Even When Washington Doesn't: The Case for Strong Mayors," *Atlantic*, April 2014.
3. Bruce Katz and Jennifer Bradley, *The Metropolitan Revolution: How Cities and Metros Are Fixing Our Broken Politics and Fragile Economy* (Washington, DC: Brookings Institution Press, 2013).
4. Benjamin Barber, *If Mayors Ruled the World: Dysfunctional Nations, Rising Cities* (New Haven, CT: Yale University Press, 2013).

5. Carla Marinucci and Lizzie Johnson, "Star US Mayors Poised to Rocket Up the Political Ladder," *San Francisco Chronicle*, June 12, 2015.

6. Quoted in ibid.

7. As Jane Mayer reports, the Supreme Court's 2010 decision in *Citizens United v. Federal Election Commission* overturned "a century of restrictions banning corporations from spending all they wanted to elect candidates." The court gave "outside groups that were supporting or opposing candidates and were technically independent of the campaigns" the right to "spend unlimited amounts to promote whatever candidates they choose. To reach that verdict, the court accepted the argument that corporations had the same rights of free speech as citizens." See Mayer's invaluable *Dark Money: The Hidden History of the Billionaires Behind the Rise of the Radical Right* (New York: Doubleday, 2016), 227.

8. For more on the smear campaign against Sinclair, see Kathryn Olmsted, *Right Out of California: The 1930s and the Big Business Roots of Modern Conservatism* (New York: New Press, 2016); Lauren Coodley, *Upton Sinclair: California Socialist, Celebrity Intellectual* (Lincoln: University of Nebraska Press, 2013); and Anthony Arthur, *Radical Innocent: Upton Sinclair* (New York: Random House, 2006).

9. The term "lie factory" was Sinclair's own. For more on the role of Campaigns, Inc., in defeating him, see Jill Lepore, "The Lie Factory," *New Yorker*, September 24, 2012.

10. Sinclair's *I, Candidate for Governor: And How I Got Licked* was self-published and, according to Sinclair's most comprehensive biographer, helped "pay off his personal campaign debts." See Greg Mitchell, *The Campaign of the Century: Upton Sinclair's Race for Governor of California and the Birth of Media Politics* (New York: Random House, 1992), 544–55.

11. Martin Gilens and Benjamin I. Page, "Testing Theories of American Politics: Elites, Interest Groups, and Average Citizens," *Perspectives on Politics* 12, no 3. (September 2014): 580.

12. See http://www.beacon.org/Refinery-Town-P1229.aspx.

13. As quoted by Emilie Stigliani and Aki Soga, "Bernie Sanders Appears After Burlington Confab," *Burlington Free Press*, June 12, 2016. Several days after these comments, Sanders gave several hundred thousand supporters a video update on his campaign that included an appeal to visit berniesanders.com/win and "learn more about how you can run for office or get involved in politics at the local or state level." About twenty thousand people responded, two-thirds of them expressing interest in becoming local candidates themselves. For more on the former presidential candidate's post-election agenda, see Bernie Sanders's *Our Revolution: A Future to Believe In* (New York: Thomas Dunne, forthcoming).

CHAPTER 1: A REFINER'S FIRE

1. Gray Brechin, *Imperial San Francisco: Urban Power, Earthly Ruin* (Berkeley: University of California Press, 2006), 272–74.

2. See "Trade Excursion to Richmond," *San Francisco Chamber of Commerce Journal* 1, no. 9 (July 1912): 11, quoted in ibid., 39.

3. Quoted in "San Francisco Bay Trail," *NBC Bay Area*, June 27, 2015, http://www.nbcbayarea.com/news/local/San-Francisco-Bay-Trail-310357431.html.

4. O. A. Knight, president of the Oil Workers International Union, in his introduction to Harvey O'Connor, *History of the Oil Workers International Union-CIO* (Denver: Hirschfield Press, 1950), v.

5. Harvey O'Connor, *The Empire of Oil* (New York: Monthly Review Press, 1955), 14.

6. Ray Davidson, *Challenging the Giants: A History of Oil, Chemical, and Atomic Workers International Union* (Denver: OCAW, 1988), 10.

7. Peter Dreier, "Radicals in City Hall: An American Tradition," *Dissent*, December 19, 2013, https://www.dissentmagazine.org/online_articles/radicals-in-city-hall-an-american-tradition.

8. Richard Gendron and G. William Domhoff, *The Leftmost City: Power and Progressive Politics in Santa Cruz* (Boulder, CO: Westview Press, 2009), 103. Business interests also sought, wherever possible, to replace district elections with at-large city council votes. According to the authors, the latter "made it more difficult for neighborhood leaders, whether Democrats, Socialists, or ethnic and racial minorities, to hold their seats on city councils because they did not have the money and name recognition to win citywide elections." In 2015, some Richmond residents unhappy about the success of the Richmond Progressive Alliance in city-wide races proposed that at-large election of city councilors be replaced by a system of geographical representation based on smaller electoral districts.

9. O'Connor, *History of the Oil Workers International Union-CIO*, 327.

10. Muriel Clausen, "This Old House," reprinted in *This Point in Time* [Point Richmond History Association] 33, no. 2 (September/October 2014): 17.

11. O'Connor, *History of the Oil Workers International Union-CIO*, 63. See also Davidson, *Challenging the Giants*, 183–91, on the 1948 strike and its aftermath, in terms of expanded contracting out.

12. Jim Payne, financial secretary of USW Local 5, quoted in David Bacon, "An Oil Worker and a Union Staffer Explain Why 1000s of Oil Workers Across the Country Are on Strike," *In These Times*, February 12, 2015, http://inthesetimes.com/working/entry/17631/oil_workers_on_strike.

13. Shirley Ann Wilson Moore, *To Place Our Deeds: The African American Community in Richmond, California, 1910–1963* (Berkeley: University of California Press, 2001), 16.

14. Ibid., 45.

15. Quoted in Richard Rothstein, "How African-Americans in Richmond Came to Be Segregated and Impoverished," draft paper presented at Richmond Housing Summit, January 27, 2015. Copy in possession of the author.

16. Alvin Bernstine, *A Ministry That Saves Lives: Sermons and Thoughts on Ministry in a Challenging Context* (Richmond, CA: ACB Ministry, 2012).

17. Lucretia Edwards, "A Short History of How the Neighborhood Councils Started in the City of Richmond, California." Undated document in possession of the author.

18. Rothstein, "How African-Americans in Richmond Came to Be Segregated and Impoverished," 21.

19. Jessica Mitford, *A Fine Old Conflict* (New York: Alfred Knopf, 1977), 128–29.

20. Jovanka Beckles, "The Gary Family of Richmond Fighting for Equality and Standing for Their Rights," *Radio Free Richmond*, February 23, 2015, http://www.radiofreerichmond.com/.

21. Moore, *To Place Our Deeds*, 96.

22. Quoted in Rothstein, "How African-Americans in Richmond Came to Be Segregated and Impoverished," 29.

23. See Lillian Rubin, *Busing & Backlash: White Against White in an Urban School District* (Berkeley: University of California Press, 1972), 93–94.

24. Tom Corcoran, the Richmond mayor who approved the transfer of refinery property so the Hilltop area could become a shopping center, also voted on a number of other Chevron-related matters. He was a retired executive of the company who owned $300,000 worth of its stock but, as current mayor Tom Butt notes, "did not understand that he could no longer represent Chevron." Corcoran's repeated conflicts of interest on the council led the California Fair Political Practices Commission to fine him $15,000—about $40,000 in today's dollars.

25. Jennings's quote is from his remarks at the August 11, 2013, ceremony renaming the Richmond Progressive Alliance office as the Bobby Bowens Progressive Center. For a longer interview with him, see Steve Early, "Q & A: Bill Jennings on Black Panther Party's Place in Richmond's History," *Richmond Pulse*, September 8, 2015, http://richmondpulse.org/2015/09/08/q-a-bill-jennings-on-black-panther-partys-place-in-richmonds-history/.

26. "Panthers Demand Independence for North Richmond Area," *Black Panther* 1, no. 3 (June 20, 1967).

27. Bobby Seale, "Community Control of the Police Was on Berkeley Ballot in 1969," *San Francisco Bay View*, September 2015.

28. David DeBolt and Robert Rogers, "North Richmond: Most Killings Go Unsolved in Tiny Enclave," *Contra Costa Times*, April 5, 2015. As DeBolt and Rogers report, between 2010 and 2014, nineteen people, almost all African American males under the age of fifty, were killed in the 1.5-square-mile area of North Richmond; charges were filed in five of those homicide cases.

29. Pierre Clavel, *The Progressive City: Planning and Participation, 1969–1984* (New Brunswick, NJ: Rutgers University Press, 1986), 1. For more on the Chicago and Boston experience, see Clavel's later book, *Activists in City Hall: The Progressive Response to the Reagan Era in Boston and Chicago* (Ithaca, NY: Cornell University Press, 2010).

30. For a perceptive insider's account of the challenges facing black mayors during this period and more recently, see J. Phillip Thompson, *Double Trouble: Black Mayors, Black Communities and the Struggle for Deep Democracy* (New York: Oxford University Press, 2006). As political scientist Adolph Reed Jr. argues, newly elected municipal officials are unlikely to pursue bolder, more progressive policy agendas in the absence of sustained grassroots pressure generated from outside city hall. See "The Black Urban Regime: Structural Origins and Constraints," in Reed's essay collection, *Stirrings in the Jug: Black Politics in the Post-Segregation Era* (Minneapolis: University of Minnesota Press, 1999).

31. Davidson, *Challenging the Giants*, 10.

32. Quoted by Antonia Juhasz, *The Tyranny of Oil: The World's Most Powerful Industry—and What We Must Do to Stop It* (New York: HarperCollins, 2008), 194.

33. Quoted in Paul Rauber, "Oiltown," *East Bay Express*, September 30, 1988.
34. For more on Clark's long career of Richmond environmental activism, see Sara Bernard, "Henry Clark and Three Decades of Environmental Justice," *Richmond Confidential*, December 6, 2012, http://richmondconfidential.org/2012/12/06/henry-clark-and-three-decades-of-environmental-justice/.
35. Quoted in Rauber, "Oiltown."
36. Juhasz, *Tyranny of Oil*, 193.
37. Ibid., 192.
38. For this summary of Chevron's past environmental law breaking, I am indebted to the editors of the *Dispatcher*, the national newspaper of the International Longshore and Warehouse Union (ILWU). See "Working with Allies to Protect the Union, Community, and Environment," *Dispatcher*, July/August 2015.
39. Quoted in *Dying at Work in California: The Hidden Stories Behind the Numbers* (Oakland, CA: WorkSafe, 2013), http://www.worksafe.org/2013/Dying_at _Work_in_CA_2013_web.pdf.
40. Joe Eskenazi, "Trust Me: Who Are You Gonna Believe, Sam Singer or Your Own Eyes?" *SF Weekly*, August 26, 2014.
41. Quoted in James North, "Ecuador's Battle for Environmental Justice Against Chevron," *Nation*, June 22/29, 2015.

CHAPTER 2: THE GREENING OF CITY HALL

1. Ian Stewart, "Years Later, Chemical Company Lot Still a Toxic Stew," *Richmond Confidential*, November 9, 2009.
2. Chris Thompson, "Burning Richmond's Race Card," *East Bay Express*, October 7, 2005.
3. In 2004, Thurmond ran and lost as an "independent" but ended up joining the council later, when he was appointed to fill a vacancy. After serving as a Richmond city councilor, he ran for the Contra Costa County school board and then gained his current state assembly seat. Later, in their own 2004 campaigns, Soto and McLaughlin also diverged over the issue of accepting business donations. Each received five hundred dollars from a local manufacturer. Soto accepted the money, while McLaughlin publicly rejected and returned her check, to uphold the RPA's policy of refusing corporate funding.
4. Rebecca Rosen Lum, "McLaughlin Proves a Pragmatist," *Contra Costa Times*, July 24, 2005.
5. Unfortunately, Richmond's municipal ID program does not currently have the backing of a financial institution, so the card obtained by undocumented workers could also be used to make bank deposits and withdrawals. This would reduce their need to carry cash, which has made some in Richmond a target for street robberies.
6. One-stop access to city services and programs is now also available to users of the City of Richmond's mobile-phone app. Via this, residents can even report streets that need to be repaired, attaching a picture of their most hated potholes if they wish. See http://4richmond.org/city-of-richmond-mobile-app-offers -one-stop-shopping-for-city-services.
7. John Geluardi, "Richmond Developer Pushes Two Ballot Measures," *East Bay Express*, November 11, 2015.

8. See John Geluardi, "The Man Behind Richmond's Renaissance," *East Bay Express*, May 18, 2011. In 2015, when the city manager's contract came up for renewal, Lindsay came under fire from critics of his compensation package. By 2013, he was receiving $288,372 in annual salary, plus an additional $123,600 in benefits, for total compensation of $411,972. "While it could be argued that city manager salaries in general are too high," noted Gayle McLaughlin, "the compensation the city council has negotiated with our current city manager is not out of line based on current levels in the Bay Area." One foe of Lindsay's, developer Richmond Poe, placed a ballot measure before Richmond voters in June 2016 seeking to cap the city manager's pay; it was only narrowly defeated.

9. The Measure T litigation settlement—negotiated by city councilors Jeff Ritterman, Tom Butt, and Jim Rogers—was denounced as a sellout by a few RPA members. Charles Smith, a retired union activist, left the organization over the issue and has continued to criticize it ever since, saying that "so-called progressives squandered this major victory." See Smith, "Bad, Bad Jerry Brown," letter to the editor, *Nation*, July 15, 2014, http://www.thenation.com/article/letters-477/.

10. For more on Kilbreth's property tax analysis and critique, see Jeff Kilbreth, "Overview of Chevron and Contra Costa County Property Taxes," presentation, November 2013, Richmond Progressive Alliance, http://richmond progressivealliance.net/Issues/Chevron/Kilbreth13-11-21.pdf.

11. David Helvarg, *The Golden Shore: California's Love Affair with the Sea* (New York: St. Martin's Press, 2013).

12. "Draft Environmental Impact Statement/Environmental Impact Report, Point Molate Mixed-Use Tribal Destination Resort and Casino," vol. 1, app. O, "Environmental Noise Analysis," City of Richmond, http://www.ci.richmond. ca.us/DocumentCenter/Home/View/7523.

13. Upstream and its tribal allies forced Richmond to spend nearly $2 million on attorney's fees in this litigation before a federal judge finally ordered them to reimburse the city for its post-referendum legal costs. The plaintiffs then appealed that fee award, but defeated casino developer Richard Levine offered to settle the case based on Richmond's acceptance of an immediately controversial plan to have Upstream build a thousand housing units on Point Molate. In mid-2016, settlement talks were continuing.

14. Nat Bates for mayor campaign mailer, 2010. Document in possession of the author. In Richmond, candidates for municipal office are identified on the ballot only by their chosen description of their occupation—not as a Democrat, Republican, Independent, or Green Party member.

15. In 2010, Whitehurst/Mosher was also hired by Richmond card club operators to campaign against the Point Molate casino project.

16. See Edward Walker, "The Uber-ization of Activism," *New York Times*, August 7, 2015, and Walker's valuable book-length study *Grassroots for Hire: Public Affairs Consultants in American Democracy* (New York: Cambridge University Press, 2014).

17. Norimitsu Onishi, "California City Savors Role in Fighting 'Big Soda,'" *New York Times*, November 4, 2012.

18. Marion Nestle, *Soda Politics: Taking on Big Soda (and Winning)* (New York: Oxford University Press, 2015), 382. In June, 2016, Philadelphia became the

largest city in the United States to embrace soda taxation after its local advocates downplayed public health as a rationale and campaigned instead on the need for new revenue for parks and recreation, public libraries, and universal pre-school programs. See Margot Sanger-Katz "Philadelphia Finds Winning Strategy For Soda Tax, and Other Cities Notice," *New York Times*, June 17, 2016.

19. In Richmond itself, city councilor Jim Rogers told me that he turned against Richmond Cares because its backers tried to convince him "that we did not need insurance to protect us from the promised industry lawsuit."

20. Rebecca Burns, "A Company Town Becomes Our Town, *In These Times*, September 18, 2013.

21. Quoted in ibid.

22. Karina Ioffee, "Bay Area Mortgage Relief Target of Mayors," *Contra Costa Times*, June 19, 2015.

23. Quoted in ibid.

24. For further details, see Local Progress and Center for Popular Democracy, *Policy for Local Progress: Case Studies and Best Practices from Around the Country* (Washington, DC: Local Progress, 2016), http://localprogress.org/wp-content/uploads/2013/09/Local-Progress-Policy-Briefs-Booklet.pdf.

25. Quoted in Steve Early, "Meet the Group of Feisty Urban Progressives Who Want to Transform the Country One City at a Time," *Nation*, December 10, 2014. See also Nick Licata, *Becoming a Citizen Activist: Stories, Strategies, and Advice for Changing Our World* (Seattle: Sasquatch Books, 2016).

26. Quoted in John Geluardi, "From Richmond to the Rainforest," *East Bay Express*, October 16, 2013.

27. Quoted in ibid.

28. Chip Johnson, "Richmond's Activist-Mayor Blurs Line over Chevron," *San Francisco Chronicle*, October 17, 2013.

29. "Time to Move on Dangerous Tank Cars," editorial, *New York Times*, May 30, 2014.

30. Jad Mouawad, "Oil Industry Asks Court to Block Rail Transport Safety Rules," *New York Times*, May 12, 2015. In September 2015 the California legislature did help curb the one-member-crew trend by requiring all freight trains operated in the state to have both a conductor and engineer. A year later, however, the Federal Railroad Administration proposed a new rule, over the objection of railroad unions, that would enable carriers to get federal approval for single-employee operations, even for hazardous-material hauling.

31. Quoted by Patsy Byers, "Protesting Crude by Rail in Richmond: The People Here Thursday Showed Some Guts," *RPA Activist*, September 7, 2014, archived at http://richmondprogressivealliance.net/docs/KinderMorganAction September4.pdf.

CHAPTER 3: RICHMOND'S COMMUNITY POLICEMAN

1. Nancy Deville and Joaquin Palomino, "The White Cop Who Embraced #BlackLivesMatter and Saved Richmond," *Pacific Standard*, December 31, 2014, http://www.psmag.com/.

2. Stacy Finz, "Fargo's Top Cop Ready for Richmond," *San Francisco Chronicle*, December 17, 2005.

3. Ibid.

4. Quoted in Wallace Turner, "Anti-Police Suit Focuses on a Town's Ills," *New York Times*, February 13, 1983.

5. Quoted in Wallace Turner, "Racial Problems Continue in a California City," *New York Times*, July 7, 1983.

6. Quoted in Joe Eskenazi, "From the 'Arm Pit of the Bay Area' to a Progressive Utopia on Earth," *San Francisco Magazine*, May 21, 2015, http://www.modern luxury.com/san-francisco/story/the-arm-pit-of-the-bay-area-progressive -utopia-earth.

7. One of the few local cops who followed the chief's example of living in Richmond was Ben Therriault, who was elected president of the Richmond Police Officers Association in 2016. Since 2011, Therriault has taken advantage of a program that enables officers to live rent free in any low-income housing project run by the city. For an account of his experiences in previously troubled Richmond Village, see Shawn Baldwin, "A Cop, and a Resident, of Richmond Public Housing," *Richmond Confidential*, September 29, 2014.

8. Elizabeth Weise, "'All Lives Matter' a Creed for Richmond, Calif. Police," *USA Today*, September 23, 2015.

9. Robert Rogers, "Richmond Police Captain Described Intimidation, Sabotage in Department in 2006–7," *Contra Costa Times*, March 27, 2012.

10. John Geluardi, "Updated: Jury Exonerates Richmond Police Chief Chris Magnus," *East Bay Express*, April 10, 2012.

11. Kevin Sack and Megan Thee-Brenan, "A Broad Division over Race in US Is Found in Poll," *New York Times*, July 24, 2015.

12. Richard Ford, "Why We Tolerate Biased Policing," *Boston Review*, January 22, 2015, http://bostonreview.net/blog/richard-thompson-ford-biased-policing.

13. Michael Schmidt, "FBI Director Speaks Out on Race and Police Bias," *New York Times*, February 13, 2015.

14. Zusha Elinson and Dan Frosch, "Police-Misconduct Costs Soar," *Wall Street Journal*, July 16, 2015.The settlement of litigation over the police shooting of twelve-year-old Tamir Rice cost Cleveland $6 million—in line with the payouts to the Garner and Gray families in New York City and Baltimore respectively.

15. Radley Balko, *Rise of the Warrior Cop: The Militarization of America's Police Forces* (New York: Public Affairs, 2014).

16. Quoted in Steve Rubenstein, "Youths Sound Off on Abusive Officers," *San Francisco Chronicle*, September 27, 2015.

17. Quoted in Robert Rogers, "Richmond Police Chief a Prominent Participant in Protest Against Police Violence," *Contra Costa Times*, December 9, 2014.

18. Quoted in Henry K. Lee, "Richmond Union Criticizes Chief for Wearing Uniform to Protest," *SF Gate*, December 13, 2014. The RPOA disputes the accusation that union officers or members have been pictured improperly in Richmond election campaign material.

19. After his direct-mail battering by the RPOA and council campaign defeat in 2004, Andres Soto invoked the same statute in his legal challenge to the RPOA's use of a departmental logo on election campaign literature. That lawsuit did not end well for him; the RPOA filed a successful counterclaim and

sought and won attorney's fees, forcing Soto to declare personal bankruptcy when stuck with a $9,000 bill for the union's legal costs.

20. David Brooks, "The Union Future," *New York Times*, December 19, 2014. For a detailed analysis of police union litigation strategies and contract provisions that can thwart reform, see Adeshina Emmanuel, "How Union Contracts Shield Killer Cops: There's a Reason Department of Justice-Mandated Reforms Don't Stick," *In These Times*, July 2016.

21. Quoted in Sarah Jaffe, "Black Labor Organizers Urge AFL-CIO to Reexamine Its Ties to the Police," *Truthout*, August 13, 2015.

22. Quoted in "Richmond Police Chief's New Approach Is Revitalizing a Tough Town," Associated Press, February 2, 2015. A year after the RPOA meeting with Magnus over his controversial sign holding, Virgil Thomas was voted out as union president. His successor, Ben Therriault, told me that "there was a lot of upset" among RPOA members over the chief's "problematic symbolism." As Therriault explained, the movement known as Black Lives Matter "is not viewed as law-enforcement friendly."

23. Quoted in Robert Rogers, "Use of Deadly Force by Police Disappears on Richmond Streets," *Contra Costa Times*, September 6, 2014.

24. Ibid.

25. According to Amnesty International, "More than 500 people have died in the United States since 2001 after being shocked with stun guns or tasers," as Nick Madigan reported in "No Charges for Officer in Miami Taser Death," *New York Times*, July 24, 2015.

26. In March 2016 California state senator Mark Leno introduced a bill, backed by the American Civil Liberties Union, to amend the 1977 Public Safety Officers Procedural Bill of Rights Act to limit its privacy protections for the personnel files of police officers. Leno argued that keeping information about police-misconduct investigations confidential erodes public trust in law-enforcement agencies. Faced with opposition from twenty-nine law-enforcement and labor groups, Leno's bill was killed in committee, as Ali Winton reported in "Cop Blocked: California Effort to Increase Police Transparency Dies at State Capitol," *East Bay Express*, June 1–7, 2016.

27. Jake Halpern, "The Cop," *New Yorker*, August 10 & 17, 2015.

28. The skepticism expressed by Chief Magnus about the need for a police commission overhaul was shared by his sometime critics in the RPOA. "The police department already has processes on top of processes . . . to improve ourselves," argues union president Ben Therriault. "How much money are we going to spend on investigations that lead to the same results?"

29. Quoted in John Geluardi, "Too Much Police Oversight in Richmond?," *East Bay Express*, March 2–8, 2016.

30. Chris Magnus, *RPD Update*, Spring 2014. Document in possession of the author.

31. Quoted in Eskanazi, "From the 'Arm Pit of the Bay Area' to a Progressive Utopia on Earth."

32. Quoted in Joaquin Palomino and Kevin Hume, "North Richmond Church Grapples with Recent Killings," *Richmond Confidential*, October 2, 2013.

33. For representative coverage of Boggan and the ONS, see Tim Murphy, "Life Is Cheap: Did DeVone Boggan Bring Down His City's Murder Rate by Paying

Kids to Stay Alive?," *Mother Jones*, July/August 2014; and Heather Tirado Gilligan, "How One California City Began Bringing Its Murder Rate Down—Without Cops," *Nation*, November 12, 2014.

34. Megan Thompson, "California Program Offers Cash to Reduce Gun Crimes," *PBS NewsHour*, May 7, 2016, http://www.pbs.org/newshour/bb/controversial-california-program-offers-cash-to-reduce-gun-crimes/.

35. See NCCD's "Process Evaluation for the Office of Neighborhood Safety," archived at https://s3.amazonaws.com/s3.documentcloud.org/documents/2178945/nccd-richmond-report.pdf.

36. Quoted in Chris Hayes, "Did Paying People Not to Kill Bring Down Murder Numbers?," MSNBC.com, July 20, 2014, http://www.msnbc.com/all-in/watch/did-paying-people-not-to-kill-bring-down-murder-numbers--482381891900.

CHAPTER 4: TUESDAY NIGHT CAGE FIGHTS

1. Eskanazi, "From the 'Arm Pit of the Bay Area' to Progressive Utopia on Earth."
2. Robert Rogers, "Could It Be Corky Time?," *Richmond Confidential*, October 22, 2010.
3. "Full Biography for Courtland 'Corky' Booze," SmartVoter, http://www.smartvoter.org/2010/11/02/ca/cc/vote/booze_c/bio.html.
4. Quoted in Carolyn Jones, "Councilwoman Perseveres Through Taunts, Rants, and Homophobic Slurs," *San Francisco Chronicle*, August 5, 2014.
5. Robert Rogers, "NAACP Richmond's Choice for Martin Luther King Jr. Peace Award Sparks Controversy," *East Bay Times*, January 26, 2013, http://www.eastbaytimes.com/ci_22455053/naacp-richmonds-choice-martin-luther-king-jr-peace.
6. Quoted in Robert Rogers, "Political Theater Rules Richmond City Council Meetings," *Contra Costa Times*, May 11, 2014.
7. Rogers later ceased practicing personal-injury law after problems with the California Bar Association. According to Stanford law professor Nora Freeman Engstrom, his license was surrendered while disciplinary charges were still pending over his operation of a "settlement mill." See Engstrom, "Sunlight and Settlement Mills," *New York University Law Review* 86, no. 4 (October 2011): 817–21.
8. Privately Jeff Ritterman and Tom Butt both suggested that the RPA's prior encouragement of vocal citizen activism at council meetings, on behalf of its favored causes, may have inadvertently paved the way for the "cage fights" of 2013–14. As Butt told me: "Gayle and her group champion grassroots movements and they turn out a lot of people at meetings. . . . Hooting and hollering in the audience—that's what movements do. They don't behave themselves."
9. For Soskin's always incisive observations about politics and life in Richmond and elsewhere, see *CBreaux Speaks*, http://cbreaux.blogspot.com.
10. Following a federal grand jury probe of alleged payoffs for city contracts, Reese pled guilty in 2001 to felony income tax evasion for not reporting tens of thousands of dollars in extra income. He was sentenced to wear a monitoring device for four months, followed by three years of probation, but he remained active in Richmond politics as a behind-the-scenes election-year strategist and

"hit piece" producer. See Will Harper, "The White Shadow," *East Bay Express,* October 24, 2001.

11. Nat Bates, "RPA Trying to Win Black Vote," *Richmond Standard,* March 17, 2014, http://richmondstandard.com/2014/03/councilman-bates-rpa-trying -win-black-vote.

12. Harriet Blair Rowan and Jimmy Tobias, "What Does It Take for One Small City to Vanquish an Oil Giant?," *Nation,* November 21, 2014.

13. As quoted in ibid.

14. Mike Parker, "A Social Policy Case Study and Follow-up on Richmond Progressive Alliance Two Years Later: Richmond Progressive Alliance: Defeating Big Money in Politics," *Social Policy* (Winter 2015), http://richmondprogressive alliance.net/docs/RPAHist2-mp.pdf.

15. Richmond's system of public matching funds was enacted in 2008, a reform championed by council member Jim Rogers and others. Under its current formula, a candidate who raises $10,000 can receive an initial grant of $5,000 in public money; each additional $5,000 raised from private donors brings in a matching amount, up to a total of $25,000 from the city election fund. To qualify, a candidate must accept what is now a $70,000 limit on total private contributions.

16. Anthony Arthur, *Radical Innocent: Upton Sinclair* (New York: Penguin Random House, 2006), 274.

17. Rory Carroll, "Chevron's One-Man Newsroom Defends His Work," *Guardian,* November 7, 2014. As Mike Aldax confessed to Carroll, "Being called a prostitute is hard. It can make you wonder about your career."

18. Michael Hiltzik, "How Chevron Swamps a Small City with Campaign Money and Bogus News," *Los Angeles Times,* October 13, 2014; Michael Hiltzik, "A Chevron PR Website Pretends to Be an Objective News Source," *Los Angeles Times,* September 22, 2014.

19. For more details of this episode, see Jimmy Tobias, "Stealth Chevron Consultants Administer Richmond News Website," *Richmond Confidential,* October 30, 2014, http://richmondconfidential.org/2014/10/30/stealth-chevron-consultants -administer-richmond-news-website. *Radio Free Richmond* cofounder Felix Hunziker contends that there was no intention to deceive readers and that he had disclosed BMWL's connection to *RFR* on Facebook and in other ways. On *RFR's* site today, BMWL is credited with providing "the initial programming of the website" which, according to Hunziker now "requires little time and money to operate" because it is primarily Facebook-based. The site is jointly owned by Hunziker and Don Gosney but is still a "partnership with BMWL, a consulting firm that includes Chevron among its list of other local clients." Hunziker insists that "*RFR* isn't funded by Chevron, nor is it pro-Chevron or engaged with Chevron in any way."

20. See Marilynne Mellander, "Community View: RPA Attempts 'Shakedown of Chevron' at Planning Commission," *Richmond Standard,* July 11, 2014, http:// richmondstandard.com/2014/07/community-view-rpa-attempts-shakedown -chevron-planning-commission/.

21. In 2014, Mellander ran unsuccessfully for the Doctors Medical Center board on a platform of closing the hospital. See Jennifer Baires, "Quiet Race for

Contentious West Contra Costa Healthcare District Seats," *Contra Costa Times*, October 6, 2014.

22. Mike Aldax, "Chevron Richmond's Latest Refinery Modernization Project Proposal Wins Community Praise," *Richmond Standard*, July 23, 2014, http:// richmondstandard.com/2014/07/chevron-richmonds-latest-refinery -modernization-project-touted-best-possible-plan/.

23. Quoted in Robert Rogers, "Richmond Approves Massive Chevron Refinery Project with $90 Million in Community Benefits," *Contra Costa Times*, July 30, 2015.

24. Victoria Colliver, "Lost Hospital Leaves Region with Big Void," *San Francisco Chronicle*, April 21, 2016.

CHAPTER 5: AN ELECTION NOT FOR SALE

1. Brett Murphy and Elly Schmidt-Hopper, "Accusations and Money Fly as Chevron Spends on Richmond City Council Races," *Richmond Confidential*, October 19, 2014.

2. Drew Weston, "Why Attack Ads? Because They Work," *Los Angeles Times*, February 19, 2012.

3. In June 2016, EMC Research conducted a survey of *Richmond Standard* readers, designed to gauge their views of its credibility as a local news source. Survey participants, including the author, were informed that "part of the function of the website is to provide a voice for Chevron Richmond." Nevertheless, the survey assured us that "the *Standard* is managed by an independent reporter," who, of course, was not identified as a senior account executive at Singer Associates, Chevron's public relations firm in San Francisco.

4. Michael Crowley and Michael Kruse, "The Foreign Minister of Burlington, Vt.," *Politico*, July 31, 2015, http://www.politico.com/story/2015/07/the-foreign -minister-of-burlington-vt-120839.

5. For more on Vermont Progressive Party history and recent activity, see Steve Early, *Save Our Unions: Dispatches from a Movement in Distress* (New York: Monthly Review Press, 2013), 264–70; and Steve Early, "Union Member Recruitment by Vermont Progressives," *Social Policy* 44, no. 2 (Summer 2014): 5-17, http://www.progressiveparty.org.2014/08/union-member-recruitment -vermont-progressives.

6. The soundness of the RPA approach to voters was confirmed in research about local elections in New Haven conducted by Yale political scientists Donald Green and Alan Gerber nearly two decades ago. "Talking to them face-to-face, the longer, the better, turned out to have a dramatic effect," according to Green and Gerber, as reported by Andrew Cockburn in "Down the Tube: Television, Turnout, and the Election Industrial Complex," *Harper's*, April 2016, 63–68.

7. For more on organizing in other states, under the "Working Families" banner, see Molly Ball, "The Pugnacious, Relentless Progressive Party That Wants to Remake America," *Atlantic*, January 2016.

8. Jennifer Baires and Robert Rogers, "Anti-Chevron Candidates Sweep to Victory in Richmond Races," *Contra Costa Times*, November 4, 2014.

9. As quoted by John Geluardi, "Chevron Bids to Retake Richmond," *East Bay Express*, October 22–28, 2014.

10. For more on this historic phenomenon, see Mary Frances Berry, *Five Dollars and a Pork Chop Sandwich: Vote Buying and the Corruption of Democracy* (Boston: Beacon Press, 2016).

11. Quoted in Samantha Cowan, "Young Journalist Fights Big Oil to Save One City's Elections," *TakePart*, October 20, 2014, http://www.takepart.com /article/2014/10/20/oil-company-spends-big-influence-local-elections.

12. Quoted in Tom Goulding, "Losing Candidates Say Money May Have Hurt Their Campaigns," *Richmond Confidential*, November 19, 2014.

13. Quoted in ibid.

14. Quoted in ibid.

15. Quoted in "Richmond Can't Be Bought Off," editorial, *San Francisco Chronicle*, November 7, 2014. As if to confirm Myrick's accusation of irrelevancy, BAPAC went out of business after the 2014 election.

16. "Chevron's Excuse," May 1, 2015, e-mail message from Public Citizen. Document in possession of the author.

17. "Dark Money's Deepening Power," editorial, *New York Times*, June 29, 2015, http://www.nytimes.com/2015/06/29/opinion/dark-moneys-deepening -power.html.

18. The case for SEC action is well argued by Kathleen M. Donovan-Maher and Steven L. Groopman, "Why Dark Money Is Bad Business," *New York Times*, May 10, 2016.

19. Eduardo Porter, "Companies Open Up on Giving in Politics," *New York Times*, June 6, 2015.

20. George Avalos, "Chevron Defends Environmental Record," *San Jose Mercury News*, May 27, 2015, http://www.mercurynews.com/business/ci_28198464 /chevron-defends-environmental-record-ecuador-sees-bright-future.

21. Clifford Kraus, "Profits Slide for Exxon and Chevron in a Brutal Year for the US Oil Industry," *New York Times*, October 31, 2015. While Chevron was not making much as a crude-oil producer, with the price of oil under $50 per barrel, its "refinery and retail profit picture, including the Richmond refinery, was relatively bright," according to George Avalos in "Chevron Sees Its Profits Plummet," *Contra Costa Times*, August 1, 2015.

CHAPTER 6: CELEBRATING OUR DIFFERENCES?

1. A year after Butt's "State of the City" report, the mall was for sale, and at least one Chevron-friendly candidate for city council, Cesar Zepeda, president of the Hilltop District Homeowners & Stakeholders Association, was making its revitalization the centerpiece of his campaign.

2. Quoted in Tim Redmond, "In Richmond, a Battle over a Council Seat—and the Role of Grassroots Groups," *48Hills* (blog), February 24, 2015, http:// www.48hills.org/2015/02/24/4174/.

3. Chip Johnson, "18 Vie for Hot Vacant Seat Dividing Richmond Council," *San Francisco Chronicle*, February 9, 2015. The RPA demanded a retraction over this column, and the paper subsequently ran the following correction: "Chip Johnson's 'On the East Bay' on politics in Richmond mischaracter-ized the Richmond Progressive Alliance. The political group has no rule

requiring its members on the City Council to clear their votes with the broader membership."

4. Redmond, "In Richmond."

5. Ibid.

6. Ibid. Redmond also reviews the relevant history of Berkeley Citizen Action (BCA), a local left-wing de facto political party in Berkeley during the 1980s. According to Redmond, "The BCA council members at times had trouble seeing other points of view. But they passed some great legislation, including the most important pro-tenant measures in the state."

7. Soon after his appointment, Pimple sided with Butt against a controversial city council resolution, which proved embarrassing to Jael Myrick and his three RPA colleagues. This resolution expressed solidarity with local residents who consider themselves to be "targeted individuals" (i.e., subjects of alleged government surveillance or mind-control efforts involving space-based military technology). Butt expressed exasperation with the council's action and, after a flurry of media ridicule, Myrick publicly apologized for his role in it. Before the flap was over, even former mayor McLaughlin agreed that the space-weaponry resolution was "a mistake" and a distraction from other council business.

8. Redmond, "In Richmond."

9. Quotes are from an RPA internal document dated April 8, 2015, titled "Restructuring Committee Analysis and Recommendations" and authored by Patsy Byers, Michelle Chan, Claudia Jimenez, Eli Moore, Jamin Pursell, Jeff Shoji, and Tamisha Walker. Copy in possession of the author.

10. No Chevron representative responded, in person, to the CSB presentation on January 28, 2015. Instead, the company issued a press statement objecting to the agency's "inaccurate depiction of the Richmond refinery's safety culture." See Jennifer Baires, "Chevron Fire Safety Culture Is Faulted," *Contra Costa Times*, January 29, 2015.

11. USW national vice president Gary Beeson as quoted in Steve Early, "Tony Mazzocchi's Spirit Haunts Big Oil Again," *Beyond Chron*, February 4, 2015.

12. B. K. White, USW Local 5 Bargaining Report on "local issues," February 2, 2015. Document in possession of the author.

13. Some angry Local 5 members questioned why their union still belonged to the CLC or allowed it to remain a tenant in the USW-owned Jeff Dodge Labor Center, a site used by several local labor organizations for office and meeting space.

14. See, for example, Paul Garver, "Striking Oil Workers Emerge Victorious, Thanks in Part to Green Group Solidarity," *Portside Labor*, March 18, 2015.

15. Chevron estimates their "average national salary, not including benefits" to be $75,620. In Richmond, according to Local 5, base pay is actually about $90,000 a year. Working twelve-hour shifts with lots of overtime, forced or voluntary, its highly skilled members have no trouble generating six-figure incomes.

16. Kory Judd, "The Power of 'Stop Work Authority,'" *Richmond Standard*, October 20, 2015, http://richmondstandard.com/2015/10/the-power-of-stop-work -authority/.

17. Smith chose to retire from the company, after thirteen years of service, rather than return to full-time work in the Richmond refinery. He remains on the

staff of Local 5, where requests for extensions of union leave, in the past, have been routinely granted by local refiners, including Chevron. Smith's former employer may have been additionally miffed by his labor solidarity tours of Australia, where he exchanged information and strategy advice with militant members of the Maritime Union, a local foe of nonunion outsourcing.

18. Malcolm Marshall, "Richmond Celebrates First Pride Family Day," *Richmond Pulse*, June 15, 2015, http://richmondpulse.org/2015/06/15/richmond-celebrates-first-pride-family-day/.

19. Jeffrey M. Jones, "In US, Confidence in Police Lowest in 22 Years," Gallup, June 19, 2015, http://www.gallup.com/poll/183704/confidence-police-lowest-years.aspx.

20. Richmond did not face this problem alone. At least thirty-five US cities reported increases in murders, violent crimes, or both after years of declines, and these "spikes" were "raising alarms among urban police chiefs." See Monica Davey and Mitch Smith, "Murder Rates Rising Sharply in Many Cities," *New York Times*, September 1, 2015.

21. For a moving profile of the deceased, see Corey Monroe, "Remembering Fontino Hardy Jr.," *Richmond Pulse*, August 2015.

22. Quoted in Mike Aldax "Ongoing Unrest Between Richmond Gangs Coincides with Uptick in Shootings," *Richmond Standard*, August 4, 2015, http://richmond standard.com/2015/08/ongoing-unrest-between-richmond-gangs-coincides-with-uptick-in-shootings.

23. Ibid.

24. Chris Magnus, "Dear Community Residents," July 26, 2015, Richmond Police Department, Facebook, https://www.facebook.com/richmondpolicecali/posts/1107722502576715:0.

25. As quoted by Caitlin Schmidt, "Tucson Police Union Makes Recommendation for New Chief," *Arizona Daily Star*, November 4, 2015.

CHAPTER 7: GENTRIFICATION AND ITS DISCONTENTS

1. As Matthew Desmond documents in his wrenching account of landlord-tenant problems in a low-income Milwaukee neighborhood, such housing insecurity is now a condition of daily life for millions of Americans. See Desmond, *Eviction: Poverty and Profit in the American City* (New York: Crown, 2016).

2. Margaretta Lin, Oakland Housing and Community Development Department, in a report titled *Oakland Housing Equity Roadmap*, quoted in Ken Epstein, "Oakland Is Losing Its Racial, Age, and Economic Diversity," *Oakland Post*, June 14, 2015. In April 2016 these trends led the Oakland city council to impose a ninety-day moratorium on rent increases and create an "impact fee" system to encourage "developers to include affordable housing in their projects or pay a fee for every market rate unit they build so the city can build its own affordable housing." See Rachel Swan, "Oakland Council OKs Impact Fees on New Housing," *San Francisco Chronicle*, April 21, 2016.

3. Randy Shaw, "Is Richmond the Next Hipster Haven?," *Beyond Chron*, August 5, 2014, http://www.beyondchron.org/oakland-hipster-haven-richmond-next.

4. As quoted in "Berkeley Global Campus: A New Bolder Vision for Richmond Bay," press release, UC-Berkeley Public Affairs, October 30, 2014.

5. Roland Li, "UC Thinks Global, Builds Local," *San Francisco Business Times*, April 3, 2015, http://www.bizjournals.com/sanfrancisco/print-edition/2015 /04/03/uc-thinks-global-builds-local-uc-berkeley-s-global.html.

6. Eskenazi, "From the 'Arm Pit of the Bay Area' to a Progressive Utopia on Earth."

7. For details on this trend, see AFSCME Local 3299 research report *Working in the Shadows: How Outsourcing at the University of California Adds to the Ranks of California's Working Poor*, August 7, 2015. Archived at http://www.afscme3299 .org/documents/reports/WorkingInShadows.pdf.

8. Ian Lovett, "University of California System Set to Raise Minimum Wage to $15 an Hour," *New York Times*, July 23, 2015.

9. Dirks was reported to be developing proposals "for reducing staff, particularly in administration" and "using real estate and branding to bring in new revenue" to address a $156 million deficit in his $2.4 billion budget. See Anemona Hartocollis, "Growing Deficit Forces Berkeley Campus to Look for Cuts and New Revenue," *New York Times*, February 11, 2016. In August 2016, Dirks also announced his resignation as chancellor, although he planned to remain in office until a successor was named.

10. After later picketing of another Richmond landlord, Butt didn't swoop in, but other rent control foes did. They accused ACCE and the RPA protestors of using "intimidation to influence government policy," thus meeting "one of the criteria used by the federal government to define domestic terrorism." See Oscar Garcia, "ACCE and RPA Unfairly Target Elderly Latina Landlord," *Radio Free Richmond*, June 20, 2016.

11. In a December 18, 2014, letter to her constituents about her dissenting vote, McLaughlin explained that she objected to how city hall staff handled the process of securing an amendment to the city's General Plan, required for this project because of the developer's proposed building height.

12. Soto's rental problems are described in Rachel Swan, "Richmond Council to Vote on Contentious Rent Control Proposal," *San Francisco Chronicle*, July 27, 2015.

13. Edgardo Cervano-Soto, "Black Families on Front Lines of Displacement in Richmond," *Richmond Pulse*, April 10, 2015.

14. From a June 25, 2015, e-mail, "Update from Council Member McLaughlin." Copy in possession of the author.

15. The RPA disputed both points, reminding the mayor that "part of balancing the budget is making sure the wealthy pay their fair share of the city's income," which the RPA has tried to do via its past campaigns to raise Chevron's business license fees, utility user's tax, and property taxes.

16. Gayle McLaughlin, e-mail message to RPA steering committee, August 25, 2015. Copy in possession of the author.

17. Karina Ioffee, "Richmond OKs Strict Protection for Tenants," *Contra Costa Times*, July 23, 2015.

18. Randy Shaw, "Richmond 1, Gentrification 0," *Beyond Chron*, July 23, 2015, http://www.beyondchron.org/richmond-moves-to-halt-gentrification/.

19. Chip Johnson, "Richmond Makes Right Call on Rent Control," *San Francisco Chronicle*, August 7, 2015. Later *New York Times* coverage of multiple Bay Area rent control campaigns in 2016 confirmed Johnson's observation that even middle-income renters were being squeezed, and responding in Richmond

fashion. See Conor Dougherty, "In Towns That Tech Made Rich, Calls to Limit the Soaring Rents," *New York Times*, June 12, 2016.

20. Quoted in Karina Ioffee, "Rent Control Is Under Fire," *Contra Costa Times*, August 28, 2015.

21. Karina Ioffee, "Richmond Petition Drive Puts Spotlight on Industry with Little Oversight," *Contra Costa Times*, December 25, 2015.

22. At the time of his death in 2012, former Black Panther Bobby Bowens served on the RPA steering committee and used the storefront office later named after him to lead a local study group on the writings of Martin Luther King Jr.

23. Like Choi and his favored presidential candidate, Bernie Sanders, Willis also "pledged not to accept any political donations from corporations and businesses." See Michelle Chan and Patsy Byers, "RPA Endorses Melvin Willis," *RPA Activist*, August 2, 2016, http://richmondprogressivealliance.net/.

24. See "Jael Myrick: Nobody's Bashing Police, My Response to Mayor Butt," *Radio Free Richmond*, February 9, 2016, http://www.radiofreerichmond.com /jael_myrick_nobody_s_bashing_police_my_response_to_mayor_butt.

25. Quoted in Edgardo Cervano-Soto, "Latino Voting Power on the Rise," *Richmond Pulse*, April, 2016.

26. Quoted in Sawant campaign press release, "Sawant Has Highest Number of Seattle Contributors," October 5, 2015. For more on the labor and political organizing in Seattle that contributed to Sawant's electoral success, see Jonathan Rosenblum's "Socialist Win in Seattle: Anomaly or Harbinger?," *Alternet*, January 8, 2016; Jonathan Rosenblum, *Not by Wages Alone* (Boston: Beacon Press, forthcoming).

27. Roots Action was also created by media critic Jeff Cohen. For more details on its valuable work, see http://rootsaction.org/about-rootsaction.

28. This was not an electoral outcome welcomed by Tom Butt. The mayor told me he would consider stepping down if the RPA achieved its first-ever four-member council majority, making cooperation and compromise with nonmembers on the council unnecessary, in his view. Butt questioned the RPA's ability to make such gains in 2016, citing polling results earlier that year showing that he was the only council member with a current favorability rating over 50 percent, based on performance in office.

EPILOGUE: MAKING LOCAL PROGRESS

1. Michael Kazin, "Promises and Limits of Progressive Cities," *Dissent* (Winter 2015): 26.

2. New York City provides a 6-to-1 match for individual donations of up to $175 for city council and mayoral candidates who agree to abide by the system's overall expenditure limits and disclosure requirements. Most candidates now take advantage of this voluntary program.

3. For details, see Will Bredderman, "City Council Sounds Defiant While Bending to Pressure From Albany on Bag Fees," *Observer*, June 6, 2016.

4. Eric Alterman, "The Real Democratic Battle," *Nation*, August 3/10, 2015, 6–7. See also Eric Alterman, *Inequality and One City: Bill de Blasio and the New York Experiment, Year One* (New York: Nation Books, 2015).

5. "Mayor de Blasio Unloads," editorial, *New York Times*, July 2, 2015.

6. Michael Grynbaum and Matt Flegenheimer, "Messes Pile Up for de Blasio in 2nd Year," *New York Times*, August 16, 2015. By year three of his first term, de Blasio also faced messes of his own making in the form of local or federal investigations of his "big-money political supporters and fund-raising efforts more broadly." See J. David Goodman and William Neuman, "Inquiries Upend de Blasio's Bid to Reboot for '17," *New York Times*, April 16, 2016.

7. *New York Times*, August 16, 2015.

8. Richmond's innovative public safety programs have received supportive funding from Sacramento. For example, the state's FY 2016-17 budget included $2,798,000 for the Richmond Police Department, Office of Neighborhood Safety, Project Safe Neighborhood grants, Family Justice Center, and the RYSE Youth Center.

9. Anthony Weiner, "Albany, Get Your Boot off New York City's Neck," *New York Times*, August 27, 2015.

10. That sorry Sacramento budget cutting deal is recalled by Steven Tavares in "Leaning Left: The Race for State Senate District 9 Pits Liberal Against Liberal," *East Bay Express*, April 27–May 3, 2016.

11. California developers impatient with construction delays resulting from state-mandated environmental reviews and local planning commission decisions are also putting their new projects directly before the voters for their approval instead. In Richmond, a controversial ballot measure like this, proposed by waterfront property owner Richard Poe, was defeated by a large margin in June 2016. For more on the developers' new strategy, see Ian Lovett, "Builders Pierce California's Environmental Shield: Speeding Developments and Sidestepping Laws Through Initiative System," *New York Times*, June 8, 2016.

12. Tom Butt E-Forum, "Moody's Throws Richmond into Debtor's Prison," October 8, 2015.

13. To raise additional revenue in the future and to reduce blight, the council considered raising city fees and possibly imposing a litter tax on local fast food outlets, liquor stores, and gas station mini-markets, an idea borrowed from badly littered Oakland.

14. Robert Reich in "Why California Should Close a Dangerous Corporate Tax Loophole," August 14, 2015, YouTube, https://www.youtube.com/watch?v=ICWx3I26An8.

15. Michael Bornstein, "Jerry Brown and Prop 13," e-mail message to *Evolve* members, October 10, 2015. Document in possession of the author.

16. For more on the big-name California multimillionaires and billionaires who spent heavily—and, in some cases, illegally—on Proposition 30, see Melody Gutierrez, "Campaign to ID Wealthy Who Donate Dark Money," *San Francisco Chronicle*, June 28, 2016.

17. Jerry Brown quotes are from Bornstein, "Jerry Brown and Prop 13."

18. "Governor Brown Wrong on Split Roll," news release, California Calls, October 8, 2015.

19. California Calls, "Next Steps in the Movement to Reform Prop. 13," e-mail message to members, October 19, 2015. Document in possession of author.

20. Jessica Calefati, "Down to Wire for Climate Bills," *Contra Costa Times*, August 30, 2015.

21. Robert Gammon, "California's Missing Climate Hawk," *East Bay Express*, September 2–8, 2015.

22. Jessica Calefati and Tracy Seipel, "Brown's Priorities Defeated," *Contra Costa Times*, September 10, 2015.

23. Justin Gillis, "Hotter Planet Fuels Drought, Scientists Find," *New York Times*, August 21, 2015.

24. See "How Long Will This Blue State Let Oil Remain King?," editorial, *Sacramento Bee*, September 11, 2015. Brown did better a year later when he overcame industry opposition to the legislature's enactment of a new timetable for cutting greenhouse gas emissions. See Jennifer Medina and Matt Richtel, "Carbon Goal in California Is 'Milestone' on Climate, *New York Times*, August 26, 2016.

25. Daniel Gonzales, Timothy Gulden, Aaron Strong, and William Hoyle, "Cost-Benefit Analysis of Proposed California Oil and Gas Refinery Regulations," RAND Corporation report, March, 2016, http://www.rand.org/content/dam /rand/pubs/research_reports/RR1400/RR1421/RAND_RR1421.pdf.

26. Letter from USW Local 5 Secretary-Treasurer Jim Payne to BAAQMD, April 8, 2015.

27. Denis Cuff, "Bay Area Air Regulators Urged to Cap Oil Refinery Emissions," *San Jose Mercury News*, June 15, 2016.

28. Among those following in Mazzocchi's footsteps is Jeremy Brecher, author of "A Superfund for Workers: How to Promote a Just Transition and Break Out of the Jobs vs. Environment Trap," *Dollars & Sense*, November/December 2015. Brecher and Todd Vachon take heart from survey data indicating that labor's rank-and-file favors environmental regulation even more than the general public. See Brecher and Vachon, "Union Members Don't Oppose Environmental Protections: They're Actually More Likely To Support Them," *Portside*, May 23, 2016.

29. Nicolas Haeringer, "The Ones We Have Been Waiting For," 350.org, http://350.org/the-ones-we-have-been-waiting-for.

30. "The Hottest Year Ever," e-mail appeal to 350.org supporters. For full text, see http://350.org/the-time-for-feeling-powerless-in-the-face-of-climate-change -is-over/.

31. See Naomi Klein, "The Problem with Hillary Clinton Isn't Just Her Corporate Cash," *Nation*, April 6, 2016.

32. Nicholas Confessore and Megan Thee-Benan, "Poll Shows Americans Favor an Overhaul of Campaign Financing," *New York Times*, June 3, 2015.

33. Bernie Sanders, "Sanders Proposes Public Funding of Campaigns," press release, August 4, 2015, https://berniesanders.com/press-release/sanders-proposes-public -funding-of-campaigns/.

34. Nicholas Confessore, "Jeb Bush Outstrips Rivals in Fund-Raising as 'Super PACs' Swell Candidates' Coffers," *New York Times*, July 10, 2015.

35. Rebecca Ballhaus, Beth Reinhard, and Christopher Stewart, "Billionaires Put Their Stamp on 2016 Presidential Campaigns," *Wall Street Journal*, July 31, 2015.

36. Quoted in Amy Chozick and Eric Lichtblau, "Facing Money Gap, Hillary Clinton Warms to 'Super PAC' Gifts," *New York Times*, August 18, 2015.

37. Columbia University law professor Robert Jackson, quoted in Amy Chozick and Nicholas Confessore, "With Issue Galvanizing Voters, Clinton Proposes Campaign Finance Reforms," *New York Times*, September 9, 2015.

38. Bernie Sanders fund-raising e-mail, June 26, 2015.
39. "Bernie Sanders' Army of Small Donors," editorial, *New York Times*, October 4, 2015.
40. Edward Sadlowski, "A Key Victory for New Politics in Chicago's 10th Ward," *Social Policy* 45, no. 2 (Summer 2015): 36–37.
41. Quoted by Paul Biasco, "Bernie Sanders Chooses Chicago's Youngest Alderman to Fire Up Crowd," *DNAinfo*, August 18, 2015, https://www.dnainfo.com/chicago/20150818/lincoln-park/bernie-sanders-calls-on-chicagos-youngest-alderman-fire-up-crowd.
42. Bernie Sanders, "Bernie 2016" e-mail blasts: "Make Them Pay," June 26, 2015; "Overturn Citizens United," June 27, 2015.
43. Laurel Rosenthal, "Money Talks: Candidates Get Schooled in Finances," *San Francisco Chronicle*, November 9, 2015. Despite the shortcomings of campaign finance reporting rules in California, they provide more information about independent expenditure makers than voters are able to access in other states, now awash in "dark money." Experts such as Chisun Lee and Lawrence Norden have hailed the state's Fair Political Practices Commission as "a model for much of what a strong disclosure regime should do." See "The Secret Power Behind Local Elections," *New York Times*, June 26, 2016.
44. Quoted by Jesse McKinley, "Cuomo Seeks Fixes to 'Rampant' Problems in New York's Campaign Contribution System," *New York Times*, June 8, 2016. Campaign finance reform advocates welcomed the governor's unexpected critique of *Citizens United* but wondered how long his zealousness on the subject would last, given his personal fund-raising history and heavy reliance on corporate donors.
45. *Richmond CA Community Livability Report, 2015*, National Citizen Survey (Boulder, CO: National Research Center, 2105), http://www.ci.richmond.ca.us/DocumentCenter/View/31307.